A Whole Which Is Greater

A Whole Which Is Greater

Why the Wisconsin "Uprising" Failed

EDITED BY PAUL GILK
AND DAVID KAST

WIPF & STOCK · Eugene, Oregon

A WHOLE WHICH IS GREATER
Why the Wisconsin "Uprising" Failed

Copyright © 2012 Paul Gilk and David Kast, Editors. All rights reserved. Except for brief quotations in critical publications or reviews, no part of this book may be reproduced in any manner without prior written permission from the publisher. Write: Permissions, Wipf and Stock Publishers, 199 W. 8th Ave., Suite 3, Eugene, OR 97401.

Wipf & Stock
An Imprint of Wipf and Stock Publishers
199 W. 8th Ave., Suite 3
Eugene, OR 97401
www.wipfandstock.com

ISBN 13: 978-1-62032-560-5
Manufactured in the U.S.A.

All scripture quotations, unless otherwise indicated, are taken from the Holy Bible, New International Version®, NIV®. Copyright ©1973, 1978, 1984 by Biblica, Inc.™ Used by permission of Zondervan. All rights reserved worldwide.

The programs that help people are the ones being dismantled by ideological zealots. The programs that help corporations at the expense of the taxpayers are being left in place. "Un-American" is not a word we are given to tossing around, nor is "fascism"—we have spent years making fun of humorless liberals who hear the sound of jack-booted fascism around every corner. But there is something creepy about what is happening here, and the creepiest thing about it is that no one is talking about it. Mussolini said, "Fascism should more properly be called corporatism, since it is the merger of state and corporate power." That's pretty much what we're looking at here, and the results are not good for the people of this country, no matter what it is called.

—Molly Ivins & Lou Dubose,
Bushwhacked: Life in George W. Bush's America

Now there's a sinister self-reinforcing quality to a culture of acquiescence and obedience. When you don't hear people talking back, when you don't see a lot of protest (or not enough, or what you do see doesn't make any sense when the media's done with it), you begin to believe that nothing can be done. That this is as good as it gets. Or as Margaret Thatcher once put it in the single word: T-I-N-A, Tina—There Is No Alternative. Acquiescence is infectious; conformity is contagious, and if everyone goes around saying TINA, then pretty soon TINA rules.

—Barbara Ehrenreich,
"foreword," in *the ralph nader reader*

I don't want to invent victories for people's movements. But to think that history-writing must aim simply to recapitulate the failures that dominant the past is to make historians collaborators in an endless cycle of defeat. If history is to be creative, to anticipate a possible future without denying the past, it should, I believe, emphasize new possibilities by disclosing those hidden episodes of the past when, even if in brief flashes, people showed their ability to resist, to join together, occasionally to win. I am supposing, or perhaps only hoping, that our future may be found in the past's fugitive moments of compassion rather than in its solid centuries of warfare.

—Howard Zinn,
A People's History of the United States

Most of us—most, at least, who have grown up in industrialized countries—have lived free from hunger with hot and cold running water, with machines at our fingertips to transport us quickly and almost effortlessly from place to place, and with still other machines to clean our clothes, to entertain and inform us, and on and on.

It has been a fabulous party. But from those to whom much has been given, much should be expected. Once we are aware of the choice, it is up to us to decide: Shall we vainly continue reveling until the bitter end, and take most of the rest of the world down with us? Or shall we acknowledge that the party is over, clean up after ourselves, and make way for those who will come after us?

—RICHARD HEINBERG,
*THE PARTY'S OVER: OIL, WAR
AND THE FATE OF INDUSTRIAL SOCIETIES*

The only wild card is whether some countervailing popular movement will step up to provide a viable alternative to this grim future. That means not just an alternative set of policy proposals but an alternative worldview to rival the one at the heart of the ecological crisis—this time embedded in interdependence rather than hyper-individualism, reciprocity rather than dominance and cooperation rather than hierarchy.

—NAOMI KLEIN,
"CAPITALISM VS. THE CLIMATE,"
IN *THE NATION* (NOVEMBER 28, 2011)

Literature is always calling in the doctor for consultation and confession, and always giving evasions and swathing suppressions in place of that "heroic nudity" on which only a genuine diagnosis of serious cases can be built.

—WALT WHITMAN,
"O'ER TRAVEL'D ROADS,"
IN *LEAVES OF GRASS*

Contents

A Note to Ourselves and to the Reader ix
Acknowledgments xi
Foreword xiii
        —David Kast
A Belated Introduction xvii
        —Paul Gilk

1 The Big Conversation 1
        —*James Botsford*

2 The End of the Myth of Progress 6
        —*Maynard Kaufman*

3 A View from the "Greatest Generation" 17
        —*Rhoda Gilman*

4 On Fascism and Democracy 24
        —*Eric Yonke*

5 Resisting Resource Colonialism in the Lake Superior Region 39
        —*Al Gedicks*

6 What's Really Going on in Wisconsin? 71
        —*Margaret Swedish*

7 Governmental Options Preferential to Corporations and Minority Wealth 88
        —*Michael Slattery*

8 Confessions of an Apostate from the Religion of "Education" 108
        —*Daniel Grego*

9 Worldwide Neo-Liberal Development: A Challenge We Must Meet 127
        —*John I. Laun*

10   Seeing Our Struggle from Distant Shores 145
             —*Jeff Leigh*

11   Can Religion Help Revive the Progressive Tradition? 152
             —*James F. Veninga*

12   Gandhi, King and 99% Spring 209
             —*Brian Terrell*

13   Who's Awake in Clark County? 212
             —*Mike McCabe*

14   Empire's Children: An Afterword 217
             —*Paul Gilk*

List of Contributors 247

A Note to Ourselves and to the Reader

THE ESSAYS IN THIS collection are not all alike in their use of capitalization, punctuation, or other literary technicalities. They reflect the styles of the contributors.

Acknowledgments

WE WOULD LIKE TO thank Erin Kast for his help with the graphs in Chapter 7 and with formatting generally. We would also like to thank Carol Ann Okite for her technical advice.

Foreword

David Kast

THE ESSAYS COLLECTED HERE, written from a progressive perspective, were prompted by the successful drive of Wisconsin Governor Scott Walker to eliminate most collective bargaining rights of state employees, the protests that drive spawned, and the culminating unsuccessful recall effort of June 5, 2012.

There is significant diversity among the essays. Some of them address particular issues, such as Al Gedick's essay which recounts historically recent resistance to large-scale corporate mining in Wisconsin including the struggle in the Bad River watershed region near Lake Superior (the Postscript to his essay discusses the state legislature's recent rejection of the Bad River Iron Mining bill proposal) and Jack Laun's which questions the neo-liberal economic model as applied in Colombia and Wisconsin and suggests the need for solidarity in resisting it. Some address more philosophical issues, such as Maynard Kaufman's essay on the Myth of Progress which questions the ideology of progress and continuous growth and calls for local sustainable living. Others are more directly political. Mike McCabe's essay discusses how the Democratic Party lost its base in Wisconsin and Michael Slattery's analyzes the economic model being pursued by Governor Scott Walker, questioning its corporate give-aways and the burden this program places on the middle class. (Slattery's essay also addresses religious issues as mentioned below.) The essay by Jeffrey Leigh views the situation here in Wisconsin from abroad and highlights what constitutes a strong public sphere in a democracy. Daniel Grego, Rhoda Gilman and Margaret Swedish relate personal histories juxtaposed with political and philosophical reflections centered in Wisconsin (Minnesota in

Foreword

Rhoda's case). Daniel Grego's reflections center on the nature of education generally and within a Wisconsin context particularly beginning with his own early political/educational adventures triggered by the assassination of Martin Luther King, Jr., Margaret Swedish's center on ecological and political upheavals against the background of her own political awakenings through the years of her youth and maturity, and Rhoda Gilman's on the need for personal and community transformation as illustrated in her own personal transformations over the years of her life. Eric Yonke gives us a lesson in the history of fascism, cautions us on its application, and warns us of its ability to insinuate itself into our political fabric. Brian Terrell questions the 99% Spring movement in the light of Gandhi and Martin Luther King, Jr.

Although most of the essays are secular in nature, some directly confront us with religious/spiritual questions: James Veninga traces the history of the Christian contribution to progressivism in the United States through the Social Gospel and asks if there is a model of Christianity that can help revive progressivism in the 21st Century. Michael Slattery makes a detailed evaluation of the politics of economics at work in Wisconsin and suggests how both the Hebrew and Christian understandings of wealth and poverty speak to the current economic atmosphere. James Botsford wonders, in a 'rough and bumpy' way, if there is an essential and larger (deeper, broader) spiritual perspective than that of secular society and purely linear scientific thinking, or of organized religions and particularly the exclusivist and anthropocentric theistic traditions.

The emotion and concern expressed in the essays is palpable; in some the frustration with our current crisis-laden state and world is clear; but the essays are *not* written in the polarizing manner we find so prevalent in much of the current political landscape. Together they ask us to seriously consider a variety of real and difficult existing problems and perspectives without rancor because the problems we face today, not only in Wisconsin but around the world, are tremendous: the growing disparity in wealth between rich and poor; climate change; the tension and conflicts incumbent upon population growth and the ensuant competition for resources; shortages in resources including clean water; environmental and ecological degradation; increasing and unsustainable consumerism; the accumulation, proliferation and use of horrific modern weaponry.

Foreword

Until people in large numbers learn to see and live beyond strictly personal and family concerns and rigid ideologies, particularly extreme individualism and collectivism, and instead embrace a humility that respects their entire environs, and in particular their immediate vicinity, that is not ashamed to respect the dignity of persons both local and foreign and the sacredness inherent in all being, we shouldn't expect conflicts and polarizations to diminish. This central perspective, so simply and convincingly suggested in James Botsford's essay, ought not be forgotten. For if we only rely on our own "correct" ideological persuasion without the humility to recognize our own *simple fitting* into a whole which is greater, more subtle and more accepting than any of our ideologies or understandings, we are bound to confront one another in rigid contrast.

Differences and arguments cannot be eliminated. That would be foolish to expect. After all, we *are* each unique as well as fallible, flawed, even contingent beings! But we should not be ashamed, either, to call greed and selfishness, hatred and abuse, what they are: egregious wrongs in a deep moral sense, minimally suggesting a pervasive illness, and to suggest the need to address and challenge them as well as immoderation, without becoming self-righteous. A number of the essays, particularly those of Al Gedicks and Jack Laun, ask us, even if indirectly, how we have failed to question corporate profit and greed, particularly when it shows itself indifferent to the good of local peoples and environments. As well, we need to challenge *ourselves* and question our own greed and selfishness, hatred, abuse, immoderation, judgments (particularly of others), their degrees and consequences.

Perhaps part of our difficulty lies in our presumption of universal solutions and "everything for everyone" (from a progressive perspective) rather than our acknowledgment of locality and local constraints which require people to work within those constraints for greater local sustainability and ecological health, as suggested by Maynard Kaufman, Margaret Swedish, and Rhoda Gilman.

Ivan Illich, toward the end of his life, spoke increasingly of people and societies in the late 20th Century becoming absorbed and integrated into systems and technologies they had created which fed their hubristic and narcissistic belief in humanly created universal solutions, and which finally controlled them, destroying their ability to live personal, neighborly, vernacular lives centered on friendship and 'conspiratio', sharing of the breath (spirit). It is the people and surroundings that we can literally see and touch that we *must* see and touch if we would more richly and meaningfully *fit* into the greater whole.

Other writers have spoken similarly, including Leopold Kohr and the Canadian philosopher Charles Taylor. They also have suggested that our desire for universal solutions, as well as our faith in universal progress and technology, is misguided; that we must think more locally, more simply, and on a smaller scale. There are many reasons for this: the tremendous diversity of peoples for whom a universal solution will require the destruction of their cultures; the tremendous diversity of natural environments that call for different local structures suitable to those environments; and perhaps most importantly the recognition that for us to know anything well and deeply requires the use not only of our disembodied intellect and ideas, but our entire selves: our corporeal selves, our bodies and senses, our emotional selves, our spiritual selves, and our mental selves. These must act directly and in concert with one another. And they are not able to do so through a mediated technological reality or at too great a distance. A body must be able to touch and see what it must work with. An emotion must be expressible directly to another being and a spiritual understanding and connection must finally pass from us and between us through direct transposition, direct transmission, unmediated, whether by 'things' or ideas or institutions or systems. To do this we must be conservative in our use of things and ideas and technologies, etc., using them cautiously and only insofar as they help our mutual communing, our local economy. Wendell Berry has written extensively in this vein. Dan Grego recalls us to some of these same ideas in his very personal essay in which he references both Illich and Berry.

It is my and Paul's hope that these essays will encourage discussion, reflection and the entertaining of ideas and convivial sharing conducive of 'awakening' and its consequentially informed action.

Dave Kast, August 4, 2012

A Belated Introduction

Paul Gilk

It was just another incident of serendipity. I was discussing the structure of this book with my friend Carol Ann Okite (who's guided my previous books through the requisite electronics and helped, in a variety of ways, with this project, too) when she showed me, for comparison, a 1977 hardback—a collection of essays—entitled *Small Comforts for Hard Times: Humanists on Public Policy*, edited by Michael Mooney and Florian Stuber. Our essays were in, David Kast was on vacation, and my job (before David's return) was to proof all essays one last time before David and I merged our corrections in the final manuscript. So I had the time, or I took the time, to skim Carol Ann's book.

Going down the list of titles on the Contents page, my eye was caught by essay seventeen, "The Lower Middle Class as Historical Problem" by Arno J. Mayer. Reading Mayer's piece clarified why my attention had been caught. It dawned on me that these present essays neglect the historical sociology of the Tea Party; and it just might be the case that without the 2010 Tea Party upsurge (which cost Russ Feingold what should have been a secure senate seat), Scott Walker would not have been elected governor of Wisconsin and the subsequent "uprising" and recalls would never have occurred. It struck me that "The Lower Middle Class as Historical Problem" contains lucid and helpful background analysis by which to more deeply understand the Tea Party phenomenon and the social forces it represents. (I very much recommend Professor Mayer's essay to the interested reader.)

There is a conceptual or ideological hinge in Mayer's piece, however, that we'll get to soon, a "hinge" that's crucial but not, in my opinion, adequately delved into by Professor Mayer. But first it needs to be said

A Belated Introduction

that after taking in a very compacted history of the lower middle class from the late Middle Ages to the middle of the nineteenth century (with reference especially to the Belgian historian Henri Pirenne), and with special attention given to the French Revolution and the European political upheavals of 1848, we are left with an impression of "the crucial swing position of the lower middle class in the battle for control of the modern state."[1] This sounds suspiciously like Tea Party to me. Or, to be clearer, Tea Party seems to be its present swing mutation.

The lower middle class in this analysis is only incidentally a designation determined by income. It is primarily a status-based construct. The lower middle class was originally composed of small merchants, traders, shopkeepers, and craft workers—not ordinary peasants or factory laborers—not what we might call the working poor—although its composition changed over time, with increasing industrialization, to include dependent clerks, technicians, and (to some extent) professionals. Its culture (or cultural aspiration) also changed over time from admiration of aristocratic high culture to an eventual saturation with commercially produced popular culture, an "incipient popular culture that, in contrast to a spontaneous folk culture, was contrived, standardized, and disseminated from on high."[2]

Mayer says the lower middle class always had a "strained relationship with the upper establishment, which it both aspires to and resents."[3] He also says that under certain "constricting conditions, the lower middle class loses self-confidence and becomes prey to anxieties and fears which, in the event of sharp economic adversity, may well predispose it to rally to a politics of anger, scapegoating, and atavistic millenarianism."[4] Yet this class has always had "difficulties jelling as a class for itself, with the result that in the end it remains a political auxiliary of superordinate elites."[5] This, too, sounds like Tea Party.

All that said, I want to focus here on what I believe is the crucial hinge: "Instead of glorifying a petite bourgeoisie that was suspended between hope and fear, Marx and Engels warned that, in the crunch of a revolutionary crisis, it would seek to save its special social position that

1. Mayer, "Lower," 225.
2. Ibid., 228.
3. Ibid., 232.
4. Ibid., 233.
5. Ibid., 234.

A Belated Introduction

had an obsolete material base, joining a coalition against the claimant underclass."⁶ (In our present circumstance, the lower middle class as Tea Party joined a coalition, not so much against an underclass, but against public sector unionized workers, teachers especially, a "class" above not below, with obvious resentment toward perceived special treatment and exclusive privileges. But, with that caveat in mind, the overall analysis remains acutely accurate.)

The crucial hinge, however, lies in the term "an obsolete material base," especially in light of the lower middle class not being able to jell "as a class for itself." Mayer goes on to reference Lenin, who said it would be fairly easy to dislodge the big landlords, capitalists, and upper bureaucrats, but that it "would be far more difficult to assimilate and control those economic and social classes that, though part of the same 'petite bourgeoisie,' broadly defined, had elements of economic independence in the form of capital, land, or tools. Although these independent strata, notably the 'small commodity producers,' would have to be gotten 'rid of,' they could not be 'driven out or crushed.'"⁷

Now I don't think that Mayer is writing from a Leninist point of view, which is (or was) a kind of totalitarian utopianism: a centralized, precisely planned, industrialized perfect system. Just as Russian peasants had to be eliminated to make room for Soviet collective agri-technology, so the "petite bourgeoisie" had to make room for a fully systemic industrialism. I've said that I doubt that Mayer was himself writing from a Leninist (much less Stalinist) perspective; but I do suspect he was immersed in the conventional intellectual stream of ideological "progress" and "development," which almost universally asserts that the small-scale—especially and particularly the agricultural small-scale, but also the vast bulk of craft artisans—constitutes an obsolete material base needing to be dispensed with.

With American capitalism, rural culture here has also been crushed by the massive imposition of agri-technology, perhaps more thoroughly than anywhere else in the world. In that respect, American agri-technology resembles, at least in principle, Soviet agri-technology: as full an application of industrial procedures to agriculture as is scientifically possible, with dismissive contempt for the "backwardness" (the obsolete material base) of all small-scale forms of farming, and

6. Ibid., 226.
7. Ibid., 231.

A Belated Introduction

certainly for rural culture as a whole. All this—the enforced mutation of agriculture into agribusiness, the virtual eradication of self-sustaining folk cultures (including the non-civilized indigenous), the forcing of craft into industry, the universal imposition of compulsory schooling, the hegemony of monopoly and multinational corporations (now legally blessed as "persons"), the emergence of global military reach with apocalyptic weaponry, the increasing concentration of power in national (and, with NATO, multinational) governments, and the polarization of a brittle theism confronting a stubborn atheism with a bewildered, mushy agnosticism trapped between—is part of the utopian, globalizing outwash that now engulfs the entire world. The perfect "no place" of utopia has finally succeeded in wrecking all the eutopian "good places," even to the point of global ecological disruptions and catastrophes.

However, American monopoly capitalism, operating in a supposedly democratic environment with a presumptive equality of persons, has always had something of an existential problem: it has had to justify "capitalism" not on the basis of its monopoly concentration (potentially leading to the rise of a post-democratic aristocracy), but on the basis of the relative small-scale, the small businessman, the mom-and-pop store, the creative "risk-taker," the entrepreneur. All this supposedly constitutes "free enterprise," framed as the heart and soul of "freedom." To this end, monopoly capitalism has had to rely on the ideological saturation of the American mind with this idealized and nostalgic perspective of the virtuous small-scale—may we call it a political mythology?—and it has always needed the lower middle class for electoral support, just as Arno Mayer points out in his larger historical context.

Insofar as we can say that the Tea Party arises from the lower middle class—and remember this is more a status identity than a strict income category—we can also say with Mayer that "in moments of social crisis, the lower middle class stood with the patriciate and also agreed that this patriciate should retain its virtual monopoly of political power and authority."[8] But it's at this point where we really need to examine the implications of saying the lower middle class is representative of "an obsolete material base," and also why it aligns with the "patriciate."

"Liberals" in classical economic terms have stood for the maximum installation of the procedures and artifacts of "progress." (This is why liberals so often call themselves "progressives.") "Conservatives,"

8. Ibid., 224.

A Belated Introduction

on the other hand, were traditionally more skeptical of unfettered "progress." The contemporary paradox is that "liberals" and "conservatives" have, with a few exceptions in the particulars (perhaps like abortion), essentially traded places. That is, "liberals" (for instance in regard to global warming and climate change) are steadily becoming more conservative—if we mean by the word what "conserve" so obviously implies. "Conservatives," meanwhile, are openly disdainful of conservation. Therefore "conservative" and "liberal" are such semantic mushballs that it's impossible to employ them usefully in their current constructions.

Nevertheless, we can in principle say that the bulk of each political constituency, both "liberal" and "conservative," certainly at their upper policy levels, continues to stand for maximized industrial growth and maximized technological applications—at least from within their respective (but hugely overlapping) ideological boundaries. Neither group addresses the crushing "externalities" looming with greater and greater menace over the entire world—a menace looming as a direct consequence and outcome of all this maximizing: climate change, peak oil, the atomic arsenal. These are the *products* of ideological fixation, of unfettered industrialism, what we might even call ideology entering into the mythological terrain of metaphysical conviction and religious belief, although it is immeasurably the case that high-level "liberal" policy makers are stuck in the utopian worldview for a variety of reasons: first, it is their own lifestyle context, outside of which they don't know how to think; second, it is the dominant lifestyle context of the "middle-class" public whose support they seek, and they don't wish to estrange that support; third, to openly acknowledge the growing ecological and cultural crises and advocate for appropriate correctives in policy is tantamount to embracing the Green and Rainbow political visions, and this embrace constitutes a personal, political, and even spiritual transformation (or crisis) that appears to promise utter political defeat, at least in the short term. Insofar as the lower middle class can be persuaded by corporate propaganda that conventional progress is untarnished by any irrational tree-hugging environmentalism or alleged resource limitation, "liberals"—politically afraid to openly confront this propaganda and personally inept and unfit to espouse the Green alternative—are cats on a hot tin roof, dancing faster and faster for escalating utopian progress and afraid to jump into the unfamiliar but healing embrace of the eutopian Green.

It's not incidental that the Koch brothers, for example, provided funding for the various "grassroots" Tea Party formations—and for Scott Walker, as well. This is perfectly in accord with Mayer's historical analysis of how elites manipulate the lower middle class. But the relative competence of the lower middle class, with its small capital, land or tools, is not in itself a "historical problem." Mayer's title skews the analysis in a false direction—or it's the first clue of a subsequently skewed analysis. There's absolutely nothing wrong with a vigorous, competent, entrepreneurial small-scale. We might even say that two of the twentieth-century thinkers who really help us understand this dynamic are the British economic historian R. H. Tawney (E. F. Schumacher's teacher) and the American historian Lawrence Goodwyn.

Goodwyn's *The Populist Moment* explores the indigenous populism of the late nineteenth-century agrarian People's Party (with its firm Omaha Platform mix of small-scale entrepreneurial freedom combined with socialism for the large-scale), while Tawney in *The Acquisitive Society* (written in the bitter aftermath of World War I) passionately argues for an entrepreneurial small-scale (both rural and urban) in political balance with a socialized large-scale composed of all entities too big to fail. Looked at through this Green lens, the lower middle class might still seem boneheaded—"prone to metapolitical appeals of a xenophobic and conspiratorial nature"[9]—while indulging in a fear of downward mobility. But we really need to quit hammering it for being a "historical problem" because its "material base" is supposedly "obsolete." Its entrepreneurial vigor is in fact critical in any possible *solution* to our overarching predicament.

What's at stake here is an issue raised by critics like Henry Thoreau, Leo Tolstoy, William Morris (and John Ruskin before him), Mohandas Gandhi, Ralph Borsodi, Martin Buber, Lewis Mumford, Helen and Scott Nearing, Leopold Kohr, Paul Goodman, E. F. Schumacher, Wendell Berry, Ivan Illich, and a whole host of others. It is, at heart, a cultural issue with spiritual content. That is, economic rationalization from the perspective of these thinkers is examined from a cultural point of view that's not immediately hostile to or inclined to jettison inherited craft patterns (whether agricultural or artisan) just because

9. Ibid., 245.

they've been labeled "an obsolete material base" by intellectual utopians. (If liberalism in its classical sense is the expression of civilizational utopianism—restless progress in constant pursuit of near perfection—then twentieth-century communism was, largely, the extreme end of such liberalism, perhaps as fascism is the extreme end of conservatism.)

For some nineteenth-century critics the issue may have been couched in artistic or aesthetic terms. (One thinks here of John Ruskin in particular.) In the twentieth, the issue was more broadly political and cultural. In the twenty-first, the crisis of utopian rationalization in behalf of eliminating the culturally evolved "obsolete material base" has reached ecocidal dimension. But the trajectory of utopian rationalization has also been *internalized* as a civilizational mandate whose moral and spiritual task is to liquidate the backwardness of eutopian folk evolution in all its "obsolete" cultural forms. We might even say that the civilizational engine, with its dominant image (and energy) of aristocratic prerogative, is in process of slamming into the wall of ecological limitation and environmental capacity, with millions upon millions of folk casualties lying in its wake, not to speak of all the ecological mayhem and species extinctions.

The really painful, difficult, and crucial step is displacing utopian mythology with a far more liveable and Earth-friendly Green eutopianism. To get beyond utopian mythology is also to get beyond the controlling influence of the "patriciate." To move beyond all this is tantamount to a religious or spiritual crisis. This, in my estimation, is the crucial test of our democratic inclination and aptitude. We need both a deepening of eutopian democracy and a shriveling of utopian "democracy." That's the point we've reached.

All in all, the following essays—consciously or unconsciously—are explorations into this spiritual paradox. Getting our heads out of Heaven and utopia, and onto Earth and eutopia, is the challenge we need to embrace and achieve. This is far less a technical problem (we have the means and the brains by which to accomplish the technical transition with relative ease) than it is an ideological, spiritual, religious, and mythological problem. These essays are a contribution to that diagnosis.

BIBLIOGRAPHY

Goodwyn, Lawrence. *The Populist Moment: A Short History of the Agrarian Revolt.* New York: Oxford University Press, 1978.

Mayer, Arno J. "Lower Middle Class as Historical Problem." In *Small Comforts for Hard Times: Humanists on Public Policy*, edited by Michael Mooney and Florian Stuber. New York: Columbia University Press, 1977.

Tawney, R. H. *The Acquisitive Society.* New York: Harcourt, Brace & World, 1948.

1

The Big Conversation

James Botsford

INTRODUCTION

I WATCHED THE RECENT election cycle in Wisconsin with an anger that turned to sorrow and then settled into ennui.

I was angry at the myopia of my fellow voters. It's hard to understand how the memory and attention span of the adult citizenry can be so short. I was angry at the selfishness reflected in the voters' choices; angry at the Dupe Masters who feed the fires of fear from their "I got mine" perspective; angry at the fickle thinking that lacks the dimensions of both time and wisdom.

And after the election it only got worse, and the worst proved true. It wasn't really about the pragmatic approaches to a balanced budget, it was more about ideology—anthropocentric, avaricious, unsustainable, dangerous ideologies that are premised on worn-out self-serving religious teachings and the phony and pushy moralities that accompany them.

And that's why the anger turned to a deepening sorrow and ennui. There is an ever increasing and really quite irrefutable body of knowledge out there telling us to think and behave more holistically, more sustainably, to temper our short-term desires, to make progressive changes that begin to heal the damage we humans are causing to the natural world; to act, as my Native friends admonish us, thinking of the best interests of those who will come seven generations from now. But do we do that? The election results and the subsequent acts of the new crop of legislators tell us no, we do not. In spite of ample evidence of the fruits of our short-term, self-serving myopia, things continue to get worse faster than they get better.

All of which makes me wonder about the religious underpinnings that ostensibly guide our culture. How can our religious teachings continue to allow for, if not encourage us to foul our own nest and poison the future? A recall election isn't going to effectuate a sea change. Electing more Democrats isn't going to usher in a new day. Unfortunately it's just more of the same old narrow vacillations, rearranging the deck chairs … though they may be a bit more artistically arranged under the Democrats.

We need to examine the religious, philosophical and moral premises upon which we base our lives and our collective cultural behavior. It seems to me that at the heart of our repetitively regressive behavior is a spiritual malaise that has been developing for centuries and is getting worse.

THE BIG CONVERSATION

All of the great organized religions of the world that claim to hold the literal truth are wrong. They are all man-made and they have all been corrupted or co-opted over time due to the desire for certainty, the zeal of leadership, the allure of power, the watering down that comes with being popularized over time, the ascendancy of rational linear thinking, and other human factors.

What I'm saying here is not to negate the intuitive, heartfelt, spiritual feelings and aspirations of people from all of the world's religions. In fact I think I'm affirming the universal validity of them in some important sense. None of us can know it all, but each of us who pay attention can sense the ineffable. We know there is something spiritual going on right here, right now, with every breath we take. What I'm saying is an affirmation of the intuitive wisdom from which that sense springs.

I am, however, in a perhaps rough and bumpy and very abbreviated way saying that the trappings that each of us are taught as a way of approaching those intuitive wisdoms are inadequate to the task and misleading. And, in fact, given how they've been manipulated and morphed over time, they are all now, in themselves, not worthy of belief.

With the possible exception of the simple experiential aspects of vipassana meditation[1] from the more or less original Buddhist teachings, the world's religions are confused and confusing. They are, on a good day, sources of valuable and helpful myths and metaphors when understood in that context.

I take a paragraph here to note that although this is a generally applicable perspective addressing all contemporary organized religions, I do feel a need to separate out this simple old vipassana meditation technique of early Buddhism. I do so because it is the only identifiable spiritual practice aimed at wisdom of which I am aware that implies no hierarchies, no dogma, no belief, no faith, no surrender, no cultural baggage, no claim of exclusivity, and no names. It is simply a technique to facilitate spiritual understanding in an innately available experiential way and as such seems consistent with the theme of this paper. (This is not true of the schools of Buddhism that encompass this practice.)

So the question comes down to this: is life or reality intrinsically, innately sacred? Is it so without any human constructs such as a Creator God, a personal God, a salvific code and any other trace of anthropomorphism? It seems to me the answer is a resounding yes. Life is sacred beyond the subjective—intrinsically sacred. The oneness that underlies everything is that sacred essence. The manifesting of this sacred oneness (the creative force) is the expression of that sacrality. Life is a holy event. God is a verb.

Life is of itself so intrinsically interwoven with propensities and creativities as to be worthy of the spiritual and wondrous word "awesome." As such it is profoundly beautiful and somewhat unpredictable (not explained by a cold-blooded reductionism of science). I use the word life to mean all of reality in the sense that it includes everything—rocks as well as the dance of cause and effect.

This truth can be glimpsed or gleaned through meditative or other experience that produces the indescribable awe of affirmation and respect. Reports from this experience have come from all corners of the

---

1. Vipassana (sometimes translated as 'mindfulness' or 'insight') meditation is enjoying a more secular, western resurgence these days as a technique for holistic healing, mental focus and deep relaxation, but its original purpose remains the unfoldment of wisdom.

world from all centuries from which we have reports. Regrettably, too often these reports have been interpreted or co-opted by the context of the prevailing religion of the time and place.

This assertion that God is a verb, that life itself is an intrinsically holy event, is not inconsistent with the highest reaches of scientific observations and understandings. But it is awkward to agree upon or even discuss because science suffers from some of the same predispositions, language limitations and anthropocentric tendencies as religion ... to say nothing of egos and other competitions.

Life is not reducible to a mechanistic (scientific) definition because creative potentialities inherent in life are not entirely predictable, and values can create change. Waves that act like particles? Particles that act like waves? Where do they come from and where do they go? There is more to this life than we shall ever fit within the bounds of our definitions. Our evolved filters, languages and other limitations keep us from understanding that eternity is here and now.

Stuart A. Kauffman in his book *Reinventing the Sacred* (a phrase he borrowed from Kiowa poet N. Scott Momaday) tries to get at this holistic sacred premise as a scientist and he makes an important contribution to this conversation (which has gone on for not only centuries but millennia). But I think he gets a bit bogged down in trying to explain the wondrous multidimensional beauty of nature and what science is discovering about it. He is on the right track but the articulation needs an injection of Taoist wisdom from Chuang Tzu and Lao Tzu, from poets like Rumi and Han Shan, from the Advaita Vedanta (beyond dualism) school of Hinduism, maybe some Meister Eckhart, something from the reports of unfettered nondoctrinaire mystics from many cultures and times, most certainly including indigenous wise men and women from everywhere. It could use a little Huston Smith, Joseph Campbell and a dose of Alan Watts. (Apologies for many omissions.)

I submit that the question becomes not whether or not life is a sacred event, but whether we can handle that knowledge without the weighty, contentious, constrictive, competitive baggage of all our inherited and accumulated isms. Can we evolve from this purer knowledge a respecting-of-all-life moral code or must we cling to these watered-down, inadequate and inaccurate dogmas to prevent a moral anarchy?

This is an increasingly important question given that these tattered old anthropocentric dogmas themselves are responsible for much of our despoliation of our planet and our violence toward each other. Given the increasing complexities and stresses we put upon life and its natural systems, and the exponentially growing potentialities of overpopulation, interconnected reliance on man-made systems, potential pandemic disasters and increasingly powerful weaponry—well, we really should get past the lazy, convenient, self-serving ideologies of the past. To anthropomorphize a little, I think that's what life is telling us.

2

The End of the Myth of Progress

Maynard Kaufman

THIS PAPER WORRIES ABOUT the myth or ideology of progress and its deleterious effect in our society. In our econo-centric society progress adds up to the expectation of continual economic growth and material improvement in living conditions. Now, as times get harder, a growing minority of people are anxious about the prospect of economic, social, and ecological collapse. Both belief systems, progress and collapse, can be seen as inadequate or even destructive visions of the future.

The myth of progress has been and remains the conventional attitude that is reinforced by popular media, by business interests, and by government as it seeks to reassure Americans at a time when questions about the future are in the air and living conditions are getting worse for many of us. The effort to maintain growth is taking wealth we need to live on, especially as the energy resources that make growth possible are getting more expensive in monetary terms. And because the myth of progress is still so strong in America, this impoverishment is denied by leaders in business and downplayed as temporary by government. As a result, the threat of economic collapse becomes more and more likely; and as the threat of collapse is made public by the prophets of doom among us, such as Chris Martenson, and reinforced by examples of ecological disaster, there is more anxiety about the future. A brief but abstract way of putting this is to recognize that as the myth of progress loses credibility it is replaced, for increasing numbers of people, by an apocalyptic myth of discontinuity and collapse.

The ideas of progress and of collapse emerged out of the notion that time moves in a linear form from an ultimate beginning to a final end. This was an innovation that came about when the ancient Hebrews experienced their deliverance from slavery in Egypt. They felt that their God was acting in history. Most people prior to this recognized the divine in the cyclical structures of nature, and time for them was experienced as cyclical return. The historian of religion, Mircea Eliade, elucidated this fundamental contrast in his influential book, *Cosmos and History*. A brief history of the idea of progress is provided in the second chapter of my book on the end of oil.[1]

The important thing is to be aware that the expectation of progress and the expectation of collapse are both destructive of the social order. Progress, understood as economic growth, demands more resources than nature can afford and can thus even lead to collapse, while the expectation of collapse can erode the incentive to build a better society, a society based on ecological respect. For those who feel that such efforts are exercises in futility, the expectation of collapse may be absolute and hopeless.

The belief in progress does have its defenders, and with cheap energy we have indeed enjoyed rising standards of living. Progress can also be understood in a relative rather than absolute manner. For example, progress could be redefined as "doing more with less" at a time when finite energy resources are becoming more and more expensive. For the vast majority, however, informed by corporate advertising, progress means having more energy and more consumer goods. This is based on the wishful thinking that the current recession is only temporary and that we have unlimited supplies of fossil fuels, even in this country, where oil production peaked in about 1970. And this wishful thinking denies any limits to growth, including the refusal to believe that the carbon dioxide given off by burning fossil fuels could be considered a pollutant that might cause global warming. My congressional representative, Fred Upton, recently introduced legislation that would have exempted carbon dioxide as a pollutant under the Clean Air Act. Apparently many Republicans now feel they must deny global warming as a matter of course, as a badge of identity. Whether Republicans can change the laws of nature by legislation remains to be seen.

HOW THE MYTH OF PROGRESS LEADS TO DENIAL

Many so-called conservative people, who do not really try to conserve resources, also resist the notion of peak oil as a geological reality. They prefer to believe that oil companies are holding back production in order to make money, or that speculators are profiteering, or that environmentalists are not letting oil companies drill. They blame such above-ground factors, and such factors may indeed contribute to the high price of oil. People who want to make money, and who are in a position to do so, can easily transform long-term shortages into short-term profit. But we may all need to rethink energy issues. The spill in the Gulf of Mexico in 2010 can remind us that the easy-to-get oil is gone, and what remains is laden with risk. Tar sands in Alberta provide oil but with high carbon emissions and very little net return over the energy invested. The same is true of ethanol which also replaces food production at a time when food is needed more than oil. And while so-called "fracking" can liberate more oil and gas, it threatens to pollute ground water, which is a more precious resource than oil or gas. It is wise to recognize oil and gas as highly concentrated sources of energy that should be used sparingly to help us move toward renewable sources of energy. And even renewables will be inadequate unless we learn to consume less, says energy analyst Ted Trainer.

The reality of global warming, which has already begun, is looming as the most intractable challenge to industrial societies. The widespread denial of global warming shows where the belief in progress leads. Until about ten years ago, informed by a consensus among climate scientists, most people generally accepted the possibility that the burning of fossil fuels was contributing to global warming. We had the Kyoto Protocol designed to reduce carbon emissions and even some half-hearted legislative attempts toward such legislation in this country. According to Nafeez Mosaddeq Ahmed, in 2004 even the Department of Defense emphasized the danger of climate change and urged that it "should be elevated beyond a scientific debate to a US national security concern."[2]

But, as Nafeez Mosaddeq Ahmed also reported, between 1998 and 2005, ExxonMobil funneled about $16 million to various groups with the aim of manufacturing uncertainty about the scientific consensus.[3] These fraudulent claims about global warming were reported by corporate-controlled media to present a so-called fair and balanced view on the topic, both for and against the reality of global warming and its effect on the climate. As a result, there is now a feeling of uneasiness about the climate, but also a growing reluctance to concede that our addiction to fossil fuels could be causing global warming. According to a poll by the Pew Research Center, there was a rapid decrease in the number of Republican voters who believed there was evidence of climate change, down to only 35% by 2009. Increasing numbers of Americans now believe climate change is a hoax.

Surely the corruption of science has encouraged this denial, but the roots of this denial are deep in the American ethos. John Michael Greer has argued that although we think of Christianity as our main religion in America, it is the myth or ideology of progress that functions as the real and effective civil religion in our society, and progress is measured by economic growth.[4] The possibility of limits to growth is resisted and denied. People are glad to feel that peak oil and climate change are a hoax. Cheap energy has given us a prosperous and easy life, and the myth of progress tells us it will continue and improve. The possibility that it could end, that the current recession may be unrelieved, generates denial and anger, along with wild and irrational outbursts blaming various alleged villains.

The problem with this denial of global warming is that it has effectively postponed action to curtail carbon emissions. Mark Hertsgaard, in his book on global warming, laments that we lost a decade during the Bush administration. Instead of reducing carbon dioxide emissions when the time for that was already long past due, the United States increased carbon emissions by 3% between 2000 and 2007.[5] Now, in mid-2011, it is still difficult to see any political will to reduce emissions, such as a tax on carbon. Throughout his book Hertsgaard reports on what poorer countries are doing to prepare for global warming, and he is aghast at the way rich countries, like the United States, are ignoring the issue even as they emit the largest amounts of carbon dioxide per capita. Blinded by the myth of progress and economic growth, most Americans are fixated on maintaining and improving a middle-class way of life. And politicians follow this majority to please the general populace as well as the corporations that profit from this myth. It is up to liberal-minded people who are concerned about saving the earth as a human habitation to make the reduction of carbon emissions central in their lives. There are many ways of doing this: fight corporate power that denies global warming, work for peace when military adventures are bankrupting the country, switch to renewable energy, raise food. But the threat of climate change must be seen as the ultimate problem.

Needless to say the delay caused by the deniers of global warming will make life more difficult. We will suffer through more hot weather, and, with warmer air and water, more violent storms on land and sea. Oceans are projected to rise about two feet, which will cost billions in sea walls near the largest cities or even more if they are actually inundated. The ecological effects are unknown, but will certainly include more loss of biodiversity. Weather patterns will be more unpredictable, with more massive floods in some areas and more droughts in others. All of this will make food production more difficult and expensive. Some of these predicaments are upon us already and most of these symptoms can be expected in 25 years or less according to physicist Joseph Romm who has written a book on climate change. The pace of climate change is accelerating.

THE COMING OF HARD TIMES

In view of these very tangible costs of delay in dealing with climate change, Hertsgaard agrees with activists who are considering the possibility of legal action against those in the carbon lobby who caused the delay with their misinformation.[6] Like the tobacco companies, who eventually had to pay billions to states to compensate for medical expenses related to tobacco, the big oil companies, especially ExxonMobil, the largest and most overt in denial, should be sued to compensate the citizens for the damage they are doing. If nothing else, this would publicize the self-interested nature of their crime. And the damage oil companies are doing to the earth just for the sake of profit is a crime of unprecedented magnitude.

Meanwhile, the elephant in the room is the bloated budget of the military-industrial complex. The military budget takes around half of the taxpayer's taxes and accounts for more than the rest of the world's militaries combined. All this is for the maintenance of the tyrannical American empire, and, as Chalmers Johnson warned us, the cost of empire is leading us to bankruptcy.[7] Hertsgaard reminded us that "The Iraq war alone will cost U.S. taxpayers an estimated $3 trillion, according to Nobel Prize-winning economist Joseph Stiglitz."[8] The cost in money is bad enough, since we have to borrow what we do not have, but the cost in the loss of democracy may be far greater. Americans, many already unemployed and suffering, have so far gone along with this drift toward empire, apparently thinking it would preserve our way of life.

As we add the cost of needless military adventures to the coming cost of global warming and the rising cost of oil, on top of a moribund economy, the expectation of progress as the engine of economic growth looks increasingly unlikely. I want to argue that this is good: we need to reduce our ecological impact on the planet, and affirming recession seems to be the only way we are capable of facing that reduction. I know this may not be acceptable to those in our society who have already been impoverished by the maldistribution of wealth. And I know that the upper 1% does have a lot of money and highly concentrated legal ownership of infrastructure and resources which, if taxed, could help to keep our country afloat. I certainly support those who fight to get that wealth redistributed "downward," especially if that money would be used to help us make a transition to a more modest and frugal way of life, with policies that might offer many of us a softer landing into a more agrarian way of life. As we plan ahead it is important to keep in mind that what we call "jobs" is the form that work took during the industrial era. In a future with more expensive energy, more workers will be self-employed in the informal economy.

Having grown up during the Great Depression of the Thirties, I also know it is possible to enjoy life in more difficult economic circumstances. When we were children, my siblings and I knew we did not have many things others had, but if any of us complained about it, another would remind us that we were poor. And that was understood as an explanation and not a complaint. Where I grew up on the Great Plains we had not only the economic depression but also a prolonged drought with its attendant dust storms and plagues of grasshoppers. We lived on a small farm, produced most of our own food, so we were mostly independent of any kind of commercial food system. My siblings and I grew up healthy and happy even though my parents were unable to pay the mortgage at times. But I was eventually able to join, through education, the great but now diminishing American middle class as a college professor—and I enjoyed it for a while.

But the disconnect between my childhood rural experience and my urbanized adult experience gradually became unsettling. With the social and cultural upheavals of the '60s and early '70s, this disconnect began to seek resolution. Energy frugality and food self-reliance were two of the ways this resolution began to take shape in my thought and life.

If we are to reduce carbon emissions we must reduce our dependence on fossil fuels and this will lower our material standard of living. I am not suggesting any particular level of poverty, but I am strongly suggesting that we should be ready to affirm recession and make do with less when there likely will be less to go around. I am suggesting an attitudinal turn-around, from expecting more to affirming less. This requires a transformation of consciousness. And as we adapt to less energy, either because prices of energy rise as demand exceeds supply or simply because we already have used the best and the easiest to obtain, or because the needed tax on carbon makes fossil fuel energy even more expensive and undesirable, we will have fewer energy slaves to do our work, and we will gradually lose our comparatively luxurious way of life. This was already clear to many of us after the energy crisis of the 1970s. My response to that was to get a half-time leave of absence from classroom teaching, at half pay, to start a School of Homesteading where young people could learn the arts and skills of self-reliance in a rural setting. This was a typical initiative during that back-to-the-land decade, but my academic colleagues thought I was crazy to try to support my family on a half-salary. Fortunately, my childhood experience during the Great Depression had prepared me for that.

MOVEMENTS THAT CHALLENGE THE MYTH OF PROGRESS

In suggesting an attitudinal turn-around I do not think I am preaching an impossible ethical ideal. There is evidence of grass-roots support for this shift away from the still-dominant myth of progress. For example, my current community activity is to help organize a Transition Initiative in my area. This movement was started in England by Rob Hopkins as a way to help people move "from oil dependency to local resilience." (This is the subtitle of his book, *The Transition Handbook*.) Our local group was the 49th to be recognized in this country where there are now over 100 Transition Towns. One of the most common activities people do is to take responsibility for raising food gardens. In this way Transition dovetails with the tremendous resurgence of local food, farmers' markets, and organic farming and gardening. I had already become a leader in the organic food and farming movement in Michigan, work which culminated in the organization of Michigan Organic Food and Farm Alliance in 1991. The Transition movement appealed to me as a continuation of my previous activities, and it now has considerable support and participation by ordinary householders quite apart from farmers.

There are, of course, many other groups that serve as a fermenting yeast in our society.

Many of them are reviewed in books like Paul Hawken's *Blessed Unrest*, which is subtitled *How the Largest Movement in the World Came into Being, and Why No One Saw It Coming*. Hawken argues that there are at least one million, or more, groups working on ecological sustainability and social justice.[9] An appendix of over 100 pages lists the types of organizations he counted, such as "community participation" (10,053) or "sustainable agriculture" (3349). Another kind of focus is in Paul Ray and Sherry Anderson's book, *The Cultural Creatives*. They calculated that there are from 50 to 70 million people who embody new values, half of them spiritual values, that diverge from both the "Moderns" (with their myth of progress as economic growth still the largest group) and the "Traditionals," which include those, especially on the Religious Right, who distrust modern values. The largely unrecognized growth of nature spirituality in literary, religious, artistic, environmental and educational contexts is reviewed in Bron Taylor's superb book of 2010, *Dark Green Religion*.

Still growing is another movement that started in the counterculture of the 1960s and 1970s as "voluntary simplicity". Samuel Alexander and Simon Ussher have published a recent update and explain that it consists of people who resist high consumption lifestyles. This represents a direct challenge to the belief that progress means having more material goods. A characteristic strategy of those who chose simplicity is to cultivate home food production. Alexander and Ussher estimate that as many as two hundred million people in the developed world share the values of simplicity, including 28% of citizens in the United States.[10] Although some adherents to these groups may be aware of the possibility of ecological collapse as a spur to action, they have not yielded to hopelessness, but are working to build a better and more ecologically sensitive society. For these groups the recognition of collapse is conditional. Few of these groups or movements have exerted much pressure to change political policies or redirect our social priorities, even though most of them express deep spiritual commitment on a personal level. But they comprise a large reservoir of potential power for social change.

There are some books that were written during the energy crisis of the 1970s that are even more relevant now than they were 40 years ago. One of these is by Warren Johnson, *Muddling Toward Frugality*. Johnson's approach differs from voluntary simplicity in that he does not emphasize personal decision so much as the ability of people to muddle through the difficulties they encounter. We can now see that the Hard Times he expected may have come about 40 years later and are upon us now. Given the anticipation that scarce and expensive fossil fuel energy would curtail industrial productivity and reduce jobs, forcing changes in the industrial food system, Warren Johnson expected a more decentralized population with more local self-reliance and household production of food.[11] This actually began to happen in what demographers described as a "migration turnaround" during the 1970s. When the price of oil was vastly cheaper again in the 1980s, this back-to-the-land movement ended abruptly. Now that peak oil is here, on a global level, the movement toward a frugal way of life on the land can once again be expected. Urban homesteading has already begun in cities, like Detroit, where land for food production is available as former autoworkers left the city. The emphasis on "reskilling" workshops, now very popular in the Transition Initiative, that help people regain the skills we had before oil did our work, was also anticipated by Johnson as people muddle toward frugality.

COLLAPSE AND TRANSFORMATION

Can these changes happen? Eventually they will be forced on us, but even then they must be affirmed. People who envision the end of progress often move on to the apocalyptic myth of the end of the world. This is an occupational hazard for those who take climate change seriously, and it can be paralyzing. We see the eventual collapse of our industrial society because the oil on which it depends is limited, along with the earth's ability to absorb greenhouse gases. Some of us yield to hopelessness and passively expect total collapse.

But apocalyptic awareness is itself a transitional phase; endings open to new beginnings. As a religious form, apocalypse is revelation;

The End of the Myth of Progress

the end of the old world leads on to visions of a new earth. This is concisely expressed in the title of a recent book on climate change: *Evolution's Edge: The Coming Collapse and Transformation of our World*. The sustainable world we hope for cannot emerge until the old industrial world has collapsed, at least as a possibility in our consciousness. Once this happens we are ready to build the new society along more energy conserving and agrarian lines. This comprehensive shift in consciousness is articulated by agrarian writers such as Paul Gilk.[12]

Let us see how this might work out in food systems, which is where so many of those who question progress are focused. Although most of our food is now produced by energy-intensive industrial methods, food prices will rise as the cost of energy rises. Anxiety about this is widely felt, and this will continue to reinforce local food production and marketing, which has already experienced phenomenal growth. It may be serendipitous that the local and organic food movement emerged even before it was needed. In fact, people who raise their own food find it deeply satisfying and enjoyable. Or it may be that ordinary people, cells in the cultural organism, simply felt the need for local self-reliance and acted on it. This seems to be what happened in the new homesteading movement of the 1970s. The back-to-the-land movement in that decade was a surprise to demographers and cultural historians.

Now, as prices for energy-intensive food rise and markets adjust to this, the structure of agriculture will adapt and land will gradually be made available for smaller farmers and homesteaders. Thus the end of the old system can make way for the new. Could such a modest change be seen as a harbinger of a more general transformation? As more and more people raise and buy food locally, food becomes a central, and centering, activity in their lives. New ways of thinking soon follow these new activities. Raising food helps people relate to nature in a new way as they learn they do not control nature but are dependent on it. Raising food can help people get off the treadmill of linear time toward a life more integrated with the cycles of nature. Thus food provides grounding for the desired transformation of consciousness, a hope we can all share with New Age visionaries.

ENDNOTES

1. Kaufman, *Adapting*, 35–52.
2. Ahmed, *User's Guide*, 33.
3. Ahmed, *User's Guide*, 19.
4. Greer, *Long Descent*, 69.
5. Hertsgaard, *Hot*, 257.
6. Hertsgaard, *Hot*, 287.
7. Johnson, *Dismantling*, 34–39.
8. Hertsgaard, *Hot*, 287.
9. Hawken, *Blessed*, 2.
10. Alexander, "Voluntary," 20.
11. Johnson, *Muddling*, 181–92.
12. Gilk, *Nature's*, 22.

BIBLIOGRAPHY

Ahmed, Nafeez Mosaddeq. *A User's Guide to the Crisis of Civilization*. New York: Pluto Press, 2010.
Alexander, Samuel, and Simon Ussher. "The Voluntary Simplicity Movement." www.simplicityinstitute.org, 2011.
Gilk, Paul. *Nature's Unruly Mob: Farming and the Crisis in Rural Culture*. Eugene: Wipf and Stock, 2009.
Greer, John Michael. *The Long Descent*. Gabriola Island, BC: New Society Publishers, 2008.
Hawken, Paul. *Blessed Unrest*. New York: Viking, 2007.
Hertsgaard, Mark. *Hot: Living Through the Next Fifty Years*. Boston: Houghton Mifflin Harcourt, 2011.
Hopkins, Rob. *The Transition Handbook*. White River Junction: Chelsea Green Publishing, 2008.
Johnson, Chalmers. *Dismantling the Empire*. New York: Metropolitan Books, 2010.
Johnson, Warren. *Muddling Toward Frugality*. Boulder: Shambhala, 1979.
Kaufman, Maynard. *Adapting to the End of Oil*. Bloomington: Xlibris, 2008.
Martenson, Chris. "Crash Course." www.chrismartenson.com
Ray, Paul H. and Sherry Ruth Anderson. *The Cultural Creatives*. New York: Three Rivers Press, 2000.
Romm, Joseph. *Hell and High Water*. New York: Harper Perennial, 2008
Taylor, Bron. *Dark Green Religion*. Berkeley: University of California Press, 2010.
Taylor, Graeme. *Evolution's Edge*. Gabriola Island, BC: New Society Publishers, 2008.
Trainer, Ted. *Renewable Energy Cannot Sustain a Consumer Society*. Dortdrect: Springer, 2007.

3

A View from the "Greatest Generation"

Rhoda Gilman

As the United States descends into fascism the mainstream media assures us that soon . . . any day now . . . we will be coming out of the great depression of the 21st century. Meanwhile the leftish bloggers and environmentalists grow more desperate in their internet rants about corporate oligarchy, buying of public officials, and denial of demonstrated facts. Mesmerized by the tube and the manipulations of the advertising industry, Americans switch channels wearily from the news to the Superbowl.

I am one of the so-called "greatest generation"—called that for what reason I cannot imagine. I do, however, have a lot of stored-up memories. I can remember quite clearly a time when I still felt hope for the country's future. That was 65 years ago. In 1946 I was a college student returning to Seattle from a six-week youth "encampment" in New York City sponsored by a whole list of progressive organizations and presided over by Eleanor Roosevelt. World War II had just ended; the United Nations was forming; old-style colonialism was clearly on its way out. I was still humming the songs we had sung that summer: "Solidarity Forever," led by the New York labor contingent, and "We Shall Not Be Moved," chanted by the Farmers Union kids from the Midwest.

As my train snaked its way across the Great Plains and the Rockies, I had time for reading and reflecting. One of the things in my bag was a copy of the *New Yorker* magazine that I had picked up in Chicago. The whole issue was devoted to the effects and implications of the atomic bombs that we had dropped on Japan the year before. It was the first real report on the subject to emerge from the mists of wartime secrecy. The magazine had sold out overnight in New York.

Its message was as dark as the bomb's own mushroom cloud. By the time we crossed the Cascades and descended into the ever-so-green basin of Puget Sound, I too had crossed a watershed. It was clear to me that what had happened at Hiroshima was not just a mega-bomb. Humanity held in its hands a destructive power that even the wisest among us only half understood, and war must be eliminated at all costs.

Those costs were too high, of course, so we froze it instead and, as years passed, the vision of a better world was encased in the ice of the Cold War. Meanwhile, my own life went on. There was work with the Quakers, graduate school, marriage to a former conscientious objector, a year at a work camp in Mexico, a move to Minnesota, and two infinitely precious girl children who would grow up into a new world of freedom and empowerment for women.

I remember the 1950s for protests against nuclear testing and the rise of the civil rights movement—all with a background of red-baiting and fear. Invisibly but permanently we were becoming a garrison society. The 1960s brought unmistakable signs of yet a new threat. This one came along with what had seemed like benign and beneficial advances. The first warning was sounded by Rachel Carson in her book *Silent Spring*, published in 1962. By 1970 the word "ecology" had become familiar, as well as the threats to the earth's living systems from pesticides, herbicides and toxic wastes. In 1972 another ground-breaking book warned us that there were *Limits to Growth* and that our capitalist economy and the world's population had almost reached them. If we had any doubts about the impossibility of unlimited expansion within a limited system, they were silently settled as we looked back from the moon at our lovely, lonely globe floating in dark space. The earth was suddenly smaller after 1969.

At just about the same time anger over the spreading war in Southeast Asia was overtaken by revulsion at our grossly swelling consumerist way of life. Thousands of young people turned their backs on affluent suburbs, high-tech jobs, and spreading freeways. They took to anarchist philosophy and living on the land, either in communes or on small farmsteads. As individuals and as families they sought an earth-friendly

A View from the "Greatest Generation"

existence through personal choices. Home births, home schooling, and handicrafts were in; shoe leather, sweat, simplicity, and spiritual search were the signs of the '70s.

Organizations took up the challenge also. Most of them addressed particular aspects of the nation's malaise, but one that proposed to change the very foundations of the system was the Movement for a New Society.[1] The MNS had radical Quaker roots. It was the direct successor to A Quaker Action Group (AQAG), which had defied the U.S. armed forces by efforts to run boatloads of medical supplies to North Viet Nam. In the mid-1970s the MNS took shape as a loosely knit network of intentional communities scattered in cities across the U.S. To its principles of decentralization, shared leadership, consensus decision-making, nonviolence, and civil disobedience it added the ringing slogan of "living the revolution now." Decoded, that meant changing the world through one's own lifestyle choices.

Times changed again after the election of Ronald Reagan in 1980. A new military push threatened to seed Europe with nuclear warheads. Peace-seekers and environmentalists there resisted with a political movement that adopted the color and the name Green as symbols. It established itself in Germany with the elections of 1983 and spread around the world like a wildfire. Globally, the Green movement rested on four pillars that echoed Gandhi and the MNS: social and economic justice, ecological wisdom, nonviolence, grassroots democracy.

In the U.S. the Greens coalesced in 1984 at a meeting held in St. Paul, Minnesota. First they took shape as a network of bioregional groups connected only by an information exchange. For more than a decade they were shut out of serious politics by a corporate oligarchy that controlled the two-party electoral system and by a national mindset that made frugality unthinkable. During that time an anarchist Left-Green Network formed and dissolved, while the mainstream of the movement struggled with its a-political structure and clung to the conviction that a vegetarian diet, a brick in the toilet tank, and a bicycle ride to work might somehow lead to change in the capitalist/military/industrial system.

Although the momentous founding conference had been held only blocks from where I lived, I was unaware of it at the time. My own life had moved to a new stage. The children had grown, and after years of illness and depression my husband had died. I now found myself trying to balance a professional career with caring at home for an aged mother and learning to cope with a computerized world. I had explored Eastern mysticism and begun to meditate, but I had also moved closer to the Quakers, drawn in part by the fact that my oldest daughter was a leader in the MNS. In looking back, I have an eerie sense of identifying my life with her generation more than my own. Was I in some sense reborn, I wonder, during all those hours of meditating with the Buddhists?

In 1988 the MNS laid itself down, and at just about the same time Soviet communism collapsed and the Cold War ended, leaving the American empire to tower alone over the world. The U.S. immediately unleashed its military power and reached to control oil resources in the Middle East. Environmental news had also become more grim with the discovery of damage to earth's ozone layer and the first predictions of global warming. I joined the Twin Cities Greens as they turned to protesting storage of high-level nuclear wastes on the Mississippi River flood plain.

Already the Green movement in the U.S. was beginning to come apart, and by the mid-1990s it split between those realists who wanted to join the political battle and idealists who shrank from the moral compromises that would entail. States, from Maine to California, were organizing Green parties of their own, independent of the national movement. Wisconsin had led the way, and Minnesota joined the trend in 1994. This time I was there at the founding. Two years later the states formed an Association of State Green Parties and overcame their distrust of centralized leadership enough to nominate Ralph Nader for president. His running mate was Minnesota's Winona LaDuke.

It immediately became clear that despite widespread support, any third party faced enormous difficulties in just getting onto the ballot. For a hundred years—ever since the rising tide of Populism—states had been putting up legal barriers to protect the two-party system. The door was closing on democracy, and it slammed shut in 2000, when Nader and LaDuke ran for a second time as Green Party candidates. Although excluded from the televised presidential debates and from nearly all other media coverage, Nader addressed an audience of 10,000 in Minneapolis alone. Democrat Al Gore won the popular vote, and that, combined with Nader's vote, beat George W. Bush by a wide margin. But the race was decided in Florida by a contested election. With the active connivance of the Democratic Party, which was fearful of

A View from the "Greatest Generation"

losing corporate support, a Republican-leaning Supreme Court ignored popular will and appointed the new president.

In 2002 the Minnesota Greens found themselves boosted by the Nader vote to major party status and embarked on statewide elections for governor and senator. Ten years earlier I had retired from my position at the Minnesota Historical Society, and during that time I had published one book and had written a second.[2] I had supported the Green plunge into electoral politics because for nearly 30 years I had watched those who practiced a Green lifestyle get exactly nowhere in changing society, although some of them had faithfully walked their talk and set examples with their lives. Even in defeat, I reasoned, politics offers a platform for reaching the public outside a committed circle. It is above all a tool for education.

Life-changing experiences are not common in one's mid-seventies, but they do sometimes happen, and one happened to me. It started with a phone call from Ken Pentel, the Green Party's candidate for governor and an old friend of mine from anti-nuclear protests. He asked if I would be his running mate for lieutenant governor. At first I said no, but when he asked a second time I felt what Quakers call a leading. I was terrified, but I could not refuse. When the election campaign was over, I was a different person, and I have been a political activist ever since.

A decade later, however, things are coming full circle. The imbalance of wealth and power in this country has gone so far that change cannot be won at the ballot box. That became clear in 2008. The rules are different now; dollars, not people, determine votes; military and business necessity will always override human rights and the U.S. Constitution.

Nevertheless, a larger force than even economic crisis or social revolution threatens the industrial system and its global stability. The environmental collapse that we assumed would be centuries in the future seems to be already upon us. Arctic ice is melting with immediate implications for climate change; our power grids, our transportation networks, and our spreading cities are vulnerable to fire, flood, and storm; food, fuel, and fresh water are already disappearing around the world; hundreds of nuclear plants are accumulating wastes that will be deadly for ten thousand years; and only yesterday we learned that ocean life as we have known it is threatened with extinction in less than a human lifetime.

A Whole Which Is Greater

Now, looking back over my own lifetime, what strikes me most forcefully is the accelerating pace of change, both in human terms and in nature. I am reminded of the words of the poet-scientist, Loren Eisley (1907–1977): "Like others of my generation, I was born in an age which has already perished . . . It [is] as though I peered upon my youth through misty centuries." At the time of his death Eisley had not known the internet, the Hubble telescope, or genetic engineering. More and more we can appreciate the insight of the Buddha, that all things are fleeting and impermanent. Even our view of what it is to be human has changed.

Should we despair? No. We also know more about the earth's past and the incredible toughness of life. We are an adaptable, inventive species. But we need to take stock of reality and determine what steps had best be taken by individuals and communities to meet the dire times that are dawning. As Bill McKibben has pointed out, the environment is already a human artifact. That does not justify more reckless technological experimenting. What it does mean is regaining control of our own lives and our ways of being together on this earth—one step at a time.

That may sound like going back to the land or to the MNS commune, and there is a certain continuity, but there is also a great difference. We are no longer a counterculture in the midst of a thriving society. All too soon it will be a matter of surviving the chaos of a crumbling civilization. Some programs, like the Transition Towns movement, have already been proposed in the face of peak oil and financial dysfunction.[3] Although their steps may seem feeble, they have the virtue of starting where people are today. And when the TV screen goes dark . . .

ENDNOTES

1. A recent book examines the philosophy and history of the MNS from an anarchist perspective. See Andrew Cornell. *Oppose and Propose: Lessons From Movement For a New Society*. A contemporary voice for the alternative movement in the upper Midwest was the *North Country Anvil*, a magazine published in Millville, MN, from 1972 to 1989.

2. See Rhoda R. Gilman, *Ringing in the Wilderness: Selections from the North Country Anvil* (Holy Cow! Press, Duluth, 1996); Gilman, *Henry Hastings Sibley, Divided Heart* (Minnesota Historical Society Press, St. Paul, 2004).

3. See Rob Hopkins, *The Transition Handbook: From Oil Dependency to Local Resilience* (Chelsea Green Publishing, White River Junction, VT, 2008).

BIBLIOGRAPHY

Cornell, Andrew. *Oppose and Propose: Lessons From Movement For a New Society.* Oakland, CA: AK Press, 2011.

Gilman, Rhoda R. *Ringing in the Wilderness: Selections from the North Country Anvil.* Duluth, MN: Holy Cow! Press, 1996.

———. *Henry Hastings Sibley, Divided Heart.* St. Paul, MN: Minnesota Historical Society Press, 2004.

Hopkins, Rob. *The Transition Handbook: From Oil Dependency to Local Resilience.* White River Junction, VT: Chelsea Green Publishing, 2008.

Meadows, Donella H., Meadows, Dennis L., Randers, Jorgen, Behrens III, William F. *The Limits to Growth.* New York: New American Library, 1972

4

On Fascism and Democracy

Eric Yonke

IS AN EXAMINATION OF fascism useful or even appropriate today? In our lexicon of political epithets, "fascist" and "Nazi" are among the most commonly abused terms. The temptation proved too great for some protesters who caricatured former President George W. Bush and Wisconsin Governor Scott Walker as Adolf Hitler; so too for some opponents of President Barack Obama. In 2011, the severe curtailment of public unions, one of the first realized goals of newly elected Governor Walker, led some on the far left of the political spectrum to recall one particular early action taken by the Nazi regime and compare it to Walker's achievement: In Hitler's first months as German Chancellor, labor unions were declared illegal and union organizers were among the first opponents rounded up. We can see immediately where the historical comparison breaks down: Protestors around the Wisconsin state capitol were not roughed up by paramilitaries or jailed by the police. This type of comparison is generally counterproductive and just bad history.

Yet we can draw useful lessons from the history of fascism, particularly in its rise to power. Fascism thrives in mass politics, appealing to the fears of ordinary citizens in a democracy, and twisting fundamental ideals such as patriotism and civic duty. As we reflect on democracy in the United States, we would do well to examine a populist movement that exploits public anxiety as well as public complacency to silence political opposition and dismantle civil rights. Fascism in the 1920s-1930s orchestrated the destruction of several republics, coming to power where defenders of democracy were politically outmaneuvered. In the end, many Europeans living in societies with the highest literacy rates in history and working in the most advanced economies traded their political liberties for a promise of order and security.

In many regards, fascism is the darkest temptation of modern civilization, because it corrupts democratic principles and republican virtues in a mass society. Fascism, as a populist movement, calls for moral regeneration and social unity. It presents itself as a viable, and even positive, alternative to the corrupt politics of the current government. Fascist ideals gain political traction in times of economic and political crisis. The temptation is to trade the often burdensome and frustrating duties of citizenship in a pluralistic democracy for a promise of social order and economic security. This essay examines fascism's core principles and the atmosphere in which those principles resonate, ultimately destroying fragile democracies.

Today, political cynicism runs high. "Public service" and "politician" are terms of dubious distinction. Many good and conscientious citizens will not expose themselves to the savage personal attacks of running for public office, even on the state or municipal level. A sense of shared civic values seems to have vanished. These are cause for concern in any democratic society. As one historian put it, "If we are going to build a better future, it must begin with a deeper appreciation of the ease with which even solidly grounded liberal democracies can founder" (Judt 221). In sum, this essay calls on us to consider carefully our obligations as ordinary citizens to defend democracy against the Faustian bargain of trading civil rights and public obligations for an elusive sense of security and prosperity.

≈ ≈ ≈

The term "fascism" originated with the Italian movement under Benito Mussolini, the first of a growing political reaction after World War I. The name "fascist" was then generally applied to political organizations in Spain, Rumania, Germany, and other countries in the 1920s and 1930s. The Italian Fascists derived their name from the ancient Roman *fasces*, the axe inside a bundle of birch sticks symbolizing strength through unity and the authority to govern.

In all of its forms, fascism defined itself through national myths. Mussolini and his followers did not look to Italy's immediate past for inspiration, but instead used Ancient Rome for political inspiration and historical mythmaking. Similarly, in Germany, the Nazi's "Third Reich" was an ideal borrowed from conservative intellectuals who spoke of a future that could be better than the Second Reich (the German Empire, 1871–1918) and as longstanding as the First Reich (the Holy Roman Empire, c. 800–1800). Just as Mussolini would rally Italians through imaginary association with the Ancient Roman Empire, Hitler pointed Germans to the thousand-year empire, or First Reich, which Germans (and other Europeans) claimed as their own from the coronation of Charlemagne in 800 A.D. to the empire's demise under Napoleon Bonaparte around 1800 A.D. The exercise in national mythmaking spoke powerfully to people who suffered terrible losses so recently in the Great War.

Use of the term "fascism" can be applied meaningfully beyond Italy and Germany in the twentieth century because its essential ideas are found in contemporary political movements around the globe. In a comprehensive recent study, the sociologist Michael Mann defined fascism succinctly as "the pursuit of a transcendent and cleansing nation-statism through paramilitarism" (17). Each term in this brief definition describes a key element of fascist ideology and will serve as an organizing theme in this essay.

THE TRANSCENDENT NATION

Nations are latecomers to human history, and yet we treat the nation as eternal and immutable. The "nation" is quintessentially a modern concept born of the American and French Revolutions. As one leading scholar has put it, the nation "is an imagined political community—and imagined as both inherently limited and sovereign" (Anderson 6).

Nationalism was the great nineteenth-century project of constructing standardized languages, folklore and mythology, and quasi-historical boundaries. Nationalists in various European states formed political movements to fight against monarchies ruling over multi-ethnic kingdoms. The new movements wanted political autonomy for their own ethnic groups and, as a consequence, allied themselves with another struggling newcomer, "constitutionalists." While it is tempting to consider nationalists and constitutionalists as one and the same, the nationalists were not wed to any particular form of government. The alliance between the nationalists and constitutionalists was murky at best, with all sides sharing only one goal in common: a desire to change sovereign power.

Establishing the historical legitimacy of the nation was critical for the nationalist movements, but most adherents would eventually accept monarchies as a historical expression of the nation. In some cases, the construction of a national monarchy required tremendous historical imagination, and only by the late nineteenth century did the ruling aristocracies accept a role in the nationalist narrative. It was a compromise position: The traditional nobilities maintained elite cultural and social status, with varying degrees of actual political power, and the modern capitalists increased their wealth and power within the national framework. The nation-state had come of age and the European nobility represented cultural tradition. Nation building was the great domestic project of the European states, and official nationalism became a cornerstone of compulsory public education across the continent (see Anderson 83–111).

The idea of sovereign nation-states thus came to full maturity only in the early twentieth century, and with devastating results. The Paris Peace Treaties after World War I enshrined the concept of national territorial sovereignty and the right of peoples to self-rule—at least for the victors. Violent struggles in Europe and throughout the European empires flared up immediately to determine what constituted "a people" and who by national right controlled the terrain.

The victors of World War I set the territorial boundaries, and the whole history of European nationalism seemed to give credence to hyper-nationalist claims in Germany and around the globe. The fascists supported the notion of national sovereignty based on a nineteenth-century concept of "sanguinity," that is, it required birth or "blood" membership in the nation. Even among the fascists we can find varying degrees of commitment to this definition. Mussolini's regime was much less fixated on it than Hitler's, for example. One historian has appropriately labeled this "ethnic fundamentalism" (see Claudia Koonz). This hyper-nationalism in the interwar period was national sovereignty taken to a logical extreme.

By contrast, U.S. nationalism is based primarily on citizenship. The individual can become a citizen and join the nation through a process of avowed commitment to the constitution and laws. Most U.S. citizens are currently members by birthright, but the United States has long had processes of "naturalization" (an interesting term) as well as a means for the individual to forfeit or renounce citizenship. Of course, the U.S. continues to struggle with immigration policy, and anti-immigration "nativist" movements ebb and flow. Yet U.S. history is a combined narrative of immigrations and the struggle to expand citizenship beyond the narrow confines of a single gender, race or economic class.

Regardless of how one defines membership, the lingering danger is hyper-nationalism and the abuse of national sovereignty. National sovereignty must be understood as a limited power rather than an absolute power. The fascists used "defense of the nation" as the sufficient explanation for almost all of their actions. They also used it to silence opposition viewpoints. To question the fascists, in their minds, was to question the nation. To oppose the fascists was to oppose true patriotism. Unfortunately for us today, this type of rhetoric appears all too frequently. U.S. political culture not only tolerates nation-worship, it maintains a series of taboos around national symbols and political debate. "True patriots" display versions of the U.S. flag in as many public venues as possible, from the inside of meeting rooms to the outside of one's personal vehicle. The careful politician must wear a flag on his or her lapel, and no sporting event begins without the national anthem. While none of this is particularly problematic and can be dismissed as trivial, what is remarkable is the extent to which nationalist symbols and rituals are cultivated in the U.S. when compared to other democratic societies.

The most serious danger of overwrought nationalism is our expansive understanding of U.S. sovereignty and rights vis-à-vis other nations. As citizens of a powerful country, we are quick to assert national prerogative in the international arena. We indulge in an all-too-common hubris of world powers, convinced that our aims and goals are synonymous with true world order and morally superior to others' claims. We are surprised when others defend their national sovereignty against intrusions by the U.S., such as in the placement of military bases or incursions into sovereign airspace or waters. September 11 (9/11) was a tremendous shock to many U.S. citizens, primarily because it was an actual attack on our soil. We then engaged in a peculiarly naïve and telling public discussion of why others hate us. Defending the territorial United States is perfectly legitimate in any understanding of sovereignty. Pursuing a War on Terror, however, with a self-proclaimed right to preemptive warfare anywhere on the globe is dangerous hyper-nationalism.

CLEANSING THE NATION

"Transcendence," in Michael Mann's definition, refers not only to the immutable nation, but to the belief that the fascist movement transcends social classes in uniting all members of the nation. The movement transcends history and class warfare, utilizing traditional symbols and espousing traditional values but within a new societal framework. To preserve the nation, shun contemporary decadence, and return to some pure form of society, "cleansing" is needed. Cleansing the nation of internal and external foes is the fascists' self-appointed duty. Political opponents are not just groups with different viewpoints; they are enemies of the nation and particularly of those who truly love the nation. Fascist "paramilitarism" is therefore, from the fascist perspective, an expression of a popular bottom-up rage against those who are destroying the nation. The fascists construe this violence as justifiable, national self-defense. As Mann argued, fascism is the most revolutionary form of nationalism in its combination of "philosophical idealism and moralistic violence" (10–11).

In contrast to the supposed amorality of democratic society, a popular theme among conservatives of the 1920s, fascists presented themselves as defenders of the moral order, a bulwark against the decadence of an overly permissive age. While their methods were decidedly populist and well beneath the dignity of the wealthy and aristocratic, the fascists claimed they would reestablish traditional values by force if necessary. This was a far more appealing goal to the privileged classes than tolerance and social "leveling" within the contemporary democratic experiments. Like the communists, however, the fascists argued that democracy was incapable of cleansing the nation or even acting decisively, trapped as it was in the fickleness of the masses, bogged down in government bureaucracy, and compromised in backroom political deals. What was needed was strong leadership. For the communists, representative democracy corrupted the working-class movement, essentially buying off the workers with a nearly meaningless right to vote. But the fascists were willing to do the dirty work to fend off godless communism and drive the socialists out of government, all while shaping up a morally bankrupt society. This morally transcendent rhetoric appealed widely even if the fascists were considered brutes. The fascist "moral narrative" cannot be decoupled from the conservatives' aversion to democracy, however, because without the claim to defend morality the fascists would have lost the critical support of conservative parties.

Along with the rejection of amoral democratic society was a somewhat weaker moralistic critique of capitalism. Fascism offered national unity as a vague but powerful slogan against the potential threat of class warfare. Rather than fighting between the classes, the fascists argued that the nation should struggle against its internal and external enemies. The worker-nation needed to unify against its exploiters, to be sure, but not as the socialists and communists would have it. The Nazis combined historical imagination with shrewd political phraseology. The "National Socialist German Workers' Party" was a name crafted by Hitler and the early party members to join "national" and "German" with socialist and worker, waging a rhetorical battle against the socialists and communists by co-opting their words and linking them to nationalism rather than internationalism.

The fascists did not reject capitalism, but they criticized its tendencies toward greed and selfishness. They argued that market liberalism and bourgeois materialism created only self-centered individualism. These were symptoms of a decaying civilization, they argued, visible to all who cared to see. The antidote was not rejection of capitalism. Rather, it was a channeling of capitalist energies to meet the greater needs of the nation. For fascists, democracy degraded the nation by pitting classes against one another based solely on economic interests. Capitalism, they argued, was partly to blame. The fascist movements spoke of traditional values but argued for a new, more socially "just" order. Theirs was a corporatist view of capitalism that allowed for private enterprise and personal wealth as long as the national economy thrived. This would require state direction, but not state ownership. They equated national well-being with social justice. The fascists claimed that, with the powers of the state, they would direct the national economy and create full employment.

THE ROLE OF THE STATE

Fascism conceives of the nation as wholly organic, part of the natural order of the world. The central purpose and function of the state, therefore, is ethnic-national preservation and advancement. In fascist ideology, only an all-encompassing state has the requisite power both civilly and militarily to defend the nation. This brand of "statism," to use Mann's term, is what an earlier generation of scholarship called totalitarianism. Most research has shown the limits of the totalitarian concept, however, and thus "statism" is a more accurate term for the extensive power exercised by fascist governments.

War is an essential corollary to the fascist conception of the state. The fascists not only glorified war, they believed war was essential to the life of nations. War purified the nation and cultivated its masculine virtues. Without war nations become soft, permissive, and eventually debased. Fascist economic planning revolved around military preparedness. The Nazis sought first economic self-sufficiency and full employment with the eventual goal of waging war. Ultimately, nations proved themselves on the battlefield. In the fascist worldview, nations fight and win, or they die out as part of the natural order.

By the dawn of the twentieth century, European civilization had generated the most powerful political and military entity on the globe: the modern nation-state. In its ability to organize people, mobilize economic resources, and build global empires, the modern state was unequalled. It is no surprise then that Europeans in the 1920s-1930s looked to the state for help in times of deep social and economic crisis. But the modern state for most of continental Europe was authoritarian and fully supported by influential sectors of society such as religious leaders. When we study Christian resistance to fascism, for example, we see that Catholic and Protestant resistance was generally not based on democratic goals. To the contrary, the Roman Catholic Church and the major Protestant churches supported antidemocratic, authoritarian regimes. Even the Protestant "Confessing Church," of which Dietrich Bonhoeffer is the most famous resistance figure, generally favored the return of an authoritarian German regime. Statism remained prevalent during World War II, and Hitler's opponents within the German military were traditional statists up until the very end. Hitler's would-be assassins of June 1944 intended to rebuild a state under the traditional elites. Statism was the norm for continental Europe, not particularly unique to fascism and certainly not premised on democratic culture.

Statism is essentially the power to mobilize the state's police authority to eliminate opposition to the government and to utilize military force in pursuit of foreign policy. The conservatives preferred a less aggressive stance than the fascists, but the conservatives fully expected obedience to their authoritarian and militaristic rule. In the early 1920s, with the European armies either depleted or dismantled through treaty agreements, paramilitarism was a ready alternative for the organization and use of violence. Like many political parties on the right and left, the fascists had their veterans' organizations as well as other overtly militaristic arms. Their function was not generally to serve as a *posse comitatus* or a militia group as we might encounter in some corners of the U.S. These paramilitary groups served as honor guards, charitable clubs, and a visible street presence for party rallies. The fascist paramilitary groups distinguished themselves from others, however, by engaging in frequent street battles particularly with communist veteran groups and committing acts of outright political violence. The street battles, often instigated by the fascists themselves, helped convince bystanders that the streets needed cleaning up. The fascists used their paramilitary organizations to demonstrate strength and unity of purpose—and to intimidate opponents.

Yet the fascists cultivated paramilitary organizations only until they gained control of the actual militaries. Then, as had happened with the Nazi rise to power, the paramilitary organizations were either subsumed into state police agencies or branches of the armed forces. In either case, an independent paramilitary arm was an embarrassment at best and a danger at worst once the fascists had control of the state.

ACHIEVING POWER

In 1920s Europe, the fascists were among the chorus of voices criticizing democracy, but the fascists only seized power in countries with very limited experience of democracy. Mussolini's Blackshirts marched on Rome only three years after the First World War. Hitler's Brownshirts attacked a German Republic that had experienced no more than five years of stability. Yet for most of continental Europe, ordinary citizens did not associate their national identity with democracy. Playing to the cultural pessimism of most conservatives and many moderates, the fascists criticized the newly arrived democracies as a foreign imposition of un-cultured mass technocracy—also known as "Americanization." Business leaders and social elites generally fought against the democratizing trends. This is not to say that all Europeans opposed democracy. On the contrary, mass movements among the working people continually pushed for greater rights. The leading advocates of democracy were the socialist parties which the fascists attacked as their most potent political enemies.

Europeans were generally willing to sacrifice democracy as they perceived it in the interwar period, but they did not turn to the fascists overwhelmingly or unreservedly. Nor did they believe that fascism was the long-term solution to their problems. In coming to power, the fascists never polled a majority in open elections. Rather, they managed a significant minority bloc of seats that were needed in some parliamentary systems to break political gridlock. Where the fascists did come to power, they did so by working within conservative blocs. In the Nazi seizure of power, for example, a coalition of conservative politicians and military leaders courted the Nazi leadership in order to form a temporary majority in the German parliament (*Reichstag*). The coalition's ultimate goal was to dismantle the German Republic in order to bring traditional elites back into permanent control of the state. Giving the Nazis key cabinet posts, such as handing the chancellorship to Adolf Hitler, was supposed to be a temporary trade-off. After the new majority voted (further) suspension of the German constitution, then—under the conservatives' plan—the cabinet's power would become subservient to a government answering to the old elites. That is, if the plan had worked, the old aristocratic general President Paul von Hindenburg would shepherd the return of an authoritarian regime. Hitler's parliamentary powers as chancellor would become insignificant and the old conservatives would shoo out the repulsive Nazis.

The German Republic died for lack of sufficient support among the middle and upper classes. The socialists could not do it alone. Most ordinary, middle-class people associated democracy and the republic with the Socialist Party of Germany and to a lesser extent with the Catholic's Centre Party. In a system of universal equal suffrage, these parties were able to mobilize large numbers of working-class voters and Catholic voters, but the fascists capitalized on the antidemocratic as well as the antisocialist sentiments of a sizable portion of the German middle classes, as well as anti-Catholicism in traditionally Protestant areas. These citizens would not defend the republic and its constitution, and would rather see a return to power of the traditional elites than see the socialists or the Catholics continue to control the parliament.

What the conservatives miscalculated were the truly revolutionary goals of Hitler's movement and the means that the Nazis were willing to employ, even with temporary state powers, in order to reach permanent control. A Faustian deal had been struck, and the Nazis came to power legally under the auspices of generally reasonable men.

LESSONS AND CONCLUSIONS

While it is tempting to dismiss fascism as an aberration or an irreproducible mutation of history, it deserves serious attention because fascism grew up in some of the most highly industrialized and generally well-educated societies of world history. Defenders of representative constitutional governance should consider seriously the conditions that allowed fascism to take hold in such "developed" nations.

The differences between then and now are overwhelmingly apparent. Democracy is not a recent experiment for us, nor have we experienced the level of political violence of interwar Europe. We have not suffered the devastation of two world wars on our main territory, or survived in the shadow of massive destruction or the trauma of postwar reconstruction. Despite the clear differences, however, we share many of the hopes and fears of early twentieth-century Europeans. Our future can look quite frightening as the U.S. teeters on the pinnacle of world power. Like the Europeans of the interwar period watching their economies and empires gasp for oxygen, we have much to worry us in the current historical moment.

Whether posed as an economic or moral question, to what extent do we worry about the future direction of our nation? As blue-collar jobs and family farms disappear from the economy, is suburbia where we find our national icons of the American citizen? When social policies are debated, how often is the argument framed as class warfare rather than a common duty? On a global scale, does the so-called War on Terror represent a violent struggle to defend the United States or to assert U.S. power around the world?

Then as now, the most vexing political tool is fear. The fascist movements thrived in an atmosphere of anxiety. World War I left destroyed industries and a starving population in its wake. Postwar reconstruction was fitful at best, hyper-inflation wiped out any modest family savings, and the Stock Market Crash of 1929 resurrected specters of economic collapse in Europe. In such an environment, should we be surprised by irrationality and desperation? The fascists utilized fear to demand limits on representative government. No time for careful deliberation, they cried, the threat to the nation was imminent. Thus "extra-legal" action must be excused. Political opponents such as the socialists, whom the conservatives already considered dangerous to the nation, must not hide behind the constitution and the laws. The fascists saw their task as cutting through the unnecessary complications of politics in a time of crisis.

The misuse of patriotism to silence political opposition or promote self-censorship is another form of antidemocratic hyper-nationalism. Our recent nativist movements have a peculiar tendency to view U.S. nationalism as "in the blood" with a clear preference for U.S. citizens of European ancestry. But more broadly in current politics, conservatives present themselves and their causes as having, at heart, a truer commitment to the United States than liberals ever could. This variant of hyper-nationalism corrodes our political culture by dismissing liberal opposition as unpatriotic or even treasonous. To question these conservatives is to question true patriots. The U.S. has had various internal battles over patriotism, censorship and government spying on its own people: The Alien and Sedition Act of 1798, the Espionage Act of 1917 and Sedition Act of 1918, the House Un-American Activities Committee of the 1950s, and the USA Patriot Act of 2001—just to name a few outstanding examples. In all of these cases, a key justification for the suspension of citizenship rights was national defense. "True patriots" were told they should have no reason to fear the government because they should have nothing to hide. But in all of these cases, we have witnessed egregious civil and other human rights abuses in the name of national security.

Since the defeat of the fascist regimes in World War II, the United States has experienced the sharp acceleration of its own military-industrial statism. The U.S. has also engaged in perpetual warfare through police actions, proxies, and outright invasions. Those who come to govern in the U.S. gain control of the largest permanent military in human history—and they gain only an illusory control of this massive apparatus. In his recent book, *Washington Rules*, Andrew Bacevich outlines the U.S. "path to permanent war" since the creation of the National Security State in 1947. In those early Cold War days, the United States expanded, further institutionalized, and globalized the system. Bacevich describes these developments up to the present day showing how, regardless of party affiliation, U.S. administrations do not question any of the National Security State's fundamental premises. Without hesitation, Congress approves annual expenditures to maintain a global military apparatus much larger than all other national militaries combined. Permanent militarism has become our quotidian. Even the fascists could not have imagined it. Yet U.S. citizens accept this permanent militarism without serious question. "Responsible" politicians do not challenge excessive military expenditures. Even in the leanest years, the Department of Defense receives budget increases even for unwanted projects. These expenditures rarely make the news. This is the extent to which the U.S. citizenry has become inured to statism and militarism in the name of national security.

But now, as the United States economy continues to constrict, losing its preeminence in the world, and after decades of a political culture promising citizens that they should pay less taxes than citizens in any other wealthy nation, the federal and state governments face budget reductions that could force a fundamental restructuring of government. We could consider tax increases, and a few members of Congress have quietly mentioned a need to examine military expenditures, but we will not seriously examine a military institution that could cut trillions of dollars and still be larger than the next ten national militaries combined. Statism and militarism have become integral to our national identity, the bulwark of our current dwindling wealth and prestige.

A vexing similarity between interwar Europe and the United States today is a democracy deficit. Facing a dismal economic future and the vagaries of representative governance, enough Europeans were then willing to trade their civil rights for a promise of security. So have U.S. citizens today. Examining the state of contemporary western democracy, one historian posed the continuing dilemma thus:

> A stable authoritarian regime is a lot more desirable for most of its citizens than a failed democratic state. Even justice probably

> counts for less than administrative competence and order in the streets. If we can have democracy, we will. But above all, we want to be safe. As global threats mount, so the attractions of order will grow. (Judt 220)

The democracy deficit in 1920s Europe differed in kind but not in effect. In contemporary America, political wisdom tells us that low voter turn-out is a sign of stability rather than a sign of troubling civic apathy or psychological disenfranchisement. To maintain our global predominance, military conscription is considered bad policy as it would dilute the professionalism of our armed forces. We pay dearly for our "defense." Political discourse treats taxation as intrinsically evil rather than a matter of civic obligation requiring constant vigilance. The level of political self-censorship is stunning. No politician wanting to keep his seat will openly advocate tax increases. "Freedom isn't free," according to one populist slogan, but what is the individual's price for democracy?

How do we as individuals pay for democracy? Military service was once considered a fundamental obligation, and most wealthy countries today have developed thoughtful alternative national service options for conscientious objectors. Yet only some U.S. citizens volunteer to serve in the professional military. We then pay exorbitantly for the supporting mercenaries, euphemistically called contractors. The concept of citizen-soldier has become deeply malformed and mercenary corporations fill the ranks of their private armies with U.S. military veterans. Under this system, current wars have further deepened a chasm between the perceived "true" Americans who serve and "support our troops"—and do not question the National Security State—and those who do not serve or who question our wars. But a citizen army could not undertake warfare as currently fought by the U.S. armed forces. This only begs the question: Are we defending the U.S. or advancing U.S. global power? Our Faustian bargain for security and world dominance is at the expense of our democracy.

Conventional wisdom now holds that U.S. citizens should pay very low taxes or perhaps none at all, should not serve in the military or perform other forms of national service, and should mostly ignore voting. The democracy deficit has only grown over the past four decades. By their nature, democracies require an active citizenry with an individually shared commitment to the common good. The commonweal must take priority sometimes over private interests. Fascism may have made a similar argument, but this is an example of how fascism perverts democracy, subjecting the individual as much as possible to the will of the state. That is not our condition, thankfully.

The threat to U.S. democracy is ultimately not from some sudden rise of an Adolf Hitler. The threat is from civic apathy, hyper-nationalism, and our quest for permanent global preeminence in the name of security, which has led to decades of U.S. citizens turning inward and away from democracy. So we are faced with a tough question: Do we value safety and order more than defending our political liberties? This is a perennial problem for citizens of any republic. With the economic uncertainties we face, the political forecast is cold and harsh. Hopefully the chilling climate will shake us out of our political passivity. It is time we exercised our republican virtues, recognizing our shared obligations to the common good within and beyond our borders, fully aware that the hard work of democracy is never truly complete.

BIBLIOGRAPHY

Anderson, Benedict. *Imagined Communities: Reflections on the Origins and Spread of Nationalism*. Revised Ed. NY: Verso, 2006 (1983).
Bacevich, Andrew J. *Washington Rules: America's Path to Permanent War*. NY: Holt, 2010.
Judt, Tony. *Ill Fares the Land: A Treatise on Our Present Discontents*. NY: Penguin, 2010.
Koonz, Claudia. *The Nazi Conscience*. Cambridge, MA & London: Harvard University Press, 2003.
Mann, Michael. *Fascists*. Cambridge U.K.: Cambridge U.P., 2004.

5

Resisting Resource Colonialism in the Lake Superior Region[1]

Al Gedicks

UNJUSTIFIED TECHNOLOGICAL OPTIMISM LED to BP's Gulf Coast oil spill and the Fukushima nuclear disaster in Japan.[2] Industry public relations snow jobs prevailed over common sense fact finding and regulation. Regulatory agencies that were captured by the industries they were supposed to police looked the other way as corporate executives cut corners on safety and environmental protection. The public is just beginning to understand the extent of the damage to the entire Gulf ecosystem and to an expanding Fukushima dead zone around the damaged reactors.

Now, proposals to deploy that same unchecked and faulty industrial logic threaten Wisconsin's water—and the Upper Great Lakes. A coal-mining company that has never developed an iron mine is proposing a gigantic open pit mine and massive waste piles that have all the makings of a future ecological disaster that would extend far beyond Wisconsin. The water that flows off the iron-rich Penokee Hills feeds the Penokee aquifer and the Bad River watershed, which flows into Lake Superior and provides drinking water for the city of Ashland and nearby towns.

The company has invested in a massive public relations offensive with radio ads proclaiming that such mining can be done safely for generations while protecting the environment. Even worse, this same company has been crafting legislation that would prevent the public and the state's Indian Nations from challenging any of these claims by excluding them from participation in the mine permitting process. Secrecy is the hallmark of this ill-conceived legislation, with total disregard for public knowledge and input, fundamental water conservation principles, safety and indigenous rights. Local government input would also be limited. This is a recipe for another technological disaster.

ANOTHER MINING BOOM-BUST CYCLE?

Soaring demand for steel, copper and nickel in the rapidly industrializing economies of China and India has led to a mining rush in the entire Lake Superior region of Wisconsin, Michigan and Minnesota. Wisconsin's historic iron mining district is confronting the prospects for a new boom-bust cycle based on the low-grade iron ore (taconite) resources of the Penokee-Gogebic Range that stretches from Gogebic County, Michigan, to southeastern Bayfield County, Wisconsin.[3] The U.S. Geological Survey (USGS) says this is one of the largest undeveloped taconite resources in the country.[4] They also note that previous resource estimates failed to consider the environmental impacts of large open-pit mines and related processing facilities which would determine whether this resource can be profitably mined.[5] Gogebic Taconite (GTac) has proposed an open pit iron ore (taconite) mine along the border of Ashland and Iron Counties. If permitted, it would be the largest mine ever seen in Wisconsin. It would also be at least as controversial as the failed Crandon, Wisconsin, mine proposal.

With a projected investment of $1.5 billion, GTac executives wanted to minimize the political risk of the project. The greatest political vulnerability is organized opposition at the earliest stage of the project. Accurate, reliable information about the social, economic and environmental impacts of taconite mining is likely to fuel the opposition. They were also worried that Wisconsin's mining regulations would not allow such a mine to be permitted. GTac executives discussed these concerns with several legislators and contributed more than $40,000 in 2010 campaign contributions to Republican candidates involved with the mining issue, including Gov. Scott Walker and Rep. Mark Honadel (R-South Milwaukee).[6] Rep. Honadel and Sen. Rich Zipperer (R-Pewaukee) had planned to have the legislature pass a major overhaul of Wisconsin's mining regulations before the end of the Spring 2011 legislative session.

When public and legislative opposition forced the bill's withdrawal in June of 2011, Wisconsin Assembly Republican legislators reintroduced the bill in December 2011.

The Iron Mining bill, drafted with the assistance of mining industry consultants, would drastically speed up the mine permitting process by denying the public and Indian Nations their right to be informed about the social, economic and environmental impacts of mining projects and to participate in the decision making process through contested case hearings and local impact committees.

WHAT'S THE BIG RUSH?

State Senator Bob Jauch (D-Poplar) was outraged when he learned that a Senate and an Assembly Committee were planning to hold a May 16, 2011 joint hearing on the controversial Iron Mining bill that had not been seen by the public. Mining proponents renamed the bill the "Jobs for Generations Act" and assigned the bill to Sen. Randy Hopper's (R-Fond du Lac) Senate Development and Veterans Affairs Committee rather than an environmental committee.

"It is an absolute insult for Senator Hopper to schedule a bill that hasn't even been released to the public. The mining company has been privately writing this legislation for five months. It is only a matter of common decency that the Chair gives the public more than five days to review the bill. I am still in the process of trying to understand what the 186-page bill does," said Jauch. "In five words I think it means 'give us what we want.'"[7] Several of the state's environmental groups, including the Wisconsin League of Conservation Voters, Clean Wisconsin and the Wisconsin John Muir Chapter of the Sierra Club successfully mobilized their membership to force the cancellation of the hearing.

The legislation came as a complete surprise to the communities most likely to be affected by the proposed mining. At a public forum in Ashland in January 2011, Matthew Fifield, managing director of GTac, assured the audience that they were not seeking to change Wisconsin mining regulations or public participation in the permit process. Four months later there was a 186-page bill that did exactly that. "Legislators are totally rewriting Wisconsin's mining laws for one out-of-state mining company that's never developed an iron mine," said Jennifer Giegerich of the Wisconsin League of Conservation Voters. "One of the things they're doing is eliminating many of the public-health and natural resource protections that we have valued here in Wisconsin."[8]

Under the provisions of this bill (LRB 2035) which only applies to iron mining, the mining company will no longer be required to do a risk assessment of accidental health and environmental hazards associated with the mining operation.[9] Existing water quality standards that protect water in the Great Lakes basin will be sacrificed if they conflict with "the need for waste sites and processing facilities to be contiguous to the location of the iron deposits."[10]

Current law has protections against water withdrawals that threaten public water supplies. The Iron Mining bill allows DNR to issue a water withdrawal permit "if DNR determines that the public benefits resulting from the iron mining operation exceed any injury to public rights in a body of water that is affected by the mining operation."[11] Current law prohibits mining companies from dumping their mine wastes on lands covered by shoreland or floodplain zoning ordinances. The DNR would no longer be able to prohibit dumping mine waste in these areas "if the activity is authorized by DNR as part of a mining operation covered by an iron mining permit."[12]

Just in case the authors of the bill may have overlooked some potential environmental obstacle, the bill states that "if there is a conflict between a provision in the iron mining laws and a provision in another state environmental law, the provision in the iron mining law controls."[13] In other words, the Iron Mining bill proclaims that the expansion of the mining industry is the official policy of the state and all other considerations are subordinate to mining.

THE CLINE GROUP OF COMPANIES

The major reason for this assault on environmental protection and indigenous rights is to accommodate the wishes of a mining company to receive a mining permit in record time. GTac President Bill Williams told a reporter that his company may abandon the project if the process takes too long.

Gogebic Taconite is a limited liability company registered on the Toronto Stock Exchange and owned by the privately held Cline Group, a coal mining company based in Florida. Christopher Cline is a billionaire who owns large coal reserves in Illinois and Northern Appalachia.

He has been called the "New King Coal" by *Bloomberg Markets Magazine*.[14] Coal industry publications describe his leadership style as confrontational. In 1999 he closed down a West Virginia mine when workers voted to join the union. He then reopened the mine without union workers. As popular opposition to the practice of mountaintop removal coal mining spread in Appalachia, Cline shifted his new investments to Illinois coal. The company's coal mines in Illinois use longwall mining to remove the entire coal seam. Once the coal has been removed the ground sinks, sometimes to a depth of more than four feet as the earth above the excavated coal fills the void.[15] Environmental groups have protested that longwall mining has disrupted stream flows, polluted aquifers and permanently damaged historic buildings. When the British Columbia government decided to protect the sensitive Flathead Watershed area by banning mining in the Flathead valley, Cline Mining sued the government for $500 million in compensation for the coal licenses it lost. The B.C. government offered to compensate Cline for sunk costs but Cline refused, seeking compensation for the full value of its proposed project. The case is headed for the B.C. Supreme Court.[16]

GTAC'S ATTACK ON WISCONSIN'S MINING MORATORIUM LAW

Senator Rich Zipperer, co-sponsor of the bill, says that mining companies need to be assured that they will get their permits at the end of the process. "The main problem they have is uncertainty," said Zipperer. "I think the current statute is, in effect, a mining moratorium in this state."[17] The main problem for GTac is not uncertainty; it is the certainty that under existing mining regulations they would not qualify for a mining permit.

The current Mining Moratorium Law does not ban mining. It simply requires mining companies to prove their proposed mine would not pollute groundwater or surface water where sulfides are present in the ore body itself or in the rock surrounding the ore body. This is also known as Wisconsin's "Prove it First" law, passed by a 29–3 bi-partisan vote in the state Senate in 1998. The political movement that was responsible for this landmark environmental legislation left an indelible impression on the entire international mining industry. The *Mining Environmental Management Journal* in 2000 portrayed the Wolf

Watershed Educational Project, one of the leading opponents of the Crandon mine, as an "example of what is becoming a very real threat to the global mining industry."[18]

THE CRANDON MINE CONFLICT: 1976–2003

Ever since the broad-based support of an Indian, environmental and sportfishing alliance defeated a proposal to build a metallic sulfide mine at Crandon, the international mining industry has considered the state among the least favorable places for mining investment. In 1996 this alliance mounted a statewide grassroots campaign to convince the legislature to pass the Mining Moratorium Law. Governor Tommy Thompson, who had opposed the legislation, nevertheless signed the Mining Moratorium Law in 1998 to insure his re-election to another term.

Acid mine drainage (AMD) occurs whenever sulfide minerals are exposed to air and water. The most serious damage occurs when the acid dissolves heavy metals that are present in the rock, metals such as arsenic, lead, cadmium, zinc, copper, mercury, etc. These toxic metals can enter the food chain and have the potential to harm people who consume fish with high concentrations of mercury, for example. Mercury can cause brain and kidney damage, behavioral disorders and other health problems. According to a recent study by the Minnesota Department of Health, one in 10 babies along Minnesota's North Shore is born with unhealthy levels of mercury in their bodies.[19] A recent report on the community health risks of hardrock mining (gold, silver, copper, lead, uranium) concludes that such mining "threatens human and environmental health because it is inherently toxic and destructive."[20] These health risks can persist long after the mining is over. "Once acid rock drainage begins," concludes an EPA study, "the chemical phenomena continue for extremely long periods of time. Some of the most problematic mine sites on Superfund's National Priorities List are sites where acid rock drainage has taken place."[21]

The mining industry has not been able to find a single example where they have mined without polluting surface and groundwaters, including the recently closed (1997) Flambeau copper sulfide mine in Ladysmith, Wisconsin. In November 2010 the Wisconsin Resources Protection Council (WRPC) notified Flambeau Mining Company and Kennecott Minerals (subsidiaries of parent company Rio Tinto in London) of their intent to sue for ongoing violations of the federal Clean Water Act, including discharging pollutants such as copper into the Flambeau River at levels far in excess of applicable water quality standards.

This same Indian, environmental and sport fishing alliance supported the Mole Lake Sokaogon Ojibwe's assertion of tribal regulatory authority over potential mine waste discharges upstream from the tribe's sacred wild rice beds on the Mole Lake reservation. Both the State of Wisconsin and the Crandon Mining Company (a joint venture of Exxon and Rio Algom of Canada) sued the U.S. Environmental Protection Agency (EPA) and the tribe in federal court, demanding that the federal government reverse its decision to let Indian tribes make their own water pollution laws. In June 2002, the U.S. Supreme Court refused to hear Wisconsin's appeal of EPA's decision and let stand an earlier federal court decision upholding the tribe's right to establish water quality standards to protect its wild rice beds.

After four successive corporate managements failed to win approval for the project, the Sokaogon Ojibwe and the Forest County Potawatomi tribes bought the Crandon mine property for $16.5 million and ended a 28-year conflict over the mine. It was a stunning defeat for the world's largest resource corporation (Exxon) and the world's largest mining company (BHP Billiton). Following the passage of the Mining Moratorium Law, a mining industry journal described Wisconsin as one of the industry's main global battlegrounds, where "the increasingly sophisticated political maneuvering by environmental special interest groups [has] made permitting a mine . . . an impossibility."[22]

However, with gold prices currently exceeding $1600 an ounce, Canadian mining companies have recently expressed an interest in the Reef gold deposit in eastern Marathon County and in the Lynne metallic sulfide deposit in Oneida County. Another Canadian company, Noranda Minerals, withdrew its application from the Lynne project in 1993 when the Lac du Flambeau Ojibwe and a local citizens group, Environmentally Concerned Citizens of the Lakeland Areas, raised objections about the impact of the mine on wetlands and the Willow Flowage, a state-designated Outstanding Resource Water.

A Whole Which Is Greater

GUTTING WISCONSIN'S ENVIRONMENTAL PROTECTION LAWS

GTac published an open letter to the people of Ashland and Iron Counties explaining why they were seeking legislative changes to the mining law. The ad stated that "the regulatory framework needs certainty." The Bad River Watershed Association responded to the ad saying "We agree. For example, local people who drink groundwater from their wells need the certainty that they can continue to count on a reliable supply of safe drinking water. We deserve a permitting process that will ensure rigorous review before a mine goes forward. . . . The permit process should not allow for a series of hurry-up exemptions to the detriment of our streams, wetlands and groundwater."[23] Unfortunately, under the provisions of this bill there will be no time for a rigorous review. If the Wisconsin Department of Natural Resources (DNR) does not complete their review of the application within 300 days the application is automatically approved.

The present review process can take several years, depending on the complexity of the mine plan and the potential environmental impacts of the project. Mining industry executives criticize the lengthy Crandon mine permit review process but fail to point out that the major reason for the many delays was because the mining companies submitted inaccurate and unscientific information about critical mining impacts. Scientific consultants hired by the tribes and by environmental groups raised questions about the accuracy and reliability of the data submitted by the mining companies and forced the companies to resubmit many studies that delayed the project timetable. This is how the process is supposed to work, especially when large-scale projects, like the proposed taconite mine, can have major effects on the environment and human health.

GTac executives say they want to hear the concerns of the community about the mine but the Iron Mining bill does not provide for local impact committees for proposed iron mines. Under current law a local or tribal government that is likely to be affected by a proposed mine can establish a local impact committee that can facilitate communications with the mining company, review reclamation plans and negotiate an agreement between the local or tribal government and the mining company. The ability of a community to negotiate a local agreement with the mining company is one of the most important powers a community has to exercise some control over the mine permitting process. This was evident during the Crandon mine conflict when pro- and anti-mining groups fought over public participation in negotiating the terms of the local agreement. Rather than provide an opportunity for any mining opposition to have a voice in the permitting process, the Iron Mining bill simply eliminates this requirement.

The Iron Mining bill further erodes community authority over the permitting process by allowing the DNR to issue a mining permit before the mining company has received all necessary zoning approvals for the proposed mining. All the mining company has to do is show that they have applied for, but not received the necessary permits. Once the mining company has the permit in hand they are in a position to dictate the terms of the zoning approvals.[24]

GTac has leases for the mineral rights on 22,000 acres of the Penokee-Gogebic Range, covering 22 miles, near Mellen and Upson in Ashland and Iron Counties. GTac proposes to mine the orebody in phases. The first phase of the project involves extracting taconite by removing about 650 feet of overburden and creating a narrow pit four miles long, one-third mile wide and at least 900 feet deep. The overburden would be dumped in massive tailings piles along the northwest side of the Penokee-Gogebic Range.

MINING AND THE THREAT TO WATER AND HUMAN HEALTH

The process of extracting taconite from the host rocks requires large amounts of water and leaves behind vast amounts of waste rock called tailings. These large tailings piles have the potential to generate acid rock drainage if sulfide minerals are present in the waste rock. GTac's managing director, Matt Fifield, denies that the rock layers covering the iron ore deposit contain sulfides. He told a reporter that "We have no expectations of making acid mine drainage."[25] However, geological evidence shows that there are sulfide minerals, mainly pyrite, in the rocks immediately above the iron formation in the Penokee Hills. This sulfide-bearing layer is called the Tyler Formation and would have to be removed in order to get at the iron ore.[26] Because of the enormous volume of waste rock that will be created from this proposed mine, even a small amount of pyrite rock could produce large amounts of acid mine drainage. Over its projected 35 year life span this mine could produce 560 million tons of tailings and 840 million tons of waste rock (overburden).[27] Does Mr. Fifield really believe that GTac is exempt from natural law? In Minnesota, sulfate pollution from iron ore waste rock has destroyed wild rice beds downstream from mining operations.[28] The sulfate comes from sulfide in rocks exposed to air and water during mining.

The entire rationale for separate legislation for proposed iron mining in the Penokee Hills is based upon the misconception that iron mining is different from metallic sulfide mining and that therefore the existing sulfide mining laws do not apply to GTac's open pit mine. Legislators in a rush to accommodate GTac have not addressed the lack of any scientific evidence to support the idea that iron mining in the Penokee Hills will not cause acid mine drainage. On the other hand, evidence recently made available from the Wisconsin Geological and Natural History Survey includes a core sample taken about eight miles from the proposed site showing sulfide mineralization.[29]

RESERVE MINING AND TACONITE TAILINGS DISPOSAL

One of the early victories of the environmental movement was the successful prosecution of Reserve Mining Company for dumping taconite tailings into Lake Superior. From 1955–1974, Reserve Mining's processing plant at Silver Bay, Minnesota dumped 47 tons of taconite tailings into Lake Superior every minute.[30] In 1974 U.S. District Court Judge Miles Lord ruled that Reserve's discharge into Lake Superior violated federal and state pollution laws and ordered Reserve to stop dumping its tailings in the lake. The key moment in the lengthy court battle was when a chemist with the U.S. Environmental Protection Agency (EPA) found microscopic fibers similar to asbestos in the water supplies of Duluth and Two Harbors, both downstream from Silver Bay. The EPA put out an advisory about the asbestos-like particles because asbestos was known to cause cancer. Concerned about possible health risks, Duluth residents switched to drinking bottled water until a special filtration plant was built.

CANCER RISKS AMONG TACONITE MINERS

The Minnesota Health Department has confirmed 82 miners have died of mesothelioma since 2003. Mesothelioma is a rare form of cancer that causes tumors on the surface of the lung and is usually fatal. Researchers concluded that commercial asbestos was the likely cause of the mesothelioma though it didn't rule out taconite dust as a factor.[31] Some scientists have suspected that exposure to asbestos might be from inhaling asbestos-like fibers in the taconite production plants or from contaminated taconite rocks. Researchers are now calling the asbestos-like fibers "elongated mineral particles" because they are not truly asbestos. Mesothelioma often takes 30 to 40 years after initial exposure before it results in lung disease.

According to Mary Manning, the director of health promotion and chronic disease at the Minnesota Department of Health (MDH), "Those fragments get into the air and there's been questions over the years about what the health effects associated with those mineral fragments are."[32] After the MDH was criticized for withholding data from the public about a dozen confirmed cases of mesothelioma among Iron Range miners, the University of Minnesota's School of Public Health took the lead role in studying the relationship between mesothelioma and taconite mining in northern Minnesota. The Minnesota Taconite Workers Health Study has confirmed a 300 percent higher rate of mesothelioma on the Iron Range than the general population in Minnesota.[33] Before Lord's decision, taconite tailings from East Range mines were used in sidewalk construction, house foundations, road building and winter sanding. After Lord's decision, taconite tailings can only be used at the mine site.[34]

The size, scale and potential environmental and human health risks of GTac's mine proposal means that the public and the Lake Superior Ojibwe have the right to be fully informed about all of the impacts of this project. Under the provisions of the Iron Mining Law, this is unlikely to happen.

UNDERMINING THE DEMOCRATIC PROCESS

During the Crandon mine permit review process the DNR held an informational hearing on the environmental impacts of the project before they wrote an environmental impact statement. This provided an important opportunity for the public to voice their concerns about the project, to learn whether their neighbors shared those concerns and to become actively involved in the permit review process. The Iron Mining Law eliminates this requirement.[35]

Under current law, the DNR must hold a hearing on the mine application which includes a contested case hearing with sworn testimony and the opportunity to cross-examine expert witnesses. The proposed law eliminates the contested case hearings for the mining permit and for any other needed approvals for the mine.[36] It also eliminates citizen suits related to damages from iron mining.

The contested case hearing is the only formal opportunity available to the public to challenge the data and conclusions of the mining company, their consultants and DNR staff about the environmental impact statement (EIS) and the mine permit applications. This right was won by the early environmental movement with the passage of the National Environmental Policy Act in 1970 and the Wisconsin Environmental Policy Act of 1973. The ability of the public to challenge the information in the EIS and the mine permit is critical because the Iron Mining bill says that the DNR "may not consider the quality of the information provided in determining whether the application is complete."[37] The prohibition on verifying whether the information submitted by a mining company is accurate is an open invitation to submit fraudulent information without fear of being held accountable or liable. The dramatically reduced permit review timelines effectively prevent the DNR from checking the accuracy of the data submitted by the mining company. If the DNR doesn't make their decision by the end of the timeline, the permit is automatically granted and the agency must refund the permit fees to the mining company.

These hearings sometimes become the most visible sign for either public support or opposition to the project. In a growing number of cases across the globe, the inability of mining companies to win the support of the local population has led the company to withdraw from the project.[38] The mining industry literature refers to this situation as a failure to obtain a "social license to operate."[39] Potential mining investors are wary of risking their capital on a project facing local opposition and uncertain profits.

IGNORING INDIGENOUS RIGHTS

The Lake Superior region is well known for its rich reserves of iron and copper. The systematic removal of the indigenous peoples from these mineral and timber-rich lands impoverished the Lake Superior Ojibwe bands and enriched several generations of East Coast copper and iron-mining families, including the Aggasizs and the Rockefellers.[40]

Beginning in the 1890s and continuing for the next 50 years or so, the iron mines of Wisconsin, Michigan and Minnesota shipped over 4 billion tons of iron ore to America's steel mills, accounting for more than three-quarters of the nation's iron ore. But all this wealth did not result in prosperous and stable communities; rather, it has resulted in widespread poverty and unemployment. In the post-World War II period, the steel companies diversified their supply sources by investing in potentially competitive sources of iron ore in Venezuela, Brazil, Canada and Australia. The investment decisions of U.S. Steel and Hanna Mining threw an entire regional economy based on mining into a severe economic depression. The last iron ore mined on the Gogebic Range in Wisconsin was from the Cary mine in 1965. A small open pit taconite mine in Jackson County closed in 1982.

Will this boom-bust cycle produce different results this time around? Bad River Ojibwe Tribal Chairman Mike Wiggins Jr. is concerned that this mine could discharge polluted water to the Bad River watershed and the tribe's wild rice beds in the Kakagon Sloughs. The Sloughs are a 16,000-acre complex of wetlands, woodlands and sand dune ecosystems that is one of the largest freshwater estuaries in the world and crucial spawning grounds for Lake Superior fisheries. The Kakagon and Bad River wetland complex has been called "Wisconsin's Everglades."

The tribe's wild rice beds are the largest in the state. Wild rice is a sacred plant for the Ojibwe and an important food source. The plant is very sensitive to water contamination as well as fluctuations in water levels. Dewatering operations at the proposed mine could lower the water table around the mine. "Our lands and water define who we are as Ojibwe people," said Wiggins.[41]

Current law prohibits a mine waste site from being located within an area specified by the law as being unsuitable for mining; within 200 feet of the property boundary; within a floodplain; within 300 feet of a navigable river or stream; or within 1,000 feet of a lake. All of these protections are removed in the Iron Mining Law.[42]

These provisions are in direct conflict with the treaty rights of the Lake Superior Ojibwe, with the UN Declaration on the Rights of Indigenous Peoples and with the recently won treatment-as-state status from the federal government allowing the Bad River Ojibwe to establish water quality standards that will protect the tribe's wild rice beds. "Water and water levels are non-negotiable," said Wiggins. "They are for our survival."[43]

This is not the first time Bad River Ojibwe acted to protect their water resources. In 1996, Bad River Ogitchida (Protectors of the People) blockaded trains supplying sulphuric acid to a copper mine in Michigan's Upper Peninsula. The Ogitchida were concerned that a spill from tankers would poison their reservation water. But they were equally concerned about the mining company's proposal to inject 550 million gallons of acid into underground tunnels only five miles from Lake Superior. Even Michigan's Department of Environmental Quality conceded that if sulfuric acid solution leaked out of the mine it could kill aquatic life in the Mineral River and damage a 50-acre section of Lake Superior.[44]

The Ogitchida made several demands, including an immediate cessation of acid mining at White Pine, Michigan until: 1) the treaty rights of the Lake Superior Ojibwe were considered; 2) there is a full environmental impact statement of the acid mine project; and 3) an inspection, report, and repair of rail lines in Ojibwe territory. The blockade drew public attention to the larger ecological threat to Lake Superior and hastened the closing of the White Pine copper mine.[45]

The blockade also caused some nervous jitters among the corporate management of the Crandon Mining Company who were already facing strong opposition from the Mole Lake Sokaogon Ojibwe. A company spokesperson told a reporter they were viewing the conflict "with a little more heightened tension."[46] If the Ojibwe and their allies could force the closure of a dangerous mine in Michigan they could do the same in Wisconsin.

WISCONSIN MANUFACTURERS AND COMMERCE: PUSHING THE MINING AGENDA

Wisconsin Manufacturers and Commerce (WMC) is the state's largest business lobbying group, representing some of the world's largest mining equipment companies like Joy Global and Bucyrus International, located in southeastern Wisconsin. If large-scale taconite mining is permitted in Wisconsin, these companies stand to profit by supplying the mining machinery for these operations. WMC was a major lobbying force for the Crandon mine and against the Mining Moratorium Law and they have assumed a major role in the current mine controversy. Even before any legislation had been introduced, GTac executives enlisted WMC to run a statewide radio ad campaign promoting the bill as a "Jobs for Generations Act." The ad states: "Iron County could be the center of record breaking job creation that will ripple through our entire state. You see, there are billions of tons of iron ore in Iron County, Wisconsin that can be safely mined for generations, all while protecting the environment."[47]

If GTac is so confident that the taconite can be safely mined, why are they pushing for legislation that will eliminate the present requirement for a risk assessment of accidental health and environmental hazards associated with the mining operation? The public cannot afford to accept the bland assurances of the company and their hired consultants. The track record of taconite mines in neighboring states challenges GTac's claim that mining can be done safely. The John Muir chapter of the Wisconsin Sierra Club has documented that all nine operating taconite mines in Minnesota and Michigan have "recent, serious air and water violations resulting in nearly $10 million in fines, stipulations and cleanup orders."[48] Nor can the public rely upon the DNR, whose budget has been cut and whose regulatory authority has been severely curtailed by the Walker administration.

ECONOMIC ENGINE OR RESOURCE CURSE?

GTac cannot sell the mining project as environmentally benign. They would much rather sell the mine as a solution to rural poverty and unemployment. But are these economic claims any more credible than their environmental claims? The evidence on job creation comes from a study done for GTac by NorthStar Economics of Madison. According to the study, if GTac's $1.5 billion mine is given the go-ahead, the two-year construction period alone would create over 3,000 jobs and $20.6 million in state and local tax revenue.[49] After mine construction there would be about 700 direct mining jobs and 2800 related jobs in the Lake Superior region.

We've heard this story before—mining as an engine of growth. Just look at the poverty in Appalachia (coal), the Ozarks (lead), the Upper Peninsula of Michigan (iron and copper) or Minnesota's Iron Range. "In the United States," says economist Thomas Power, "the historic mining regions have become synonymous with persistent poverty, not prosperity."[50] Economists call this the "resource curse." This refers to the paradox that countries (and communities) with an abundance of natural resources have less economic growth than countries (and communities) without these natural resources. Over the last several decades the evidence shows that dependence on mining did not enable U.S. mining communities to perform better than other U.S. communities. "In fact," says Power, "mining-dependent communities lagged significantly behind the average for the rest of the nation."[51]

During the controversy over Kennecott's proposed Flambeau copper mine in Ladysmith, WMC released an economic study of the potential benefits of the mine that predicted enormous employment gains for Rusk County. The actual economic impact was quite different, as documented by Roscoe Churchill and Laura Furtman:

> While the mine was in operation, there was no real improvement in *any* of the important economic indicators, including unemployment rate, average per capita income, number of people living below the poverty level or population growth. For example, before, during and after the mining years Rusk County's annual unemployment rate remained among the highest of any county in the State of Wisconsin.[52]

Modern mineral mining is very machinery-intensive, creating far fewer jobs than promised. The most competitive mines extract more minerals with fewer workers. GTac's major competition comes from Australia, the leading mining country in the world. Australia has more new iron ore mines than any other country. Eleven out of the 20 largest mega-mines in Australia are for iron ore and all require investments exceeding $1 billion.[53]

The two largest mining companies in the world, the British/Australian Rio Tinto and the British/Australian BHP Billiton are heavily invested in iron ore production in Australia. In response to the expansion of the world market for iron ore and the need to increase production and efficiency, Rio Tinto's iron ore mines in the Pilbara region of Western Australia have invested heavily in robotics, including driverless trucks and automated drilling. Rio Tinto's mine is the largest civilian robotics project in the world and is promoted as the company's "Mine of the Future."[54] GTac's Matt Fifield has said that his taconite mine could compete with established mines despite the difficulty of mining such steep and narrow deposits by operating more efficiently and relying heavily on automation.[55]

If GTac's job projections are overstated, they completely ignore the impact of the proposed mine on existing jobs in tourism, forestry, the Lake Superior fishery and the subsistence economies of the Lake Superior Ojibwe tribes that have treaty-protected harvest rights in the ceded territories of Wisconsin, Michigan and Minnesota. The Bad River Watershed Association, a group of local people who care about the local rivers and surrounding lands, have raised some of these long-term economic concerns in an open letter to the community:

> Gogebic Taconite's potential mine development in the Penokees will bring greater change to the Bad River watershed and the region than anyone has seen in the past 100 years. Quite simply, you can't dig a hole nearly 1,000 feet deep, and pile the waste rock elsewhere without making big changes. There will be impacts to streams, fish, groundwater, forests and wildlife—the questions we are asking are 'What will those changes look like? How will they affect us, the rivers we enjoy, the water we drink . . . ?' It would be a shame to make the mistake of rushing into a mine without a thorough evaluation of potential long-term impacts to our region. This is our home, our past and our future. Let's think carefully about what we do with what we have.[56]

Potential pollution discharges into the Lake Superior ecosystem makes this mining project an international environmental issue under the authority of the International Joint Commission and the Lake Superior Binational Program to Restore and Protect the Lake Superior Basin. The largest source of mercury in the Lake Superior basin are air emissions from taconite plants.[57] The Lake Superior Lakewide Management

Plan currently has a Zero Discharge Demonstration Program to prevent any new or additional sources of critical pollutants from entering Lake Superior.

In a recent letter to Governor Walker and members of the Wisconsin Legislature the Binational Forum recommended that the Iron Mining Bill "require that any company proposing a ferrous (iron) mine in the Lake Superior basin must first demonstrate how the company will prevent the discharge of any mercury-containing materials that may enter Lake Superior or the streams, rivers, and wetlands within the Lake Superior basin."[58]

INDIAN AND ENVIRONMENTAL ALLIANCES BEFORE AND AFTER CRANDON

The Lake Superior region has not only been a site of extractive resource exploitation but the granitic bedrock of the region has made it a potential dumping ground for the nation's high-level nuclear waste. High-level waste is spent fuel from commercial reactors and waste from the manufacture of nuclear weapons. The nation's first major nuclear waste disposal site at Yucca Mountain in the Nevada desert, located on the treaty lands of the Western Shoshone, was not designed to store all the high-level wastes that have and will be produced by the nuclear industry.[59]

The DOE predicted that by 2010, commercial nuclear power plants will have generated the entire amount of high-level waste that is allocated for disposal at Yucca Mountain. A second repository was needed. A 1979 report for the U.S. Department of Energy (DOE) ranked the Lake Superior region as the "most favorable for further study" as a potential radioactive waste disposal site."[60] In a 1983 statewide referendum, 89% voted against a nuclear waste disposal site in Wisconsin.

In January, 1986 the DOE recommended the Wolf River batholith in northeast Wisconsin as the site for a second repository. The 1,094-square mile area within the Wolf River batholith includes parts of seven Wisconsin counties, the land of three tribes (Stockbridge-Munsee, Menominee and Ho-Chunk) and the off-reservation treaty lands of six other tribes where the tribes retained hunting, fishing and gathering rights.

The proposed site also contains the upper portion of the Wolf River, a state-designated Outstanding Resource Water. Studies of numerous water wells in the area have shown that much of the batholith is extensively fractured and contains substantial groundwater which could reach the hot waste. According to the DOE's own guidelines, these geological and hydrological characteristics should have eliminated the site from further consideration.[61]

Part of the attraction of the Wolf River batholith was the tribal sovereignty of Native Nations, which makes their lands exempt from state law and many environmental regulations. Indian lands are also some of the most isolated and most impoverished, making them ideal targets for nuclear dumps.

Ironically, it was the termination policy of the federal government that created much of the impoverishment that made the Menominee reservation such an attractive target. The Menominee Nation had a sustainable forest-based economy when the tribe was "dissolved" by Congressional passage of the Termination Act in 1955. The Menominee, along with the Klamath of Washington State, were selected as test subjects in this social policy experiment. Both tribes had significant timber resources attractive to private companies. With termination came the reluctant sale of valuable tribal property to pay for the services previously financed by the federal government. The Menominee restoration movement, under the leadership of Ada Deer and Lucille Chapman, finally convinced Congress to restore tribal status in 1973.[62] The tribe is still recovering from the impoverishment of this period.

At every stage of the nuclear fuel cycle, from uranium mining and milling, to the testing of nuclear weapons over native lands, to the disposal of radioactive wastes, Native Americans have disproportionately borne the brunt of the impacts of these destructive activities which are appropriately characterized as "radioactive racism."[63] While DOE recognized tribal sovereignty in the siting process, they did not recognize tribal sovereignty when funds were given to the state, but not the tribes, to review and comment on siting studies.

Following the DOE's announcement in January 1986, the agency conducted several public hearings in the potentially affected communities. These hearings brought together Indian tribes and non-Indian rural communities in strong opposition to DOE plans. Hilary J. "Sparky" Waukau, Vice Chair of the Menominee Tribal Legislature, testified at several of these public hearings and objected to DOE's invasion of tribal sovereignty by gathering information on siting without the tribe's knowledge or permission and desecrating their sacred land.

Laura Coyhis, a Stockbridge-Munsee representative, testified that federal treaties could protect non-Indian portions of Wisconsin from being chosen as a site for a nuclear dump. Because a repository could leak radioactive waste into the Wolf River Basin, that would violate the trust responsibility of the federal government in the treaties.[64] After massive public and tribal opposition at the public hearings the DOE said it would indefinitely postpone the search for the second nuclear waste site.

Two recent developments have brought renewed interest in the Wolf River batholith. First, President Obama fulfilled his campaign pledge by ordering the DOE to withdraw the construction license for the Yucca Mountain site from the Nuclear Regulatory Commission. That means there is no federal facility for high-level waste disposal. Second, a recent report warned that American reactors are more vulnerable to the threat of a catastrophic release of radioactive waste from spent fuel pools than was Japan's Fukushima plant because such pools in the U.S. are typically filled with far more radioactive material.[65] What if the tornado that recently destroyed part of the city of La Crosse had hit the spent fuel pool at the defunct La Crosse nuclear reactor just south of the city at Genoa?

If Wisconsin's common sense moratorium on the construction of new nuclear power plants is lifted, as proposed by Rep. Mark Honadel, the chair of the Assembly Committee on Energy and Utilities, the DOE will have all the more reason to reconsider the Wolf River batholith as a suitable site for a permanent waste repository. Under the current law, passed in 1984, Wisconsin has placed two important safeguards on new nuclear reactors. First, there has to be a federally licensed repository for the high-level radioactive waste generated. Second, the power generated must be economically advantageous for state ratepayers. So far the industry has not been able to meet either condition.

Why, after the Fukushima nuclear catastrophe in Japan, does Rep. Honadel want to repeal Wisconsin's waste and cost safeguards on new nuclear reactors? He told Wisconsin Public Television reporter Frederica Freyberg the reason was that "Right now the nuclear energy people don't even have a seat at the table. If we were to want to build a new plant, we cannot because of a moratorium."[66]

Just as with the Mining Moratorium Law, the Nuclear Moratorium Law does not prohibit new plant construction; it simply places conditions for granting a construction license. The real complaint is that the nuclear and mining industries can't or won't play by the rules in Wisconsin, rules that are the result of hard-won environmental victories. Rep. Honadel wants to put the profits of mining companies and nuclear utilities above protecting the environment and respecting the rights of indigenous peoples in Wisconsin. This move has already sparked the beginnings of a new Indian and environmental alliance to resist resource colonization in the Lake Superior region.

On June 9, 2011, environmental activists and organizations gathered at the Sigurd Olson Environmental Institute at Northland College to organize the Penokee Hills Education Project.[67] Inspired by the Wolf Watershed Educational Project that helped defeat the Crandon mine, this coalition of Indian and environmental groups will serve as a statewide resource for organizations, service clubs, media and others interested in learning more about the Lake Superior region and the GTac mine proposal.

POSTSCRIPT

Despite a media campaign featuring statewide radio ads sponsored by WMC, GTac failed to secure support for its overhaul of Wisconsin's mining regulations by the end of the spring 2011 legislative session. The company said they would put the project on hold until state legislators passed the Iron Mining bill.

In December 2011, Wisconsin Assembly Republicans introduced Assembly Bill 426, a nearly identical version of the bill that failed in the last session. The first public hearing on the bill was in West Allis, more than 300 miles from the mine site, but near the corporate headquarters of mining equipment companies like Bucyrus International. Many northern residents got in their cars or caught a bus at 5:00 am to make the long trip to testify at the hearing. Opponents of the legislation outnumbered supporters 2 to 1. Even supporters of the proposed mine, like the editorial board of the *Milwaukee Journal Sentinel*, condemned AB 426 as "a travesty of legislation that will significantly weaken environmental protections and reduce citizen participation in the permitting process. It's almost as if children had replaced Republican legislators and had dared each other to see how outrageous they could make this bill."[68]

One of the big unanswered questions raised at the West Allis hearing was "who drafted the Assembly's Iron Mining bill?" In response to a reporter's question, Rep. Mark Honadel (R-South Milwaukee) made no apologies: "Of course we worked with getting ideas from the mining company," he said. "If a biotech company came here, we would sit down with them and get all their ideas, too."[69] This same logic of consultation apparently did not apply to the Bad River Ojibwe Tribe, which is a sovereign nation with treaty rights in the lands and water that will be most directly affected by the proposed mine. Republican legislators did not consult the tribe about the legislation or about their position on the proposed mine. Nor did the DNR consult with the tribe before it authorized GTac to do exploratory drilling in the Penokee hills. The exclusion of Wisconsin tribes from the decision-making process over mining is a classic case of environmental racism. "If we didn't stand up and exert ourselves, and sound our voices, we are going to be railroaded," said Bad River tribal chair Mike Wiggins.[70]

In September 2011 the Bad River Ojibwe tribal council held a 90-minute news conference before meeting with the governor at the state Capitol. Tribal members told reporters that the proposed mine presents an imminent threat to their air and water quality. "This is our land. This is where we live. We just can't pack up and move," said council member Frank Connors. "Our land is our culture, our history, which runs deep. We came here to protect it."[71] The state's other 10 tribes appeared alongside Bad River at the press conference and the meeting with the governor. While the governor listened to the tribe's concerns, he was upset that the tribe had not chosen to meet with him prior to expressing their concerns in a news conference. The governor told Mike Wiggins that he had read the press release and wondered what else there was to discuss?[72] The governor's dismissive attitude toward tribal concerns was part of a pattern that prompted the U.S. Bureau of Indian Affairs to inquire whether Wisconsin violated treaty rights by not consulting with tribal governments that could be affected by a state mining bill.[73]

After Assembly Republicans ignored citizen requests to hold a public hearing in the mine-affected communities, Democratic legislators (Sen. Robert Jauch, D-Poplar and Rep. Janet Bewley, D-Ashland) agreed to hold their own public hearing in Ashland. Suddenly, Assembly Republicans decided to hold their own hearing several days later in Hurley. At that point Sen. Jauch and Rep. Bewley cancelled their hearing and urged people to testify at the Assembly Jobs Committee in Hurley.

By the time of the January 2011 Assembly hearing in Hurley, local citizens concerned about mining had met with tribal members on the Bad River reservation several times and renewed the bonds of solidarity between Natives and non-Natives that had developed out of the Ojibwe spearfishing conflict and the successful 28-year struggle to oppose the Crandon mine.[74] One of the enduring lessons that came out of that struggle was the recognition that Ojibwe treaty rights were a powerful legal tool to protect the resources in the ceded territory of Wisconsin for everyone. "From just north of the Penokee Mountain area to Lake Superior, our tribe is ready to stand up and protect Nibi (water) for all peoples and future generations," said Mike Wiggins.[75]

Tom Maulson, tribal chairperson of the Lac du Flambeau band of Ojibwe and one of the veterans of both the spearfishing and Crandon mining struggles, reminded the members of the Assembly Jobs Committee:

> You haven't consulted us. Some of you are old enough to understand the fish wars . . . We will decide this issue. We the Anishinaabe have the right in the treaties. It's not a threat, it's a promise . . . We share the resource, but we have the right to identify what the resources are going to be. When you back us in a corner, when you say, 'We don't wanna listen to you Indians,' then I become an activist, a hell-raiser. Are we going that route?[76]

The mobilization of Native and non-Native against the proposed mine was not confined to northern Wisconsin. On January 25 and 26, 2012, Madison for the Penokees hosted a "Bury the Bill Rally" and "People's Tribunal" on AB 426. More than a dozen groups co-sponsored the rally and tribunal, including the Mining Impact Coalition of Wisconsin, Wisconsin Network for Peace and Justice, SaveTheWatersEdge.com, Wisconsin Democracy Campaign, Sierra Club, Wisconsin Resources Protection Council and Midwest Environmental Advocates. Members of the Bad River and Red Cliff bands came to the rally in two chartered buses. During a ceremonial prayer song, Lincoln Morris, a member of the Red Cliff band of Ojibwe, who had brought his drum into the Capitol rotunda, was told by Capitol police he could not finish his drum song. He was evicted from the rotunda and issued a citation for disorderly conduct for drumming even as the Solidarity sing-along group was being allowed to sing during the noon hour as a protest. Two Capitol police officers handcuffed Morris and took him to the basement of the State Capitol where he was locked in a room for about thirty minutes and prevented from talking to his attorney, Glenn Stoddard. Morris has filed a federal civil rights court case over the incident.[77] When the Assembly was ready to vote on AB 426, Republican Pro Tem Bill Kramer ordered state troopers to remove all members of the public who voiced their opposition to the bill and unfurled a banner that said "Bury the Bill." The Assembly then proceeded to pass the bill 59–36 on a party-line vote.

The Wisconsin League of Conservation Voters (WLCV) responded by announcing their first statewide television advertising campaign in opposition to AB 426 as it was then headed to the senate. The ad showed the human health consequences of weakening Wisconsin's current environmental regulations on mining and urged citizens to contact their senators to oppose the bill. "If given the choice between a clean glass of water to drink or one that is potentially contaminated with arsenic, lead and mercury, I'm going to choose the clean one," said Kerry Schumann, executive director of WLCV. "But the real point here is that Wisconsinites shouldn't have to choose. We all have a right to clean, safe drinking water."[78]

While the Republicans dominated the Assembly they held only a one-vote majority in the Senate (17–16) after they lost some Republican senators in recall elections the previous year. Senator Neal Kedzie (R-Elkhorn), chair of the special senate mining committee, made some changes in the Assembly version of the bill in hopes of winning votes from Democrats and moderate Republicans opposed to AB 426. Among the changes in the senate bill (LRB 4035/1) were provisions for extending the time for DNR's review of the mine permit, restoring the contested case hearing process and providing for seventy percent of the mine tax proceeds to be invested in a mining impact fund for local communities. Wisconsin Manufacturers and Commerce immediately criticized the bill for requiring the mining company to pay more in mining taxes.

Senate Republicans scheduled a hearing on the bill for February 17, 2012 in Platteville. The hearing was never held because Senate Majority Leader Scott Fitzgerald dissolved Kedzie's committee and assigned the Assembly bill to the Joint Finance Committee which would make its own changes and hold a hearing. Fitzgerald was concerned that the process was taking too long and he was determined to pass the legislation before the end of the legislative session in March 2012.

Senator Bob Jauch (D-Poplar), who had been part of the special Senate mining committee, called Senator Fitzgerald's decision "nothing short of a declaration of war on responsible government" that will "disenfranchise the hundreds of citizens who are eager to testify at the Platteville and Ashland hearings."[79] Jauch also warned Fitzgerald that taking up the Assembly bill would make it difficult to win the votes of Democrats and moderate Republicans. "The bill the Assembly wrote behind closed doors with significant input from the mining company is unrealistic, it's unfair to the north and it makes Wisconsin government look like some Third World country."[80]

Senator Dale Schulz (R-Richland Center), whose district includes iron ore deposits in the Baraboo Bluffs area, announced that he could not support the Assembly bill because it did not allow for a contested case hearing and exempted iron mines from several environmental protections. Schulz was also opposed to the latest Republican version of the bill that came out of the Joint Finance Committee. Senators Jauch and Schulz proposed their own mine permit bill which restored the contested case hearing and provided that 100% of mining tax dollars go to local communities affected by a mine.

After several unsuccessful attempts at compromise between the Schulz-Jauch and the Republican bills, Senator Dale Schulz joined all 16 Senate Democrats in voting, 17–16, to kill the iron mining bill. Shortly after the vote, Bill Williams, president of GTac, said "We get the message. We are ending plans to invest in a Wisconsin mine."[81]

GTac may have temporarily abandoned its proposed mine but company spokesman Bob Seitz says the firm still wants Wisconsin's mining law changed. Efforts are under way to develop a new "consensus" on legislation that failed to pass the Senate. George Meyer, executive director of the Wisconsin Wildlife Federation, has met with Tim

Sullivan, president of the Wisconsin Mining Association, to develop a compromise bill. According to Meyer, WWF and the mining association "agree on 90 percent" of the issues.[82]

This attempt to bring interested parties together to work out "consensus" legislation that would allow GTac and other mines to go forward, rubs many grassroots activists the wrong way. That process would elevate an unrepresentative group over broad, thorough discussion and scientific investigation.

When Wisconsinites last saw this "consensus" approach to mining legislation, it resulted in regulations allowing groundwater contamination beneath and around mine sites. That ill-advised legislation was the result of a 1980s push by mining companies (Exxon, Kennecott and Inland Steel) and the Department of Natural Resources to overturn the previously existing policy of nondegradation of groundwater. Kennecott then obtained a permit for its Flambeau open pit copper and gold mine at Ladysmith in the early 1990s. Kennecott's own monitoring wells now show the groundwater there is highly polluted with sulfates and various metals.

Wisconsinites thoroughly rejected the lax regulation that "consensus" developed. In 1998 a broad-based alliance of conservation-minded citizens and tribes succeeded in passing Wisconsin's "show me it is safe first" mining moratorium law. A 29–3 bipartisan vote in the state senate reflected the depth of support.

This wise law reflects a high regard for citizen oversight and reasonable prudence. The Iron Mining bill, largely written by GTac, would have exempted the company from the requirements of the mining moratorium law. Any compromise legislation that allows GTac to mine where sulfides are present would threaten both Ashland's drinking water and the Bad River Ojibwe's renowned wild rice beds. One overwhelming message came out of public hearings on the bill written by GTac: the citizens and tribes of Wisconsin will not trade mining jobs for long-term contamination of their water.

Furthermore, the secretive process that produced GTac's bill reconfirmed a broad truth: an informed and assertive public is the watchdog that guarantees the public's ability to question and block ill-advised industrial schemes. When GTac returns, the opposition will be ready to resume the battle.

ENDNOTES

1. This is a revised and expanded version of an article that appeared in the September 2011 issue of *Z Magazine*.
2. I am grateful to Eric Hansen for help in framing this issue.
3. For an excellent overview see Sack, 2006. Gogebic and Penokee come from the Ojibwe word for iron.
4. Cannon et al., 2007, p. 31.
5. Ibid. p. 33.
6. Wisconsin Democracy Campaign, 2010.
7. Jauch, May 11, 2011.
8. Wisconsin League of Conservation Voters, May 2011.
9. LRB 2035, Iron Mining Law, 2011.
10. Ibid. p. 9.
11. Ibid. pp. 16–17.
12. Ibid. p. 22.
13. Ibid. p. 18.
14. Lippert and Parker, October 12, 2010.
15. Rushton, 2006.
16. *Northern Miner,* May 30, 2012.
17. Bergquist, 2011a.
18. Khanna, 2000, p. 19.
19. Marcotty, 2012.
20. Boulanger and Gorman, 2004, p. 10.
21. U.S. EPA, 1997, p. 8.
22. *North American Mining*, 1998, p. 3.
23. Bad River Watershed Association, May 11, 2011.
24. LRB 2035, p. 126. I am grateful to Dave Blouin of the Mining Impact Coalition of Wisconsin for calling this to my attention.
25. Kaeding, 2011.

26. Cannon et al. 2007, p. 12
27. GLIFWC, 2012, p. 2.
28. Hemphill, 2010.
29. Seely, 2012
30. Hemphill, 2003.
31. Associated Press, August 6, 2005.
32. Mador, 2007.
33. Myers, 2012.
34. Bloomquist, August 26, 2002.
35. LRB 2035, 2011, p. 5.
36. Ibid.
37. LRB 2035, 2011, p. 6.
38. Boyd, 2002.
39. Joyce and Thomson, 2000.
40. Gates, 1951
41. Stein, April 12, 2011.
42. LRB 2035, 2011, p. 14.
43. Wiggins, 2011.
44. Myers, July 23, 1996.
45. Grossman, 1996.
46. Imrie, 1996.
47. Simonson, June 7, 2011.
48. Sierra Club, 2011.
49. Newman, April 12, 2011.
50. Power, 2002, p. 20.
51. Ibid. p. 21.
52. Churchill and Furtman, 2007, pp. 884–85.
53. Ericsson, 2011, p. 28
54. Grad, 2010, p. 34.

55. Duncan, 2011.
56. Bad River Watershed Association, 2011.
57. GLIFWC, 2012, p. 2.
58. Lake Superior Binational Forum, June 8, 2011.
59. La Duke, 1999, p. 99. The U.S. has about 72,000 tons of civilian spent fuel and tens of tons of military waste.
60. Yucca Mountain cannot hold this amount of waste.
61. Dames and Moore, 1979.
62. Shames, 1972.
63. Public Citizen, n.d. Also, see Churchill and La Duke, 1986.
64. Gruberg, 1988, pp. 12–14.
65. Alvarez, 2011.
66. Freyberg, 2011.
67. Penokeehillseducationproject@gmail.com
68. *Milwaukee Journal Sentinel*, December 18, 2011.
69. Bergquist, 2011b, p. 1A.
70. Bergquist, 2011a.
71. Richmond, 2011, p. A3.
72. Personal conversation with Mike Wiggins, March 2012.
73. Simonson, February 2, 2012.
74. Grossman, 2005.
75. Bergquist, 2011c, p. 5B.
76. With, 2012
77. Broman, 2012.
78. Ashland Current, 2012.
79. Jauch, 2012.
80. Bergquist, Marley and Stein, 2012.
81. Marley and Bergquist, 2012.
82. Simonson, 2012.

BIBLIOGRAPHY

Alvarez, Robert, 2011. *Spent Nuclear Fuel Pools in the U.S.: Reducing the Deadly Risks of Storage*. Washington, D.C: Institute for Policy Studies.

Associated Press, 2005. "Scientists Wary of Expanding Taconite Tailings Use." (August 6).

Bad River Watershed Association, 2011. "Community Concern for a Shared Resource: Mining and the Bad River Watershed," *Daily Press* (Ashland, WI). (May 11).

Barbour, Clay, 2011. "$1.5 B mine project put on hold," *Wisconsin State Journal* (June 23).

Bergquist, Lee, 2011a. "Republican plan would speed mining permit process," *Milwaukee Journal Sentinel* (May 12).

———. 2011b. "Mining company says project on hold until Legislature changes law," *Milwaukee Journal Sentinel* (June 21).

———. 2011c. "Can jobs, pure water coexist?" *Milwaukee Journal Sentinel* (July 3).

———. 2011d. "Lawmakers got help on mining bill," *Milwaukee Journal Sentinel* (December 20).

———. 2011e. "Water quality authority OK'd," *Milwaukee Journal Sentinel* (October 6).

Bergquist, Lee, Patrick Marley and Jason Stein, "Fitzgerald alters path on mining," *Milwaukee Journal Sentinel* (February 16).

Bloomquist, Lee, 2002. "Study to revisit taconite tailings," *Duluth News Tribune* (August 26).

Boulanger, Aimee and Alexandra Gorman, 2004. *Hardrock Mining: Risks to Community Health*. Bozeman, MT: Women's Voices for the Earth.

Boyd, Stephanie, 2002. "Tambogrande Referendum Has Domino Effect in Peru," Americas Program, Silver City, NM: Interhemispheric Resource Center. (July 16).

Broman, Claudia. 2012. "Morris Files Charges in Federal Civil Rights Case in Drum Incident," *Ashland Current* (May 3).

Cannon, W.F., G.L. La Berge, J.S. Klasner and K.J. Schulz, 2007. *The Gogebic iron range – a sample of the northern margin of the Penokean fold and thrust belt*. Reston, VA: U.S. Geological Survey. Professional Paper 1730.

Churchill, Roscoe and Laura Furtman, 2007. *The Buzzards Have Landed: The Real Story of the Flambeau Mine*. Webster, WI: Deer Tail Press.

Churchill, Ward and Winona La Duke, 1986. "Native America: The Political Economy of Radioactive Colonialism." *The Insurgent Sociologist* 13:3 (Spring): 51–84.

Dames and Moore, 1979. *Crystalline Intrusions in the U.S. and Regional Geologic Characteristics Important for Storage of Radioactive Waste*. Cincinnati, OH. (December).

Duncan, Casey, 2011. "Public Meeting Held on Proposed Penokee Iron Mine," (February 1).

http://Headwatersnews.net/feature/public-meeting-held-on-proposed-penokee-iron-mine/ (Retrieved 5/20/11).

Ericsson, Magnus, 2011. "E & MJ's Annual Survey of Global Mining Investment," *Engineering and Mining Journal* 212:1 (January/February): 28–30.

Freyberg, Frederica, 2011. *Here and Now*. Wisconsin Public Television (March 18).

Gates, William G. Jr., 1951. *Michigan Copper and Boston Dollars*. New York: Russell and Russell.

Grad, Paul S., 2010. "Running with Robotics," *Engineering and Mining Journal* 211:1 (January /February): 34–36.
GLIFWC (Great Lakes Indian Fish and Wildlife Commission), 2012. "Iron mining in the Lake Superior region," *Mazina'igan Supplement* (Spring/Summer).
Grossman, Zoltan, 2005. "Unlikely Alliances: Treaty Conflicts and Environmental Cooperation between Native American and Rural White Communities," *American Indian Culture and Research Journal* 29:4:21–43.
———. 1996. "Chippewa Block Acid Shipments." *The Progressive* (October).
Gruberg, Martin, 1988. "Wisconsin Tribal Activity Regarding Nuclear Waste Siting." University of Wisconsin-Oshkosh, Department of Political Science. Unpublished paper.
Hemphill, Stephanie, 2010. "Mining pollution may be hurting Minnesota's wild rice." Minnesota Public Radio (November 29).
———. 2003. "The legacy of the Reserve Mining case." Minnesota Public Radio (October 29).
Imrie, Robert, 1996. "Rail blockade not solely about acid shipment," *St. Paul Pioneer Press* (August 5).
Jauch, Bob, 2012. "Statement from Senator Bob Jauch in response to the announcement that the Senate Mining Committee has been disbanded." (February 15, 2011). "Jauch Blasts Hearing on Secret Mining Bill." Press release. (May 11).
Joyce, Susan and Ian Thomson, 2000. "Earning a social license to operate: social acceptability and resource development in Latin America." *The Canadian Mining and Metallurgical Bulletin* 93:1037 (February): 49–53.
Kaeding, Danielle, 2011. "Penokee iron mine environmental impacts." News from 91.3 KUWS (January 6).
Khanna, Tracey, 2000. Editorial comment. *Mining Environmental Management* 8:3 (May).
LRB 2035, 2011. Madison, WI: Legislative Reference Bureau. 186 pages.
La Duke, Winona, 1999. *All Our Relations: Native Struggles for Land and Life*. Cambridge, MA: South End Press.
Lake Superior Binational Forum, 2011. "Letter to Governor Scott Walker and Members of the Wisconsin Legislature." (June 8).
Lippert, John and Mario Parker, 2010. "New King Coal." *Bloomberg Markets Magazine* (October 12).
Mador, Jessica, 2007. "Taconite a suspect in Iron Range cancer deaths." Minnesota Public Radio. (March 29).
Marcotty, Josephine. 2012. "High levels of mercury found in North Shore babies," *Minneapolis Star Tribune* (February 2).
Marley, Patrick and Lee Bergquist. 2012. "Mining firm drops out," *Milwaukee Journal Sentinel* (March 7).
Myers, John, 2012. "Iron Range lung cancer study advancing," *Duluth News Tribune* (June 4).
———. 1996. "Greens protest train, method," *Duluth News-Tribune*. (July 23).
Newman, Judy, 2011. "Mine seen as economic boom," *Wisconsin State Journal* (April 12).
North American Mining, 1998. "Troubled times; brighter future." 2:4 (August/September).
Northern Miner. 2012. "Cline Mining Sues B.C. government for $500 million." (May 30).

Power, Thomas Michael, 2002. *Digging to Development: A Historical Look at Mining and Economic Development*. Boston, MA: Oxfam America (September).

Public Citizen, n.d. "Radioactive Racism: The History of Targeting Native American with High-Level Atomic Waste Dumps." Washington, D.C.

Richmond, Todd. 2011. "Tribe pushes to kill mine," *Wisconsin State Journal* (September 22).

Rushton, Bruce, 2006. "The Return of King Coal," *Illinois Times*. (March 23).

Sack, Carl, 2006. "Potential Environmental Impacts of a Penokee Mine." Ashland: Northland College. Unpublished paper.

Seely, Ron. 2012. "Back to work on mining bill," *Wisconsin State Journal* (June 17).

Shames, Deborah (ed.), 1972. *Freedom with Reservation: The Menominee Struggle to Save Their Land and People*. National Committee to Save the Menominee People and Forests.

Sierra Club. 2011. "The Environmental Track Record of Taconite Mining." (December). http://www.sierraclub.org/documents/TheEnvironmentalTrackRecordof TaconiteMining.pdf

Simonson, Mike. 2012. "Groups search for Wisconsin mining law compromise," Wisconsin Public Radio (April 12).

———. 2012. "Feds to look into state's handling of mining bill with tribes," Wisconsin Public Radio (February 2)

———. 2011. "Pro-mining ad running statewide from WMC." News from 91.3 KUWS (June 7).

Stein, Jason, 2011. "Ojibwe tribal leader warns of proposed mine," *Milwaukee Journal Sentinel*. (April 12).

U.S. Environmental Protection Agency, 1997. "Risks posed by Bevill Wastes." Washington, D.C.

Wiggins, Mike, 2012. Personal interview. (March 16).

———. 2011. WORT-FM radio interview. (May 27).

Wisconsin Democracy Campaign, 2010. "Mining Project Execs Gave Walker $10,000." Press release. (December 15).

Wisconsin Geological and Natural History Survey, n.d. "Granitic batholiths: A brief history of DOE's 1980s search for potential high-level radioactive waste disposal sites in Wisconsin." Madison, WI: University of Wisconsin Extension.

Wisconsin League of Conservation Voters, 2011. "WI Conservationist: Mining Legislation is Flawed." Press release (May).

With, Barbara. 2012. "The Anishinaabe Speak: There Will be No Mines in the Penokees," (January 17). http://wcmcoop.com/members/the-anishinaabe-speak-there-will-be-no-mines

6

What's Really Going on In Wisconsin?

Margaret Swedish

My great-great-grandfather, Michael Blommer, helped build the City of Milwaukee. He arrived in Wisconsin from Germany when the state was still the Northwest Territories. According to the genealogy report, he was a carpenter who built boats and helped construct the original Watertown Plank Road, which runs out to the western suburbs. Back then it was a route into the city from the farms that raised the grains for the breweries downtown. He also had a farm in what is now the inner city and, as the report states, "traded with the Indians."

That was my mother's mother's side of the family, deep roots in the geography of Wisconsin. My German ancestors did very well. Two of Michael's sons built small businesses (my great-grandfather, John, was a wagon-maker and his brother, Conrad, founded the Blommer Ice Cream Company) rising up into the middle and upper-middle class.

My mother's father made his living in banking and real estate, creating a fine life for his wife and four daughters—until the depression catapulted his proud family into the misery of urban poverty, marked by cruelties like eviction from their home and repossession of property by the bank. My mother was only ten when the descent began, tough age for a kid to see her world fall apart.

My father's family trajectory was quite different. His father, Janko (John) Cvitaš, left an economic depression in Croatia in the 1880s when he was just nineteen years old to work in the copper mines around the town of Calumet in the Keweenaw Peninsula of Upper Michigan. He later sent for his girlfriend, Ana Pupich. They married in Calumet, had nine kids, and became naturalized citizens. In 1906 he moved his family to Milwaukee hoping for better options for his sons than life in the mines. He died of typhoid fever four years later, leaving my Croatian grandmother with nine kids to raise on her own. The older boys had to go to work to help support the family. My father did not finish high school.

But my father had a great musical talent which he translated into a successful career in Milwaukee through the vaudeville and Big Band eras, and on to weddings, conventions and large civic events, becoming one of the city's biggest music contractors. Steve Swedish and His Orchestra became iconic in the city, part of Milwaukee folklore, a guy whose presence marked some of the most important moments in people's lives—weddings and graduations, New Year's Eve parties and summer park concerts. He was still working out music contracts at age 83 from his deathbed in his office at home. That was 1988.

My parents met when my father hired my mother out of high school to sing with the band (stage name, Maureen Rosay; real name, Mary Rose Reichard). She sang for ten years until marriage and kids finally kept her off the stage. We grew up in a lovely home in the suburb of Wauwatosa. Down the street were a meandering river, parks, a county swimming pool, and plenty of room to play.

My father was also a friend of Senator Joe McCarthy, whose name was spoken with reverence in our household. I met the entire Richard Nixon family when I was eleven years old, on a stage on the tarmac at Milwaukee's airport. It was Nixon's one Milwaukee campaign stop in his 1960 run for president and my dad's band was hired for the event. I was thrilled and honored to shake their hands. My father played all the Republican gigs (some of the Democratic ones, too), and I still have my 1964 "If I were 21 I'd Vote for Barry" button, and my "AU H2O" button, a real collector's item, along with my 1968 Young Republican membership card, which I keep in a little box in my desk drawer to remind me of my roots.

By June of 1968 I was a passionate Bobby Kennedy fan and mourned with the rest of the world when he was killed. That was the beginning of my own personal "great turning." I think of the assassinations of Martin Luther King, Jr. and RFK that year as one of the bookends of that turning, the other being the massacre of students at Kent State University in May, 1970. After those two tumultuous years, there was no going back to my old cultural framework. I had seen too much.

But my roots go deep here in my home state both in terms of these generational origins and then how deeply my parents were embedded in the local culture because of the music. Though I spent twenty-six years working in the Washington, D.C. area on issues of human rights and Latin America policy, I never really left Wisconsin, returning often to be with family, go to baseball games, hear my dad's band, spend time with old friends, finally returning in earnest in 2007. I came back to a state I fully recognize, with all its warts and blessings, for both are in my blood, part of my inheritance. And I came back just in time for the political upheaval of all upheavals, the crashing together of seemingly irreconcilable trajectories in terms of addressing the transitional moment at which we have arrived as a nation. We are a reflection of national trends, national battlegrounds for the soul of the culture, competing visions for how we move through an unprecedented moment in the human experience.

For we are dealing here with a terrifying combination of ecological and economic breakdowns, the two deeply connected, manifesting far greater transitions in both the earth's history and the global economy than most of us realize and that few if any political leaders are willing to articulate, and the life-and-death struggle is on for who will have control over how the future unfolds out of the crisis.

THE GREAT UPHEAVALS

When I was born in 1949, just under 2.5 billion human beings were living on the planet. By the end of the year 2011, we crossed the seven billion threshold on our way to 9–10 billion by mid-century. The population in the U.S. has more than doubled during that sixty year period. In my lifetime, we have seen the greatest industrial expansion in all history, driven by several factors, among them: the post-World War II economic recovery; the rivalries of the Cold War that spurred rapid innovation and technological development, especially in the defense industry; and the emergence of a huge middle class of military veterans and their spouses ready to go to work in the factories. Industry fostered the growth of a consumer culture and paid workers well enough to buy

A Whole Which Is Greater

and consume what industrialists were producing, and the economy kept on churning and growing, woods were bulldozed, housing tracts were bought and filled, streets were paved and highways built, suburbs and then exurbs expanded rapidly beyond the cities, and pretty soon everyone owned a car—or two, or three.

And the baby boom continued. My parents had seven kids. We lived pretty frugally, shared bedrooms with siblings, ate around a crowded dinner table every night. My father paid college tuition for all of his kids because higher education was beginning to be seen as a birthright for the sons and daughters, and the grandsons and granddaughters, of immigrants who were "making it" in this country.

I was raised Roman Catholic and this drive for higher education was especially true for us since Catholics still encountered a good deal of discrimination in our overwhelmingly Protestant culture. One of the ways my parents' and grandparents' generations wanted to prove their mettle was to attach schools to parishes and offer quality education for parish families staffed by willing and available nuns working pretty much for free. Vocations to religious life blossomed in those days.

Education and civic participation were highly valued in that culture. I knew the basic workings of government by fifth grade, and my responsibility as a citizen in a democracy was really drummed into me.

Higher education was affordable then and offered a broad liberal-arts program usually for two years before we were asked to declare majors, no fast-tracking along career paths back then, especially from babyhood on as we so often see today. Universities became fonts of learning, of critical thought, of broad inquiry and questioning about the world (undoubtedly one of the reasons they came under such withering assault from the right in subsequent years).

Both my parents loved history (accurate or not) and they passed that on to their children. I grew up hearing screaming political arguments between my father and his siblings and in-laws because they were all Democrats, union members who benefited from the good life—the wages, work hours, benefits, paid vacation days—that unions had won for them. Politics was a passion, but you didn't stop being family because of it, unlike now when so many families and friendships are becoming victims of the heated polarization.

In many ways this was the typical, even mythic, middle-class America, stuff of folklore and legend, a mythology most of us bought

What's Really Going on In Wisconsin?

hook, line, and sinker. We knew there was a dark side—the Korean War, the atom bomb, the Cuban missile crisis, Soviet Premier Nikita Khrushchev banging his shoe on the table at the United Nations, military coups and uprisings—but that was all background noise for the rise of white middle-class America.

In just the span of my one lifetime, this way of life boomed, this standard of living that spread deep and wide across the country; and in my one lifetime it is all beginning to crash down around us. We are reaching tipping points in many aspects of this unsustainable growth that supports our unsustainable standard of living. These tipping points represent limits to the earth's ability to restore or regenerate what we take from it and to absorb the waste we put into it as the inevitable by-products of industrial development. The result is that the earth's ecosystems are beginning to show signs of unraveling, of becoming unstable, and the future for the species (and millions of other species) is looking troubled indeed.

We have surpassed the earth's biocapacity, its ability to absorb the costs of our extraction, consumption, and waste. We are in what is called "ecological overshoot." In 1986 we crossed over that limit and now need 1.5 earths to continue current levels of human consumption and waste. For everyone to live to the levels of technology and consumption in the U.S. would require four more planets.

So these aspirations of rising wealth across the globe, the endless quest for a standard of living more closely matched to that of the U.S. and other western countries as a measure of human progress, are not only not sustainable, but are in reality impossible. And so is the model of economic "growth" which has driven us to this crisis point, however well-intentioned its original motives may have been.

The environmental shocks that come from overshoot are becoming obvious now, not just from impacts of climate change, but from depletion of aquifers and other water sources, toxic contamination of water, air and soils from the thousands of synthetic chemicals that we have put into our environment and that now invade our bodies and make us sick, from breakdown of ecosystems and habitats causing a sharp acceleration in species' extinction rates, from our development craze that has covered over farmland and wetlands, shifted groundwater flows, preparing the ground for future "natural" disasters.

A Whole Which Is Greater

We have dammed rivers and cut down forests. We have engineered nature and then become economically dependent on that engineering, so that when nature responds to the abuse, we are shocked over and over again—by floods and wildfires, extreme storms and extreme drought, by tsunami waves that can humble the most brilliant plans of nuclear engineers.

Building "The American Dream" has cost the planet dearly. Problem is, we're kind of used to it now, we sort of expect it—this, and more: that's the America in which I grew up. And for the boomer generation and the ones that have followed, this is the world we know. We don't remember another world. Our parents and grandparents did not even want us to know another world, especially the one in which they suffered degrading poverty. But the massive industrial project required to build and support these expectations of growing affluence (unreasonable, as it turns out, for a host of reasons) has taken more from the planet than it had available for this one species, and the price we pay is mounting.

Unfortunately, that doesn't mean the industrialists or their financiers are prepared to alter course, not when trillions in profits are involved. Corporations have shareholders, and shareholders are not likely to respond warmly to a message from the CEO that says: For the sake of the earth, and for the sake of the human prospects of continuing to live within it, we need to plan for the dissolution of the company, or find another way to make a living.

GLOBAL MARKETS CRASH INTO ECOLOGICAL LIMITS

It would be challenging enough if the ecological crisis was all we were dealing with, but there is more. The global economy is also crashing into limits and a major restructuring is underway. In recent decades multinational corporations have freed themselves from national roots, denationalizing markets, investment, and production as trade barriers have fallen and financial markets have opened across the globe. The world has become for them one enormous investment pool and their capital moves around in search of the best possible return in the shortest amount of time. Markets have become more volatile as a result, and nations are losing their ability to make decisions over their own domestic economies. In order to be a player in the global market, countries must play by the rules that are being set by large corporations and their most powerful backers, particularly the so-called G-8 countries (U.S., France, United Kingdom, Russia, Germany, Italy, Japan, and Canada). The combined clout of these economies and big corporate players means that any nation trying to go its own way will find itself shut out of markets altogether.

Now this global economy is facing the same stresses described above—a world in ecological overshoot, meaning diminishing or deteriorating sources for everything they need to continue extracting, producing, and consuming to feed the growth idol. In a world of rising population and rising expectations, we are crashing into the ultimate planetary limit—there is simply not enough available from this precious planet to go on as we are, much less to "grow," even less to grow at the current scale and pace. Everywhere we turn we are running into limits of available water, arable land, minerals, natural resources of all kinds needed to feed industry and even our survival. As these resources become stressed, they also become more valuable. When they become more valuable, they become bigger targets for investors, and the competition is heating up for who will control access to the things we need for life—not only food, water, and energy, but breathable air, *healthy* food, medicine, even nature itself as font and source of culture, art, and spiritualities.

As competition for water, land, minerals, metals, energy sources, and other crucial inputs of industrialization heats up, the voracious global economy meets the ecological crisis and ratchets it up a few notches. The urgency is simply to produce more to meet consumer demand, and at the lowest possible cost in labor, taxes, and regulations. As countries like China and India see a rise in incomes and an emergent middle class, resources must be found to make the stuff they will consume (cars, homes, cell phones, computers, meat . . .) and more pressure is put upon this poor planet and its ecosystems. As industry makes more waste and urgently needs to dispose of it—into the air, water, soil—the pressure to reduce or eliminate environmental protections increases, and that translates into powerful industry lobbying firms at work on legislatures at state and federal levels, and in various international arenas (International Monetary Fund, World Bank, World Trade Organization, Inter-American Development Bank, etc.).

A Whole Which Is Greater

This global market crashes into the earth's limits—and it is not a pretty picture. As these two powerful forces run into each other in increasingly dramatic and destructive ways, we are beginning to get a glimpse of how impossible this is—to use the global economy and its ideology of "growth" to create a sustainable, democratic future in which the basic needs of people and ecosystems are met. Under the model we have now, an era of increasing scarcity and rising demand will move us rapidly towards a world in which we will endure human suffering on a scale never seen before by the human species. In order to have abundance (defined as basic well-being for all on a healthy planet) we will have to address scarcity in a wholly new way.

In order to do that, we have to address the stranglehold of corporate power over our state and national politics that is one of the greatest threats to democracy this nation has seen since at least the 1950s, the era made so famous by our own Senator McCarthy. In order for us to have the urgent conversation about how we are going to proceed in this new global context, we have to strengthen every available tool of democracy, including access to information, vital and relevant education, media that are up to the standards required for this discourse, and an activated, engaged community of citizens willing to put their hands to the plow (because we won't be able to use gas-guzzling tools anymore) to move the culture of this country into a new economic/ecological era. As stresses increase and more of our fragile "security" falls apart, urgency will sadly be our teacher in a way that thirty to forty years of available (and usually dismissed) information and research was never allowed to be by the dominant culture.

WISCONSIN AS BELLWETHER

What does all this mean for Wisconsin? Here's one example. Shortly after Governor Scott Walker was inaugurated in January 2011, Koch Industries, Inc., opened a lobbying office in downtown Madison. One of the first items on their agenda was to meet with the Walker administration to negotiate an easing of phosphorous pollution regulations for Wisconsin's waterways. The paper giant Georgia Pacific is a subsidiary of Koch Industries and has been a major source of phosphorous pollution in the Fox River. Another of Walker's more generous campaign contributors was the road-building lobby. Upon taking office, Walker rejected $810 million in federal funds to build high-speed rail from Milwaukee to Madison to connect with the existing Chicago-Milwaukee route. Over time, the federal plan was to continue on to Minneapolis. Walker wanted none of it, despite the vast potential for job generation and a shot of adrenaline into local economies all along the train line. But his first budget has plenty of funds to build more roads for more cars.

Decisions like these are commitments, transparent certainly in political terms, to our unsustainable, destructive, self-defeating economic path, the very one that has led us to the ecological/economic crisis into which our world is crashing headlong. But these decisions are not surprising given the interests Walker represents. Charles D. and David H. Koch, the now infamous Koch brothers, heavily fund organizations that supported Walker's campaign. They are founders of Americans for Prosperity (AFP) and major supporters of the supposedly grassroots Tea Party. These groups were active voices in the early days of Walker's administration trying to muster a competing presence to the tens of thousands of protestors that took to the streets of Madison and the State Capitol Rotunda in February, March, and on into the spring of 2011. These groups largely failed to inspire much enthusiasm; however, AFP and other Koch-funded groups (Club for Growth is another) made their presence known through ubiquitous TV ad campaigns throughout the winter budget debate.

Karl Rove is another outside player moving aggressively into Wisconsin politics. His political operations, American Crossroads and the secretive Crossroads GPS, receive almost all their funding from billionaires. Rove's groups pour massive amounts of money into campaigns around the country, purchasing TV ads sadly short on truth but high on scary drama. In the heat of the debate around proposals in Wisconsin to end the collective bargaining rights of public sector unions, Crossroads GPS spent $750,000 to air an ad nationwide smearing not only the unions but public sector workers themselves as greedy and selfish.

So what's going on here? What is the agenda of Wisconsin Republicans and their corporate backers, and how does this piece fit into the larger puzzle of the nation's great corporate power grab?

Over the past two to three decades, as the power of corporations over the global economy has deepened, we have seen a shift in our nation's politics. While business interests have always had an inordinate amount of weight in skewing our nation's laws and regulations in their favor, in recent years corporate money has also been skewing the democratic process itself. Corporate money pays for political campaigns, founds and funds a broad array of organizations to represent its interests, develops the computer machines on which we all cast our votes now, machines that have proven to have significant security flaws, and has seeped into the media (most notably in the creation of Fox News, or the AM radio giant, Clear Channel). These groups are waging battles on many fronts, from environmental regulations to tax laws to anti-labor laws to patents on life forms to often pseudo-scientific reports on everything from climate change to the safety of pharmaceuticals, cell phones, and genetically modified organisms.

They can say and write what they want and none of it need be based in fact or truth. And now, thanks to the Supreme Court and its ruling in the Citizens United case, unlimited corporate money floods our electoral process. One result is that it now requires a billion or more dollars to run for president, hundreds of millions for the U.S. Senate, millions for legislative or governors' offices, millions also for a seat on many judicial benches—hardly a good prospect for broad, representative democracy.

The Republican Party became an available target and convenient conduit for rightist corporate interests, especially those representing the endangered fossil fuel industries (endangered for all the reasons outlined above), chemical industries, BigPharma, telecommunications industries, mining interests, and more. These interests have built powerful alliances with social conservatives (even though one can assume that many corporate leaders could care less about issues like abortion and gay marriage) to build a bloc within the Party that has taken over its infrastructure and decision-making. This highly disciplined cadre iterates and reiterates talking points and political positions that are in lock-step across the spectrum of this network of groups and the elected politicians who receive money from them. It does not matter that so much of what they are pushing in terms of policy is deeply unpopular and will cause harm to growing millions of Americans—the messaging is evocative, sensationalist, and effective. Rather than reveal their underlying intentions, the messaging tends to demonize opponents, often in very personal terms, appealing indirectly (and sometimes directly) to some of the worst of our deep-seated cultural baggage, like racism, classism, sexism, and hatred of immigrants who are not wealthy.

When private sector workers—who have lost union representation, who have seen their wages fall, benefits disappear, or who are on unemployment roles and can't find work, while corporate bosses are making record profits and incomes—are voting for right-wing politicians because they oppose gay marriage and support concealed carry, one gets a sense of the incredible success of this strategy.

What does the corporate right want? It is not enough to say they want access to resources, fewer regulations and limits on their corporate practices, and lower taxes on corporate wealth. The heart of this political agenda is to gut government itself, to take as much money as they can out of the public sector and make it available for private investment, for corporate profit. What they want is to privatize more and more government services. What they want to get their hands on are huge pools of money, like the Social Security Trust Fund, an enormous potential source of investor wealth. What they want is a corporate state. In these times it is not too much to say that they want unfettered power over the lives of you and me, over the global economy, over the State of Wisconsin, to put our labor and our resources, and even our small savings and retirement funds, at the service of their financial interests.

In Wisconsin we are seeing expression of this national trend, and indeed we have become a key testing ground to see just how far corporate interests can go, a central battleground for the future of the nation. The 2011–2013 state budget made this abundantly clear. The size of government is being reduced through budget cuts effecting state and local services. More and more of the public sector is being dismantled, state services are being put into the hands of private contractors and subcontractors whose wages lag well behind government workers, with fewer protections and benefits (if any benefits at all). Regulations are being eased so that businesses have a freer climate in which to operate, fewer constraints, fewer labor rights to restrict their production practices, lower taxes—all of this at the expense of wage earners, the environment, and the well-being especially of those on the margins of society—the poor, kids, elderly, disabled, and the unemployed. It is largely these "marginal" populations who are seeing vital services cut and who have few if any resources to make up for those losses.

A Whole Which Is Greater

What is happening in Wisconsin is not unique to us, but rather part of a national strategy of the corporate right and states' rights advocates to undermine government itself, erode the authority of the federal government, and free up more public money—as in taxpayers' money—to be made available for corporate investment. They want more of our money freed up from government services to be made available to financiers and corporations for private investment and the benefit of their stockholders.

When we understand this, it is easier to understand, for example, Representative Paul Ryan's (R-WI) plan for Medicare. His plan would change Medicare from a government program, paid into by our tax dollars over the course of our working lives then paid back to us with health care in our elder years for a small premium, to a voucher program that will put that public money into the coffers of the health insurance industry. This is why the health insurance industry supports politicians who will back privatizing programs like this one, and why they spend millions of dollars every year for lobbyists in Washington, D.C., and in our state capitals. Health insurance and private capital investors are behind a good deal of disinformation regarding a publicly funded single-payer system. Sadly, the scare tactics and distortions work.

This is also why Social Security is in the bull's-eye for financial institutions and the corporate right—imagine the glee when they consider the possibilities of getting their hands on the Social Security Trust Fund, the retirement funds of all Americans who paid into it over the course of their working lives!

As the corporate right and the politicians who represent their interests use budget deficits to create fake alarm scenarios about government being "broke," a favorite Walker sound bite ("broke," by the way, is when you have no money, not when you have lots of money but expenditures exceed revenue—a budget deficit is not the same as being "broke"), the real point here is to starve the government of revenues, and then use deficits as an excuse to privatize services, which motivation and logic has then changed the public mandate completely, from delivering services to making a profit.

Governor Walker wants to make it easier for business to operate in Wisconsin. In the context of this scary evolution of concentrating corporate power combined with the ecological crisis, the crisis of looming scarcities and the global economic crunch as the economy tries to meet accelerating demand, one gets a sense of what the politics of his administration will mean for this state in a fiercely competitive world of shrinking resources and a large pool of cheap labor.

Here in Wisconsin, the unraveling of the democracy we once knew has become apparent. This is not simply a matter of rightist government being elected into office in 2010, of conservative politicians backed by special interests taking control of all three branches of government in an election marked by low voter turnout. The strategies that brought about this result have been at work in our system for a long time, only those who tried to ring the alarm bells were often ridiculed or accused of excessive partisanship.

Evidence of the decline of the middle class has been around for some time, as has the arrival of a kind of politics marked by extreme polarization and incivility. It's just that when it became our turn, and then when the turnover in state government was so total and the opposition rendered so powerless, we were taken a bit by surprise. And now, as with the weather, we are stunned by shock after shock as we see the political culture of our state go into steep decline. While an inspiring opposition has emerged to show itself in the streets of Madison and elsewhere in the state, it came too late to change the power trajectory within our state government. The 2011–2013 budget has put in place programs and policies that will be difficult to reverse in the short or medium term, even in the event that another election shifts the power balance in Madison.

While 2012 turned out to be an historic political year in the state with the successful campaign to force a recall election of Scott Walker, the end result was to keep everything pretty much in place politically. And the effort did nothing to ease the polarization that has heated up the state's politics. Meanwhile, redistricting under a Republican-controlled state government means that Democrats will have a hard time taking back political power any time soon.

This political impasse is happening at a time when we face challenges of changing climate and depleted resources, as we move into an era of long-term scarcities all around the planet, as we face the urgent need to reflect deeply and quickly on how we are going to live within the balance of nature before it can no longer hold us as we shred its carefully balanced ecosystems—and as more and more economic and political power is being taken away from the voter, the citizen, the worker, the folks, and given to the corporate and financial sectors that simply do not have our interests at heart. As resources become scarce, the question of who will control how they are used, and to whose benefit, has become one of the most important questions of our time.

We need remind ourselves—and it is sad that we need to do so—that government and business are not the same. They do not serve the same functions in society. We often hear the mantra that government should operate more like a business. Actually, no, it should not. Government should *not* operate like a business. Business exists to make money; in its best expression it combines that motive with a useful service, with vital innovation, with production of goods or services actually useful to the human endeavor. But business is not a democracy; business is beholden to its owners, its CEOs, its stockholders. It doesn't represent me or my interests until I am an investor of some means. Even a small stockholder has no power over corporate decisions.

Government, on the other hand, exists to provide services like schools, roads, courts, elections, firefighters, police, libraries, and a social safety net for vulnerable populations; to ensure protection of the rights of its citizens whom it is supposed to represent, sometimes in the face of threats from the corporate sector (e.g., violation of labor and environmental laws, malfeasance or corruption); to provide laws and regulations to guide the social life of the society and then ensure that they are enforced.

To confuse these two roles is dangerous. It is also disingenuous. And it is also one of our most important cultural debates at this moment. For two or three decades now, we have been witnessing a fierce assault on the legitimacy of government itself. This is usually followed by an affirmation of the wisdom and genius of private markets and the need to cut them free from government rules and regulations.

In Wisconsin we are getting a glimpse of how this assault translates into policy, but not only from the Walker administration. Previous governors of both parties have been anxious to promote business, often at the cost of union rights and the wages and benefits of workers. With Walker this tendency has taken a giant step by virtue of the fact that all three branches of our state government are in the hands of corporate-backed rightwing politicians and judges. Not even the record crowds at rallies and protests all through the first six months of 2011 could impact this direction. Democracy, depending as it does on our system of checks and balances and a basic fairness in the electoral process, is in grave jeopardy in Wisconsin as we have seen corporate money pour into the state, as elections themselves are called into question, as computer voting and partisan control of local voting procedures has obviously become subject to corruption and doubt.

This is not a pretty picture. It is actually rather frightening. However, it is not the only thing that is going on, and this, too, is something special about Wisconsin.

WISCONSIN'S POSSIBLE TRUMP CARD— A REBIRTH OF POPULAR DEMOCRACY

For all this very bad news, of course, something else happened in Wisconsin in 2011. Citizens did not take all this lying down—and then some. With many people saying they never saw this coming, with thousands of people expressing buyers' remorse, or regretting that they just couldn't make it to the polls in November 2010, and with not only basic rights but also well-being suddenly threatened, Wisconsin's long tradition of popular democracy suddenly reawakened. What happened is that citizens of the state began to realize what lethargy, inertia, and complacency can do, what can happen when we are not paying attention.

In mid-February 2011 hundreds of protestors occupied the Wisconsin State Capitol and refused to leave—for weeks. Outside, masses of protestors numbering in the tens of thousands began gathering weekend after weekend, their numbers growing in response to fourteen Democratic state senators who stopped a senate vote on a budget repair bill by leaving the state, denying the body a needed quorum. While the immediate trigger of these historic protests was Walker's move to eliminate the collective bargaining rights of public sector worker unions, it became clear quickly that something more was at stake—Wisconsin democracy itself, the state's deeply rooted history of open government, and a sense of basic fairness and decency in the democratic process that the new Republican regime was throwing out the capitol windows.

But when the Republicans attempted to close the doors of the capitol to Wisconsin's citizens—a move actually prohibited in the state constitution—something else was triggered: a passionate, angry, deeply felt reassertion of Wisconsin's democratic culture.

Democrats in the assembly brought desks and staff outside in the mid-winter cold to meet with their constituents. Some opened first floor windows so that food could be passed into the building for the protestors inside. Then the police began locking down the windows.

I stood in a large crowd in front of one of those doors one cold March day when one of the assembly Democrats came storming out the door crying out, "Food! We need food in here!" Seconds later, food was being passed over the heads of the masses—bunches of bananas, oranges, bread, a jug of juice, whatever people had on hand—and the fearless state representative returned through the door with his arms full of food.

I will never, ever forget the chant that day: "Let us in, please! Let us in, please!" Such was the spirit of Wisconsin citizens protesting the takeover of their democracy.

Then there were the pizza orders that came from all over the world (seventy countries by one report)—pizzas for the protestors. Every now and again, a van would pull up in the midst of the crowd and start handing out slices to the folks in the streets. Most of the orders went to a place called Ian's, which reported that it handed out more than 60,000 pizza slices over the course of those several weeks of weekend mass gatherings.

Democracy became a community of solidarity in the streets, an experience that few of us are likely to forget. But inside, something else was going on. The doors to our state capitol were closed. There were secret meetings and surprise late day and late night votes. State Republicans shut down the democratic process because they did not want to hear from their opponents—and why should they? They could now do whatever they wanted, and it was clear they wanted to get as much of that *whatever* done in the shortest amount of time before the public backlash would become political backlash that would come to haunt them.

But after the damage was done and the protestors went home, much of that popular energy was translated into political organizing, resulting in a series of recall efforts that gained more national notoriety for the state. Many political battles were lost in 2011, but the work of restoring popular democracy had just begun. However, given the imbalance of power right now, this incipient democracy movement is going to have to mature quickly, to move beyond sector interests to a broad solidarity among all the communities, including eco-communities, under attack from the state's GOP.

The only thing that can defeat unlimited corporate money is people, lots and lots of people.

This is Wisconsin's trump card and it is not yet clear how well it will be played. But first it is important to know what one is up against, what the real battle is so that the struggle is not being waged on the side issues, the distractions. The soul of the state is at stake—what kind of people we are, who we want to be, and what quality of life we want to have for our kids and grandkids.

As I ponder the lives of my ancestors these days, I try to imagine myself in their shoes facing the daunting challenges they confronted to survive in the new land, how hard they worked, what they built, the spirit that drove them. We could learn something from this. That energy was translated into building an "American Dream" that turns out not to be sustainable, no longer realistic on our beautiful but finite planet. But what made it possible for them to survive and thrive was a dedication to building a new way of life that would be better than the old way of life.

And that is where we are right now, faced with the challenge of creating a new way of life. What do we want our Wisconsin to be? Who will determine its future? I know that I would rather pose those questions to the people in the streets, chanting politely to be let in to their state house, passing food over their heads to feed the hungry inside, than to the Kochs and other corporate billionaires who simply do not see, or even care to see, the Wisconsin that I see—and cherish.

I would rather hear from the teachers, the firefighters, the folks getting BadgerCare, the seniors whose lives are so deeply rooted in this state, the trash collectors, the family farmers, the folks in our cities struggling to hold their families and neighborhoods together, the conservationists and ecologists, and the true lovers of democracy. From these people, *my* people, a vision for a sustainable, beautiful, just, and democratic Wisconsin might well emerge.

7

Governmental Options Preferential to Corporations and Minority Wealth

Michael Slattery

Paul Tillich, the famous Protestant theologian from New York Theological Union Seminary, advised that to be a Christian in today's society you need to have the Bible in one hand and *The New York Times* in the other. Christian living is not something that is mere replication of literal biblical interpretation of the life and sayings of the historical Jesus, but requires an understanding of the intricacies of and interaction within contemporary society (sociological, economic, political, religious, anthropological, etc.). Reality devoid of biblical meaning often sinks into immorality, just as biblical exegesis without the reality of the world around us results in fundamentalist interpretation and empty spiritualism. The creation of a public fiscal budget is unquestionably a moral act because the collection of revenue and the appropriation of that revenue relies on value choices based on one's moral commitments and faith application, whether conscious or not.

INTRODUCTION

With barely one month into his four-year term as Wisconsin governor, Scott Walker upended a $120 million fiscal surplus for 2010 (according to the Wisconsin Legislative Fiscal Bureau) and converted it roughly into a $140 million deficit (a) by authorizing anew more than $140

Governmental Options Preferential to Corporations and Minority Wealth

million in corporate tax credits and (b) by accelerating some payments for taxes and public works delayed for payment in 2011 into FY2010, an accounting gimmick not unfamiliar to the Democratic Party. The Walker Administration and its allies in the Republican-controlled legislature cleverly used this self-manipulated budget crisis for launching its primary objective of undermining the largest organized basis for state Democratic Party funding—public-sector union support. Inserted into the 2010 "Budget Repair Bill" to address this contrived deficit, Walker and cronies included several clauses that clearly run counter to twentieth-century moral thinking with regard to labor rights. Appearing to place the cause of fiscal deficits on the largest facet of public-sector expenditure, i.e., labor, they proposed to eliminate the rights of labor to bargain for anything besides actual wage rates, provided that any raises remained less than the rate of inflation; labor unions annually would be required to collect their own dues and not have the state or local government entities withhold them, and would have to annually re-certify. This strategy was clearly implemented to weaken the Democratic Party base in future elections.

By the second month of the new Walker administration, more traits concerning its philosophy and that of its legislative allies revealed their basic premises, *weltanschauung*, objectives, and policy measures. Basically, this administration and the ruling party in the legislature are clearly promoting policies that benefit the profits of corporations over the social needs of individuals. The administration and legislature are attempting to accomplish this through increasing corporate tax credits, reducing capital gains taxes, combining tax reporting, effective lowering of corporate tax rates, declaring tax holidays for certain qualifying corporations, eliminating or gutting regulatory reporting and compliance, favoring large-scale operations and their interests over those of struggling smaller entities, etc.

Few people questioned the reasons for the exploding deficit; even Walker and the Republican-controlled legislature never publicly acknowledged the projected biennial deficit was attributable as much to the results of a severe recession since 2007 as to the expenditures to which the state had committed. The expected slow recovery and the jobless recovery probably factored more into causing the deficit than the level of public-sector wages.

BACKGROUND

Fiscal and Budgetary Issues Related to Deficit Financing

Wisconsin's biennial budget of roughly $66 billion has been funded lately by sources with the following ratios. Of taxes collected, individuals provide the state with more than 90 percent of tax revenue (individual, excise, and the majority of sales and utility taxes) and corporations a scant 6 percent; but, taxes comprise roughly only 40 percent of Wisconsin's revenue for financing the budget and 30 percent is received from the federal government. As an approach to resolving projected state fiscal deficits, though, this administration and the legislature have trapped themselves and their supporters in a funding bind by refusing to raise new revenues through taxes or to issue greater amounts of public debt (general or revenue).[1] Thus, with overall effective corporate tax rates expected to decline and the administration's refusal to raise taxes in the face of expected decline in federal financing, the deficit can only be covered by reducing state expenditures, by shifting the tax burden to individual income tax payers (proportionately, more middle-income), by some combination of these two approaches, or by issuing more state debt that will surely push bond ratings lower (and thereby raise funding costs) and avoid confronting resolution of the problem for the moment.

Deficit resolution through reducing expenditures can only partially fix the problem. Under the proposed biennial budget, reductions of $1,600 million for public primary and secondary education, $470 million for state-funded Badgercare and other Medicaid-related uses, $322 million for University of Wisconsin system and tech colleges, and over $300 million for shared revenue with local government, etc. would still leave a gap of about one billion.

---

1. We can speculate on the ineptness and inexperience of these politicians who seem not to know how to run a business. Any business, whether large or small, always searches for ways to improve its income position by (a) finding ways to increase revenue and (b) reducing expenditures through elimination of redundancies and unproductive activities. Any entity that merely attempts to improve its income position through expenditure reduction only is bound for self-extermination.

Governmental Options Preferential to Corporations and Minority Wealth

Wisconsin Estimated Budget Revenue Sources, 2011-2013 (US$1 BB)			
Tax Sources for General Fund (a)			
Individual Income	14.2		21%
General Sales & Use	8.7		13%
Excise (Tobacco & alcohol)	1.5		2%
Public Utility	0.7		1%
Corporate Income & Franchise	1.8		3%
Insurance Company	0.3		0%
Miscellaneous Taxes	0.1		0%
Subtotal	27.2		41%
Federal Revenue	19.4		29%
Program Revenue	8.7		13%
Segregated Revenue	7.7		12%
Bonding authority	3.4		5%
TOTAL	66.4		100%

(a) Legislative Fiscal Bureau, Table 7 for General Fund Taxes, pa. 13.

Source: Legislative Fiscal Bureau (Govenor's Budget)

Walker and others argue that reduction in corporate tax rates and increased credits will generate more investment, stimulate commerce, promote employment, and result in economic expansion that will raise revenue to be captured by increased tax receipts.

This administration and the state Republican Party have cleverly enflamed support for these policies by capitalizing on base feelings of fear of the unknown, petty blue-collar jealousy, and unrealistic delusory greed among its voter base.

The fallacy in this approach to fiscal management lies in the belief that increased benefits and income to corporations, especially larger entities, and wealthy individuals will trickle down to smaller firms and lower-income households. Further, they contend, deregulation of corporate activity will result in reduced costs, higher net income and resulting higher tax revenues. This did not work in the policies initiated by Donald Regan during the Reagan administration whereby (a) supply-side economics promoted by Arthur Laffer, whose theories on tax rates and tax revenue effectively supported reduced tax rates, were supposed to accrue ultimately to lower-income earners or (b) the laissez-faire economics of deregulation and reduced or limited government involvement in economic management promoted by Milton Friedman and the Chicago School of Economics were supposed to allow the free market to stimulate the economy. These approaches to government failed ultimately in the U.S., just as they were thrown out finally by the Pinochet and successor governments in Chile. The deregulation promoted by Reagan was the principal cause of the near meltdown of the financial sector in 2007; that meltdown precipitated a severe recession bordering on national depression.

Why have Walker and the Republican legislators resurrected these flawed policies? The beneficiaries of such policies were unabashedly corporations, the larger the better, and wealthier classes of individuals. We increasingly are confronted with oligarchic government that controls the media. The idea that government is to serve the common good, particularly where the private sector is unwilling or unable to adequately meet the needs of that good, is considered by these individuals to be anathema to free-market modus operandi. Despite the creationist and traditional religious thinking espoused by many, if not most, of their supporters, Walker's approach to government would leave individuals and classes who are the weakest and least capable to social Darwinist exploitation and further marginalization. The recession of 2007 to 2009 has only been countered by a toothless and jobless recovery, whose beneficiaries are concentrated in larger corporations and wealthier individuals, not unlike the anemic expansion following Japan's 13-year recession of the 1990s. If there are no or few jobs in a recovery, there will be minimal increased tax revenue and increasing, prolonged impoverishment, no growth in consumption that drives expansion, a hollowing of the economy, and heightened mal-distribution of income and wealth.

Corporate Income and Taxes

Corporations often perceive themselves as unfairly maligned citizens of the U.S. democracy—paying their taxes, employing residents and thereby supporting the economy through household income, and as market participants developing U.S. domestic and foreign policy interests for the betterment of the U.S. consumer and citizenry. As such, they have argued on their own behalf before the U.S. Supreme Court, as have some of the judges themselves, for a right to unlimited monetary participation in the political process through *Citizens United vs. Federal Election Commission* in 2010.

Governmental Options Preferential to Corporations and Minority Wealth

With regard to taxes on a federal level, in the 1950s corporate income tax receipts constituted about 30 percent of all federal income tax receipts, but as of 2009 constituted only 6.6 percent.[2] In fact, in the 1950s, when the highest U.S. tax rates approximated 84 to 91 percent (87 percent of statutory income), corporations seem to have paid proportionately as much in taxes to the central government as individuals. Today, however, individuals are paying more than quadruple what corporations are paying and paying roughly triple what corporations are paying for FICA welfare taxes for social security, healthcare, and unemployment.[3] (Please see attachment hereafter.)

The Congressional Budget Office analyzed the corporate tax burden for federal taxes paid in the U.S. and compared it to tax regimes in other G-7 countries and members of the Organization of Economic Cooperation and Development, the 30 most industrialized countries in the world exclusive of Russia and the Peoples Republic of China.[4]

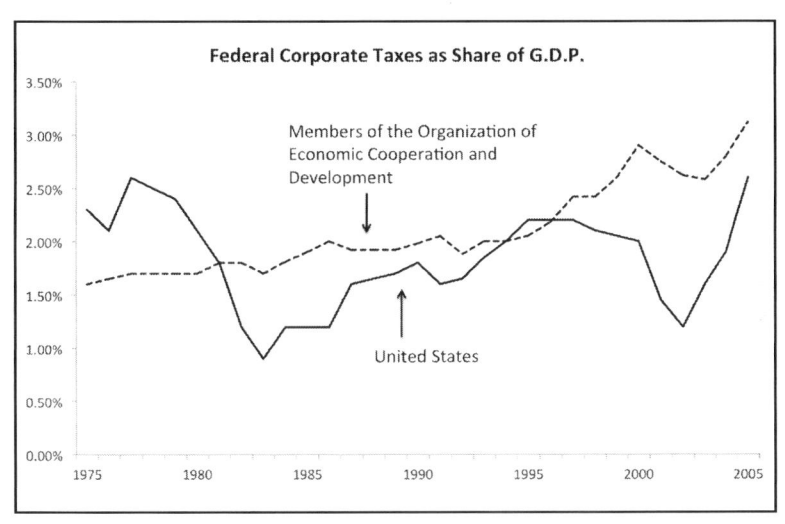

Source: Organization of Economic Cooperation and Development,
The New York Times, **May 2, 2011**

---

2. David Kocieniewski, "GE's Strategies Let It Avoid Taxes Altogether," *New York Times*, Mar. 24, 2011. I hereby inform the reader that I was an employee of GE Capital for six years as a low-level executive who was responsible for business development of new operations and products in Japan; I still own GE stock and receive a pension from the company.

3. See line graph in Appendix.

4. "Corporate Income Tax Rates: International Comparisons," Congressional Budget Office, 2005.

A Whole Which Is Greater

As of 2002, the Congressional Budget Office in its study found that, as a percent of Gross Domestic Product, the percent of all income taxes paid to central government and respective local governments (state, municipal, etc.) constituted 1.8 percent for the U.S., 2.8 percent on average for the other G-7 countries, and 3.4 percent for all OECD countries on an un-weighted average, but 2.5 percent on a weighted average.[5] The above line chart comparing OECD central government corporate tax revenues as a percent of Gross Domestic Product with those of the U.S. also indicates that for the larger part of the past 30 years, the U.S. clearly remains below their peers in the OECD for taxes as a percent of GDP, which means the U.S. corporate tax burden is not so onerous that it provides a competitive disadvantage to U.S. companies.

A recent series of articles published by *The New York Times* analyzed that multinational corporations reduce their tax liabilities by employing various sets of strategies. Large firms hire hundreds of tax experts (lawyers and accountants), many of whom previously worked for the IRS or congressional committees responsible for tax formulation.[6] They know the peculiarities of the various federal and state tax codes and are able to facilitate the means to reduce tax payments. These firms also will book their profits offshore, rather than repatriating capital and paying their U.S. parent. They often will avoid U.S. taxes by reducing their U.S. profits through illegal discounted sale of parent-owned patents and materials to their foreign subsidiaries. The IRS attempts to discover these non-arms-length transfers and below-market pricing. This becomes a cheap sale of royalties. Multinationals will also share their U.S. domestic research with their foreign subsidiaries by licensing at a discount patents developed domestically. They then might move manufacturing offshore where labor costs are cheapest, pollution controls are weakest, etc., and royalty payments are paid to the foreign subsidiary with the lowest tax rates abroad. When these foreign subsidiaries then pay dividends to the U.S. parents, they will reduce U.S. tax liabilities by as much as 65 percent, depriving the U.S. and state governments of morally receivable taxes but legally avoidable payments. Regardless of the corporate tax credits, the aforementioned means deprive U.S. and state

5. "Corporate Income Tax Rates: International Comparisons," Congressional Budget Office, Nov. 2005, x.

6. See David Kocieniewski, for a series entitled "But Nobody Pays That," *The New York Times*, Mar. 24, May 2, and June 19, 2011.

Governmental Options Preferential to Corporations and Minority Wealth

governments of revenue that must be filled by either more debt issue or increasing the burden on individual tax filers.

With rising deficits looming in the future and the need to fund previously generated deficits, primarily attributable to financing the U.S. war machine that annually consumes 25 percent of the federal budget and 58 percent of discretionary spending, the call for deficit reduction accompanied by lowered corporate tax rates and increased corporate tax credits will fall most heavily on the backs of the middle class to fund both their federal and respective state budgets. What is true with respect to corporate tax revenue, tax rates, and tax credits at the federal level is unquestionably true when applied to the state of Wisconsin.

The rationale used by opponents of corporate taxation relies on a theoretical reason that reduced or non-existent taxation of corporate income will benefit the government because companies will be enticed to move their operations to that state and invest in start-up or expansion of their operations. Such is simply not the case. Based on my own experience of having worked for years in strategic planning and business development for the two largest institutions in the world (operations of Japan's largest bank in the U.S. in the 1980s and finance operations for the U.S.' largest company in Japan), the issue of national or state corporate income tax rates is hardly on the radar screen when strategizing and developing businesses. Factors such as labor costs, healthcare costs, proximity to resources and end markets, pollution controls, regulatory and legal protection, even-handedness of the judicial system, quality of and access to necessary labor market, etc., are paramount in the relocation or establishment of a business or operation. The level of taxes and the ability to repatriate income are much lower priorities of consideration.

My experience in working for and with Japanese institutions has revealed a fundamental flaw in our U.S. corporate and capitalist system. In Japan, corporations would be embarrassed and have their reputation rightfully attacked if they did not pay their share of taxes. Not so in the U.S., where corporations regularly help legislators devise the means for corporations to significantly reduce or avoid the payment of taxes! The lack of social commitment and responsibility to support the public good, not just the interest of the capitalist or shareholder and enrichment of senior management, is frightfully appalling in this country.

A Whole Which Is Greater

ECONOMICS OF INCOME DISTRIBUTION IN TAXATION OF CORPORATIONS AND INDIVIDUALS IN WISCONSIN

Wisconsin corporate income tax constitutes between five and seven percent of state general fund collections and is a flat 7.9 percent, below the national state corporate income tax average and alleged to be second lowest in the U.S. Wisconsin appears generous in providing handsome corporate tax credits which allow corporations to subtract these credit amounts from their gross tax liability, credits that are over and above federal corporate tax credits. Before calculating taxable income, corporations are permitted to apply various income deductions.

Regretfully, data on gross taxable corporate income and corporate tax credit by type for Wisconsin-registered corporations could not be obtained for this analysis. Thus, I am unable to analyze the appropriateness of the Wisconsin corporate tax regime. We can surmise, based on the below-noted facts, however, that Wisconsin corporations in all likelihood, similar to other U.S. corporations, have seen their stock values appreciate multi-fold over the past 30 years, while private individual households have only inched upward. Further, the amount of corporate tax credits has significantly reduced Wisconsin corporate tax revenues and shifted the burden of deficit financing to individual households.

Clearly, the types of business credits presently available to corporations are multiplying and are applicable to an increasing number of diverse industries and their interest groups. Presently, more than 25 types of business credits exist (from job creation, water-use, livestock expansion or modernization, film production, bio-diesel production, ethanol and bio-diesel pump use, dairy processing, healthcare risk, meat processing, dairy cooperatives, electronic medical record processing, woody biomass harvest and processing, beginning farmer, etc.), not to mention (a) exclusion of Wisconsin capital gains, (b) expansion of venture capital gains tax deferral, (c) elongation of loss carry-forwards, (d) more favorable treatment of combined reporting, and (e) preferential real estate taxes for farmers in land-use-valuation tax. While individual filers may utilize many of these tax credits, the vast majority of individual filers can only avail themselves of tax credits related to being married, real estate (home) ownership, earned income (to be reduced), and homestead credits (to be de-indexed). One cannot fail to notice the number of corporate tax credits related to agriculture (35 percent of all credits), although agriculture only accounts for one-fourth of the gross state product. That corporate tax credits enhance the expansion of business and result in job creation is not disputed. The questions that should be addressed are: (a) At what cost and at whose cost? (b) Are the majority of the jobs created low-wage jobs? The cost to the individual taxpayer is effectively increased while the wealth is shifted to the shareholder. Given the above delineated Wisconsin corporate tax credits, most jobs would appear to be low-paying.

In 2008, for example, Wisconsin's gross state product amounted to $240 billion. Yet, adjusted gross income for individuals accounted for $128 billion and corporations for at least $89 billion ($7.003 billion/7.9%).[7] The latter number raises questions about the actual net income of corporations in the state. Of all corporate tax filers, 66 percent pay no tax at all. This is attributed to a number of reasons—effectively dormant entities, severity of the recession, corporations used as tax shelters, or unprofitable firms. Given what is occurring at the federal level in the payment of corporate taxes, corporate tax rates, and corporate tax credits, there remains more than a strong suspicion that Wisconsin corporations are similarly paying a state corporate tax rate well below the 7.9% flat rate and are generously subsidized by corporate tax credits.

Individual Income and Taxes

Distribution of Individual Income and Wealth

Contrary to politicians' lament that we are broke in our governmental fiscal operations, we have ample wealth and income whose ownership/ beneficiaries have not been paying their fair share of governmental expenditures; despite getting all of the benefits of the government, their share of income and wealth continues to increase.[8] U.S. corporations

7. Ron Shanovich, Wisconsin Legislative Fiscal Bureau, "Corporate Income/Franchise Tax," Jan. 2011, 37.

8. On a federal level, we waste billions of dollars annually. The cost of two wars in Afghanistan, Iraq and Pakistan has exceeded 2.3 trillion dollars and will eventually cost more than 3.7 trillion U.S. dollars (in line with Nobel laureate Joseph Stiglitz's projections of 2008), not to mention more than 224,000 people killed, 365,000 wounded and more than 7.8 million displaced persons and untold injuries, (according to "Cost of War" compiled by Brown University's Watson Institute for International Studies,

continue to break records in increasing their annual net income and their stock prices have multiplied more than 10-fold over the past thirty years, but the median and average household income has not even doubled during the same period. (Stock prices rise because of market assessment of the worth of a company and the company's expected or potential income-generation, among various factors.) More than 163 Wisconsin corporations annually had taxable net income approximating five billion dollars over the past few years.

As of 2009, the bottom 60 percent of U.S. households owned only 2.3 percent of total U.S. wealth, less than the Fortune 400 wealthiest individuals, nine of whom reside in Wisconsin.[9] This means that the upper 40 percent of the U.S. population hold more than 97 percent of the wealth (net worth). The GINI coefficient, a scale that indicates the gap between the wealthiest and poorest classes in a group or in a country, indicates that, as a country, the U.S. has one of the worst distributions of income and wealth in the industrialized world and this has annually worsened over the last 35 years. (N.b., the higher the coefficient, the worse the distribution of wealth.) The U.S. (57 index score) ranks poorly in categories approximating those of Mexico, Brazil, and Colombia; even Russia (40) and China (44) have better income and wealth distribution than the U.S. The E.U. (33), Germany (28), U.K.(37), France (33), Canada (33) and Japan (38) all had better GINI indices by as much as 25 percent for disparity in income distribution as the U.S.[10] In wealth distribution, the U.S. has a GINI index coefficient of 87, meaning U.S. wealth distribution is one of the worst in the industrialized world.[11]

---

and carried by MSNBC and Reuters on June 29, 2011).

We annually spend one trillion dollars in military-related expenditure (25% of our federal budget), more than the rest of the world combined. (See CIA World Factbook.) If we would cut annual military expenditure in half and avoid imperialist wars for resource control, the federal budget deficits would be more than manageable.

As we shall see later, the expenditure and waste of the fiscal budget at the federal level, especially on military and war efforts around the world, are probably the principal cause of federal deficits which adversely affect Wisconsin's state budget now and in the future as federal subsidies decline in order to pay for past and future wars.

9. Edward Wolff, "Recent Trends in Household Wealth in the United States: Rising Debt and the Middle-Class Squeeze—an Update to 2007," 33.

10. Source: CIA, *World Fact Book*, 2006. CIA-calculated coefficients.

11. Arthur B. Kinnickell, "Ponds and Streams: Wealth and Income in the US, 1989 to 2007," 2009-13, Federal Reserve Board, 34.

Governmental Options Preferential to Corporations and Minority Wealth

The lowering of the highest tax rates on individuals initiated by the Reagan administration and further pushed by the Clinton administration has not resulted in a more equitable distribution of income or wealth. In fact, trickle-down effects of supply-side economics, while corporate profits rose geometrically and stock prices multiplied, have only resulted in wealth transfer from lower- and middle-income to upper-income individuals.

Contrary to Laffer's projections anticipated by the Reagan government, there was virtually no trickle-down effect to poorer classes from a reduction in taxes; rather, income and wealth effectively exploded upwards whereby poorer and middle classes transferred their wealth to richer classes. In a 2005 Bureau of the Census report, over a 25 year period, between 1979 and 2004, the change in real after-tax income for individuals by quintile grouping reveals that the bottom 20 percent of income earners saw a gain of nearly 6 percent, with gains for higher quintile groupings rising respectively per grouping by 17, 21, 29, and 69 percent. The top one percent of income earners, however, saw a gain of 176 percent. We are certain that these discrepancies in real take-home income have been further magnified since 2004, particularly in light of the severity of the recent recession.

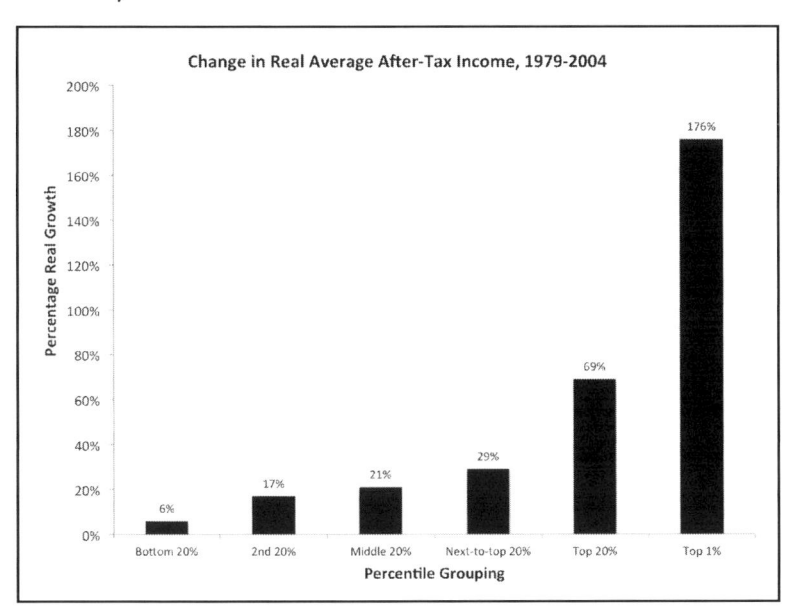

Source: Bureau of the Census, 2005.

A Whole Which Is Greater

When we look at nominal amounts of average adjusted gross income in 2004 by income grouping, the bottom 25 percent of income tax filers had average AGI of $4,777, the bottom 50 percent had $11,379, bottom 75 percent had $16,045, but the top 10 percent of filers showed average AGI of $181,098 and the top one percent had AGI of $605,510. (Kindly see table below.) Although this data represents 2004 nominal income distribution, any conclusions drawn from this comparison remain just as true today.

As of the tax regime of 2009, Wisconsin uses a five-scale individual tax system; individual tax rates rise from 4.6 percent (on taxable income less than $10,070 for single filers or $13,420 for joint filers) to 7.75 percent (on taxable income of $221,660 for single filers, but of $295,550 for joint filers), with increased taxable income. This can hardly be considered progressive taxation. That is, for an individual with only $10,000 in taxable income, 4.6 percent is the tax rate, but an individual with 22 times that level of income would be taxed at a rate only 3.1 percent greater than the lowest rate. Tax rates for joint filers witness the same trait. The average effective rate for all individual taxpayers, though, is 4.8 percent after accounting for tax credits of more than $1 billion or 16 percent of gross tax income before reduction of these credits. Filers with AGI greater than $80,000 utilize more than 50 percent of all tax credits. For filers with more than $200,000 of AGI, this on average has reduced their effective tax rate from 7.75 to 6.2 percent, a sizable benefit.[12]

---

12. Please see Rick Olin, "Individual Income Tax," Wisconsin Legislative Fiscal Bureau, Jan. 2011, 23.

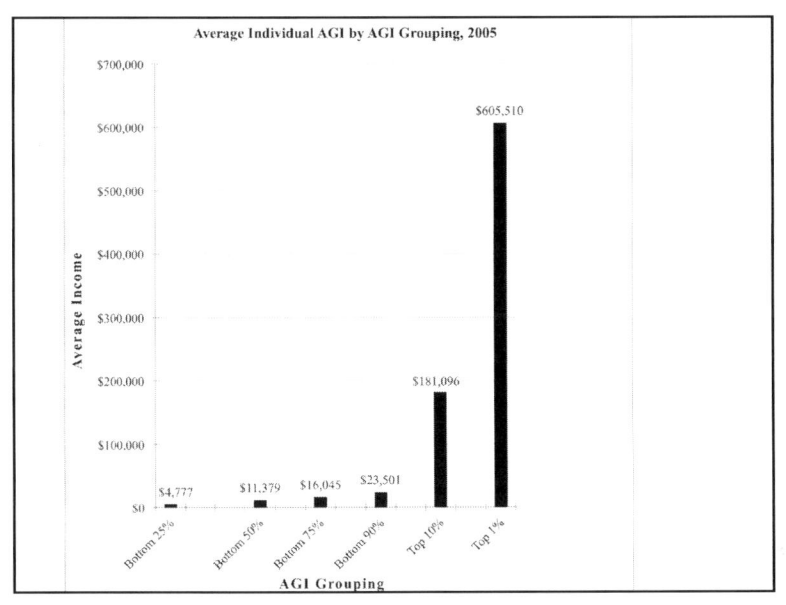

Governmental Options Preferential to Corporations and Minority Wealth

Average Individual AGI by AGI Grouping, 2005

AGI Grouping	Average Income
Bottom 25%	$4,777
Bottom 50%	$11,379
Bottom 75%	$16,045
Bottom 90%	$23,501
Top 10%	$181,096
Top 1%	$605,510

Source: "Individual Income Tax, All Returns: Sources of Income, Adjustments, and Tax Items, in Constant 1990 Dollars, by Size of Real Adjusted Gross Income, Tax Year, 2004," Internal Revenue Service, 2005.

As of 2009, in Wisconsin 15 percent of the state's individual income filers (AGI greater than $80,000) controlled more than 52 percent of the income (AGI-basis of aggregate of $66.8 billion of total state individual AGI of $128 billion), but they also benefit from 57 percent of the tax credits ($615 million of total credits of $1.1 billion). While some may argue that these 15 percent of filers paid 64 percent of the individual filers' taxes, they certainly have more resources available for such payments, and their net after-tax income affords an easier life style. Sixty-one percent of the filers (inclusive of individual and joint), with AGIs less than $40,000, theoretically have an income less than the national median household income. This class of taxpayers has an effective tax rate of two percent. An effective difference of four percent in the tax rates between the poorest and wealthiest income classes is hardly considered progressive, but should be considered regressive. Two dollars for a loaf of bread for this group, however, is far dearer than two dollars for the same bread purchased by the highest class noted above.

The Walker biennial budget would increase various corporate tax credits and business credits for high net-worth households and individuals, but would eliminate tax credits on the poorest classes of society—earned income credit, etc., in addition to reduction or elimination of (a) aid per student in public schools, (b) assistance for medical care and medicines for seniors and poor classes, (c) inflation-indexing of homestead credit, etc. The administration and legislature would effectively engage in racial discrimination to satisfy its base by prohibiting undocumented immigrants, even though born in the U.S., from benefiting from food assistance and tuition as state residents, despite the fact that even illegal residents pay federal, state, and FICA taxes.

SCRIPTURAL AND MORAL BASIS FOR EVALUATING BUDGETS

Many politicians approach the drafting of a budget and appropriation of revenues as if religion and faith are devoid of guidelines to facilitate such decision-making.[13] Both the Hebrew and Christian scriptures, however, are replete with stories that rouse our consciousness to make moral judgments with regard to extracting goods and services from people and how we are to treat each other, even as a government.[14]

Do the Hebrew or Christian scriptures comment on the issues of income distribution and taxation? No! Just like these scriptures do not comment on who pays and who may benefit in healthcare, on the issue of abortion, or on marriage of people of the same sex, etc. Nevertheless,

---

13. Along with eight others persons under the auspices of the Wisconsin Council of Churches, we visited Sen. Frank Lasee, state senator of our district, in March 2011. He attempted to persuade us that it was only natural for laborers to be jealous in unilateral determination of wage rates based on a faith story in the Christian scriptures (Mt. 20:1-16) wherein the vineyard keeper paid the same rates to all laborers no matter what the length of time worked in the vineyard. This sort of literalist reading of faith stories typifies so-called fundamentalists baptized as Christians. The story has no meaning whatsoever concerning labor rates or treatment of employees. To interpret it as such distorts the meaning of the text. Lasee was oblivious to the hermeneutical meaning of this scripture that really concerns the belief that the God of the scriptures rewards all persons equally, no matter when they worked for realizing their faith. (This Christian story really attempts to influence the early Christian community to recognize that not only their predecessors, the Jews, but also Jesus' disciples, will receive no better reward than the Christians who followed and changed their Jewish faith.)

14. I personally regret that I am not well-versed enough to provide commentary from the perspective of the Quran concerning these issues.

Governmental Options Preferential to Corporations and Minority Wealth

one can interpret these scriptures in various analogous cases and also judge the spirit of these scriptures.

The Hebrew and Christian scriptures are all about politics—the allocation process for distributing scarce resources.[15] In the Hebrew scriptures, Jeremiah (22:13) castigates Jehoiakim and the Judah leadership for extorting from the poor and not paying just wages. (Poverty increased dramatically under the Hebrew monarchy as it engaged in warfare and edifice-building.) The eighth-century (BCE) prophet Isaiah (Is. 61:2) strongly demanded that the Hebrews enact according to their laws a year of favor, i.e., all debts and whatever was owed on them (e.g., interest) were forgiven periodically, if unpaid, and the relationship between the owner and the renter began completely anew. Isaiah also emphasized that the enactment of their laws did not advocate in favor of social band-aiding and personal contrition for exploitation of poorer classes but, rather, demanded that wealth be shared in what is needed for life (Is. 58:6-7, 10). Amos, like Jeremiah, criticizes the Hebrews for oppression of the poor (Amos 2, 4, 5). Exodus (Ex. 22:20-24) claims that oppression of the poor is criminal.

Based on the spirit of the Hebrew scriptures, the Christian canonical scriptures from Matthew through Revelation passionately witness the economic imperatives of discipleship in the way of Jesus. Particularly like the eighth-century prophets, the Christian scriptures emphasize not just special concern for the poor, but how the Christian believer treats those who are oppressed or marginalized in society. Sharing of wealth necessarily underlies Matthew's gospel story of the Last Judgment (Mt. 25:31-46) and Mark's gospel story of the rich young man (Mk. 10:17-22). Luke also proclaims God's liberating power on behalf of poorer classes and advocates sharing all one's possessions with these classes so that the poor cease to exist (Lk. 1:52-53 and 4:18-19). The Deuteronomic mandates are witnessed in the Lukan Magnificat of Mary whereby the rich and powerful (who are always a minority) lose their wealth and power and, in a reversal, those who are oppressed and poorer benefit.

The Hebrew and Christian scriptures have a preponderant focus on the issue of poverty. The poor (*ptochos* or *ptochoi* in Greek) is the word most commonly found in these writings. In the Hebrew

---

15. Robert McAffee Brown, *Unexpected News: Reading the Bible with Third World Eyes* (Philadelphia: The Westminster Press, 1984).

scriptures, particular concern is shown toward the *anawim* (widows who had no one to care for them since their bread-earner left, orphans, and foreigners—those who are different from the dominant value class) and *anayim* (those who are politically marginalized and economically disenfranchised) as those who are oppressed or inequitably treated.[16] The prophets of the eighth century BCE and particularly the Christian writings give preferential treatment to the poor. The apostle James writes, "You have lived on earth in luxury and in pleasure; you have fattened your hearts in a day of slaughter" (James 5:1-6). Expanding on Luke 6:24, James here assures us that God will harshly judge those with wealth and those who have exploited the labor of poorer classes.

A preferential option for poorer classes permeates the Christian scriptures. The treatment of these classes or groups does not just demand passing interest, a prayer on their behalf, or a few coins in the Salvation Army kettles at Christmas. Rather, as in the prayer taught by Jesus, it requires that we make the reign of God realized in the here and now. "Your kingdom come on earth as it is in heaven." As the faith story of the vineyard keeper paying the same wage to all his laborers as the reward for a good life, the equitable sharing of the world's goods and fairness to all must be realized in this world, not just in some afterlife. Thus, these scriptures call us to seek an equitable distribution of the goods of the earth so that no one is suffering from want and no members of the community are benefiting at the expense of others, at least not egregiously.[17]

How do we as Christians, Jews, or whatever religious affiliation, live in this manner when the rapidly growing disparity between

---

16. See John P. Meier, *A Marginal Jew: Rethinking the Historical Jesus*, vol. 2, (New York: Doubleday 1994), 334. Matthew effectively equates these two groups in his beatitudes (Mt. 5:3 and 5:5).

17. One can be amazed at the pre-eminence in the political statements of the Tea Party members and the religious right. Included in this group in contemporary USA are found traditional Catholics and their spokesperson politicians. Their concern about deficit spending seems to be fostered by blue-collar jealousy for teachers and others with incomes higher than their own, by unrealizable greed that hopes that they or their offspring will be able to control enormous wealth some day, and by fear of any person or group with values different than their own. They seek to reduce present deficits by cutting expenditures for those who are most vulnerable in society and supporting benefits for those who sit at the top of the economic pyramid. While they espouse Christianity for the most part, they can be considered to be nothing more than non-Christian baptized.

Governmental Options Preferential to Corporations and Minority Wealth

wealthier and poorer classes is growing? One of the ways to address this is through income redistribution by the taxation system. The system that we have in both Wisconsin and the U.S., though, is failing miserably at this because we have effective wealth redistribution from poorer classes to wealthier. The elimination, reduction, or gutting of programs such as Wisconsin state healthcare, public education, tax credits for home ownership, etc., while granting tax credits to corporations and wealthier classes, is a preferential option for the rich! This is anti-Christian.

As an early Church father, Ambrose, said, "You are not making a gift of your possessions to the poor person. You are handing over to him what is his. For what has been given in common for the use of all, you have abrogated to yourself. The world is given to all, and not only to the rich."

Since Pope Leo XIII's *Rerum Novarum* ("The Condition of Labor") in 1891, at least Catholic social teaching acknowledges that moral law has to be part of every economic system and has at least three criteria—(a) justice, demanding equity in exchange and bargaining, (b) balance between various economic sectors, and (c) organization of the constituent economic units.[18] Ninety years later, Pope John Paul II in 1981 issued *Laborem Exercens* ("On Human Work"), a consideration of the role of labor in the twentieth century, from the perspective of a Polish cleric who had experienced the limitations of Soviet-style communism. The dignity of the human person is the focus of any consideration of labor and the treatment of labor in contemporary society. The objective of labor and its remuneration is to make life more human for the public good, not just for a select minority. Thus, labor is not be viewed as one other factor in production of goods and service, but rather the key to the Christian understanding of labor resides in the premise that the laborer is the subject of the exercise, not the capitalist or the goods and services generated in that exercise of production. *Laborem Exercens* also stresses that labor unions are an appropriate means to achieve the dignity of the worker in negotiating the terms of labor—something that the Walker administration is attempting to eliminate by structurally weakening public-sector unions.

---

18. David O'Brien and Thomas A. Shannon, eds., *Catholic Social Thought: The Documentary Heritage*, Orbis Books, Maryknoll, NY: 1998, 13.

A Whole Which Is Greater

As a result of the second Vatican Council of 1965, ecclesial leaders were again made conscious of the real world in which we live. The need for implementation of social justice according to the teachings and the practice of the historical Jesus, as seen through the gospels, focused on just distribution of possessions of the earth. Thus, *A New Catechism* clearly called for a redistribution of the world's resources and wealth:

> It is all a question of justice—not only of "commutative justice" which says that each one must be given his own in business and the like, but of "social justice". Social justice demands that the goods of this world should be distributed rationally. Mankind possesses the world in common. And just as there is a certain equality among men—so too men have a right to a certain equality in the distribution of the world and its goods. It is not good that some should be very rich while others are very poor. It is a matter of justice that this should be changed.[19]

This does not mean that the goods of the world are distributed without each person working to his/her ability to partake in the joy of creation. Labor by all is required. However, the New Catechism cautions that "a society where constant struggle and vigilance are needed to preserve the right of all to a fair distribution of property is not a truly human society and certainly not a redeemed one."[20]

RESPONDING TO NARROW INTEREST POLITICS DETRIMENTAL TO THE COMMON GOOD

Fiscal management of public-sector budgets is a moral issue. The projected Wisconsin biennial fiscal deficit cannot be viewed as solely or even principally the result of excessive expenditure, but must also be evaluated as an effect of a severe recession since 2007 and poor political management by elected officials. To manage the projected deficit by only reducing expenditure demonstrates a lack of sound managerial expertise. Contrary to the statements of politicians and government officials, neither the state of Wisconsin nor the federal government is broke. It is as important to seek to raise revenues as much as to control and reduce expenditures. This is sound business practice. To reduce the

---

19. *De Nieuwe Katechismus* ("A New Catechism: Catholic Faith for Adults"), New York: Herder and Herder, 1969, 431.

20. *A New Catechism*, 432.

Governmental Options Preferential to Corporations and Minority Wealth

effective tax burden of wealthier classes of individuals and households and of corporations and to increase the tax burden of low- and medium-income households is effective wealth transfer from the poorer and middle classes of individual households to wealthier classes and effective subsidy to corporations. The massive shift in wealth and income to wealthier classes and corporations away from more equitable distribution of income is myopic at best, but devious and immoral at worst. Clear national and statewide trends over at least the past 30 years indicate rapidly growing disparity in income and wealth distribution that can only foster class warfare and antagonism.

It behooves the citizenry to wrest power and influence away from corporations who now control both major political parties in the state and in the U.S. We the citizenry need to demand both legislative and judicial reform of the treatment of corporate "personhood." We will need to reverse the trend toward regressive taxation where effective flat tax rates are enforced and we must require that corporations, whose incomes and wealth have so multiplied, pay their fair share of the tax burden. Otherwise we face increasing deficit financing through individual taxes, particularly with enhanced burden placed on the middle class. Real effective progressive tax reform with elimination of caps and tax credits for wealthier classes and corporations is absolutely necessary.

APPENDIX

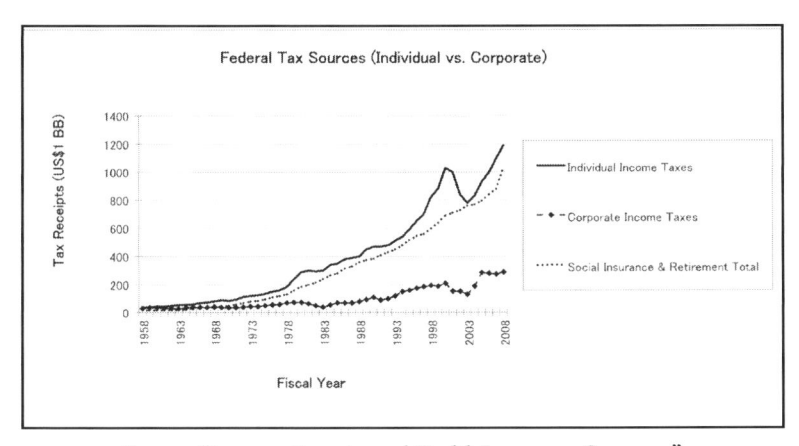

Source: "Income, Poverty, and Health Insurance Coverage,"
US Census Bureau, 2005.

8

Confessions of an Apostate from the Religion of "Education"

Daniel Grego

"School has become the world religion of a modernized proletariat, and makes futile promises of salvation to the poor of the technological age."[1]

IVAN ILLICH

1

ON FEBRUARY 9, 2011, just two days before releasing his now infamous "budget repair bill," in which he proposed eliminating the ability of most public employees to bargain collectively, Wisconsin Governor Scott Walker was interviewed along with U.S. Secretary of Education Arne Duncan on Wisconsin Public Radio.

The Secretary congratulated the Governor on the concessions he had been able to obtain from the Wisconsin Education Association Council (WEAC), the State's largest teachers union. The union had agreed to allow students' scores on standardized tests to be one of the factors taken into consideration when evaluating teachers' performance and in determining their compensation. The latter is known as "merit

1. Illich, *Deschooling*, 10.

Confessions of an Apostate from the Religion of "Education"

pay." The headline in the *Wisconsin State Journal* that day read: "In a reversal, teachers union backs proposals to reform education."[2]

As I listened to the interview on the radio, I thought of the distinction the philosopher Alan Watts once made between what he called "the prickles" and "the goo." "Prickly people are tough-minded, rigorous, and precise," Watts wrote. "The gooey people are tender-minded romanticists who love wide generalizations and grand syntheses."[3]

When it comes to "education," the only thing about which the prickles and the goo can agree is that our schools are not producing the results we want. The prickles blame the unions for protecting incompetent teachers and interfering with best practices and attempts to innovate.[4] The gooey group points to the problems of poverty and racism and to the "savage inequalities" that exist in the way schools are funded.[5]

Clearly, Secretary Duncan and Governor Walker were promoting a prickly approach to "education reform." It was not difficult to imagine them wearing lapel buttons calling for national standards. Predictably, there was a gooey response. People like writer Alfie Kohn, who had published an article in 2003 entitled "The Folly of Merit Pay," could be depended upon to label the Governor's efforts and the union's concessions misguided.[6] (I'm being polite.) Schools need to be more than test-prep centers as the website of Rethinking Schools (a mostly gooey group) makes clear: "Schools are integral not only to preparing all children to be full participants in society, but also to be full participants in this country's ever-tenuous experiment in democracy."[7]

The prickles and the goo have been battling over schooling now for decades, perhaps since the first compulsory attendance law was enacted in Massachusetts in the middle of the nineteenth century. Since there

---

2. The proposals supposedly backed by the union were actually reforms to "schooling," not "education." I think it is a mistake to use the terms interchangeably, as I hope will become obvious below.

3. Watts, *Book*, 146.

4. Steven Brill recently summed up the prickly position in *Class Warfare*.

5. See Kozol, *Savage Inequalities*. A recent gooey critique of the prickly agenda can be found in Alfie Kohn's *Feel-Bad Education*.

6. Kohn, *Folly*.

7. Rethinking Schools.

A Whole Which Is Greater

has never been a consensus about the purpose of schooling—what it is we are trying to do—the battles rage on.[8]

I'm inclined to be more gooey than prickly myself, but I have come to believe that both sides in the schooling wars are misguided. (I'm being polite.) In fact, I have become an apostate from the religion of "education." To explain how I eventually lost my faith, let me begin by telling a story.

2

On Thursday, April 4, 1968, I stopped by the Park Ridge Bookstore in the early evening on my way home from the library where I had just returned the copy of Martin Luther King's *Strength to Love* that I had borrowed. (The shops stayed open late in Park Ridge, Illinois on Thursday nights.) *Strength to Love* had so impressed me that I wanted to buy my own copy.

The clerk was listening to the radio as I approached the counter and handed her the small volume of sermons.

"He's just been shot," she told me.

"Who?" I asked.

"Martin Luther King."

At first, I thought she was joking. The voices from the radio soon convinced me that she was not. I bought the book (it probably cost me fifty cents) and ran the five blocks from town to my house. Inside, I found my family huddled around the television. No one said anything. I don't remember my parents being supporters of Dr. King, but all of us sensed that America had lost a great man that day.

The television replayed his speech from the night before in which he told of going to the mountaintop and seeing the Promised Land. "I might not get there with you," he prophesied. "But I want to tell you tonight that we as people will get to the Promised Land." He finished with the rhetorical flourish for which he was so well known: "Mine eyes have seen the glory of the coming of the Lord!"

After his death, what came were riots in cities all across the country. President Johnson expressed his sorrow and asked for calm. Mayor Daley issued his "shoot to kill" order. The next day, the news reports

---

8. See Salomone, *Visions*.

Confessions of an Apostate from the Religion of "Education"

were that Chicago was in chaos and flames. But that night, Friday, April 5, 1968, folksinger and topical songwriter Phil Ochs was scheduled to perform at Orchestra Hall. My friend Michael Majewski and I had tickets. Given the news reports, it was not surprising that our parents told us we could not go downtown for the concert. But, we were fifteen. We wanted to be involved. So, we went anyway.

There was an eerie silence in the train as we rode downtown. There was none of the usual banter of an evening commute. The only sound was the clacking of the train's wheels along the tracks. When we emerged from the Chicago & North Western station, the city seemed deserted. We walked right down the middle of Madison Street the ten blocks to Michigan Avenue.

Only a couple hundred people showed up at Orchestra Hall for what had been a sold-out concert. We moved down from our cheap seats in the balcony to the main floor. Phil Ochs appeared. Before his first song was finished, he vomited on stage. He apologized. He had been up all night he said. He asked for our patience. He wanted to go back stage and clean up. He promised he would return and do his show.

While we waited, activists Staughton Lynd and Rennie Davis, who were in the audience, announced that a memorial service was planned for the following noon at the Civic Center Plaza. After the service, there was to be a march to the National Guard Armory on Chicago Avenue where a "teach-in" would be conducted to encourage Guardsmen not to shoot rioters.

Ochs returned and sang for two hours. When he sang "Too Many Martyrs," there were tears in his eyes and on the cheeks of most of us in the audience.

Michael and I had been engaged in an on-going conversation about justice and peace since the day we first met. We had stayed after a last-hour freshman theology class to continue an argument and kept talking as we walked to his house about four or five blocks from the Catholic boys' prep school we attended. By then, I had studied the writings of Mahatma Gandhi and Martin Luther King. Michael had read Thoreau and Tolstoy. Before long, we were together so often that some people assumed we were brothers. We used to say: "We are. We just have different parents."

We complemented each other in remarkable ways. If I were stuck on some school problem, Michael would invariably know the answer.

A Whole Which Is Greater

And conversely, whenever he was at a loss, somehow, almost magically, I would have the solution. We became so close that more than once when we were walking along in silence, suddenly, simultaneously, we both started singing the same song in the same place.

We became so confident in our ability to support each other that we challenged our teachers to allow us to take tests as a team. We agreed that they could dock us quadruple for any mistakes we made. No one took us up on it.

As we rode the train home from the Phil Ochs concert that night, we agreed that we should participate in the rally and march the following day. That Saturday was to be one of the most important days of my "education."

On Saturday, April 6, 1968, between four and five hundred people, mostly black, mostly women and children, gathered at noon at the Civic Center Plaza for a memorial service for Martin Luther King, Jr. Ministers led the assembled in prayer. Gospel choirs gave voice to our sorrow. Speakers denounced the violence that had erupted after Dr. King's assassination—both the violence of the rioters and looters and of the police. We linked arms and sang "We Shall Overcome."

When the service ended, the march began. We were to walk east to Michigan Avenue, then north up the "magnificent mile" to Chicago Avenue, then east again at the Water Tower to the National Guard Armory at Seneca Street.

Michael and I acted as marshals near the front of the line. People sang as they walked. Small children rode on their parents' shoulders. We carried leaflets that we intended to give to members of the National Guard, in the hope that they could be dissuaded from shooting first and asking questions later as they had been ordered to do by Mayor Daley.

The police were extremely courteous to us as we moved along. They stopped traffic at the various intersections as we progressed. When the message of nonviolence was communicated to them, they nodded and smiled.

When we reached Chicago Avenue and turned east, the police escort stopped. There was a little park north of Chicago Avenue west of the Armory. After everyone in the march had turned off of Michigan Avenue, two armored vehicles pulled behind us preventing our retreat. The front of the line where Michael and I were walking had reached Seneca Street when we noticed television cameras atop news vans.

Confessions of an Apostate from the Religion of "Education"

Suddenly, the Armory doors flew open and National Guardsmen emerged in a "V" formation with rifles lowered and fixed bayonets. People in front of the line began backing up as the Guard approached. Two more armored vehicles and a paddy wagon appeared from the east on Chicago Avenue. From those vehicles, uniformed Guardsmen hurled canisters of tear gas and mace into the crowd. There was panic. People were screaming and running into each other trying to retreat. Children were crying. People in the front of the line were jabbed with the sharp blades of the bayonets. Some fell as they backed up and tripped on the curb. Many of these were picked up by the police and arrested, we later found out, for "assaulting officers."

Michael and I began helping people up off the street and leading them into the park away from the confusion and the gas. The gas made us nauseous. It felt like pins and needles sticking in our mouths and nostrils and down our throats and into our lungs. But we kept going back until everyone had been carried from the corner of Seneca and Chicago.

When we were sure everyone was safe, we snatched some of the leaflets and went north to Pearson Street and tried to sneak around behind the Armory and reach the Guardsmen from the rear. We were met by policemen, "peace officers" as they are sometimes called, who prevented us from reaching our goal. We gave up and, without knowing what else to do, started for home.

We were fifteen years old then, so it is understandable, I think, that when we arrived at my house, we switched on the television to see whether or not we had "made it" on the news. And indeed, we had. The cameras captured the crowd being dispersed, the confusion, the panic. After a few seconds of this footage, however, the coverage cut to an interview of the commander of the National Guard. He claimed that a group of rioters (we were marching to advocate an end to the riots) had entered the Armory (we had never made it to the Armory itself) and had attacked the Guardsmen with sticks (no one had sticks or weapons of any kind) in an effort to prevent them from carrying out their duty (I have already stated our purpose). No one else was interviewed or quoted. The newspaper stories the next day reported the same story in the same way.

I learned firsthand that night as I retched from the mace and rubbed alcohol where I had been poked with a bayonet what I was later told by a college history professor: "History is something that never happened written by someone who wasn't there."[9]

The nature of Michael's and my conversation changed that day. We became active in CADRE (the Chicago Area Draft Resistance) and the Chicago Peace Center. We participated in other demonstrations that spring and summer. Some of them have been forgotten; others are more widely remembered. By the end of the summer, we decided that something important was missing from our schooling. The war in Vietnam was escalating. We and all of our classmates would soon be subjected to the draft. The effects of racism and militarism were everywhere apparent. Yet none of this was being discussed in our classes.

As we approached our junior year in high school, we decided to start what we called the Midwestern Institute for the Study of Nonviolence. Our goal was to bring people of all ages together to discuss the issues of war and peace, violence and nonviolence, racial and economic justice. We persuaded the administrators of our high school to allow us to meet in the school building in the evenings if we found a faculty sponsor. John Norris, the head of the science department, agreed to work with us.

In the fall of 1968, we offered our first course, which we called "The Nature of Man" [sic]. Classmates, faculty members, students from other schools, and others participated in our weekly sessions. We studied Frantz Fanon's *The Wretched of the Earth,* Eldridge Cleaver's *Soul on Ice,* King's *Strength to Love,* Thoreau's essay on civil disobedience, excerpts from Tolstoy and Gandhi, Richard Gregg's *The Power of Non-Violence,* Erich Fromm's *The Art of Loving,* among other texts.

Given the typical prickly proposals for "education reform" from people like Governor Walker and Secretary Duncan, what happened at the Institute all those years ago is inexplicable. No national or state standard or mandate was invoked. The Institute's organization and curriculum were not designed by "experts" from a school of education or a central office bureaucracy. The conveners did not have teaching licenses or college degrees or even high school diplomas. The program was not evaluated or endorsed by any accrediting agency. No board or panel approved the texts. No credits were awarded. The participants were not

---

9. To this day, I am astounded when I hear grown men and women argue in favor of television by claiming that it is an important way to get "the facts" about what is happening in the world.

subjected to standardized tests. No credentials were conferred. Yet, I maintain that more crucial learning occurred each week than often occurs in years of conventional schooling.

Over forty years later, when I have run into people who participated in our discussions, I have often been told that while they cannot remember anything they "learned" in high school, they still think about the conversations we had at the Institute. We were a group of people trying to educate ourselves by coming together in a study group started by two (by then) sixteen-year-old boys.

3

Given my experience with the Institute, one might have expected that I would have been able to see through the illusions (and delusions) of "education" and even the prickly or gooey proposals for "education reform." However, I was too "schooled-up" (I'm being polite) and it took twenty-five years for me to understand what was really going on. Perhaps, it took me so long to wake up because I did not have enough critical distance from "education." Most of my life has been spent in and around schools.

After graduating from college, I taught for a few years in high schools in Chicago. Then, while visiting Michael in Manhattan, where he had moved, first to study philosophy, then law, and to be with his girlfriend who was a dancer, I met choreographer Debra Loewen. Deb and I fell in love and, after living in New York for a year, we married and moved to Milwaukee when she received a fellowship to do graduate work at the University of Wisconsin.

On our first day in town, I was hired to teach math at Shalom High School, a small, private, independent, alternative school for young people who were failing and dropping out of the large, comprehensive high schools in Milwaukee. Shalom had been founded in 1973 and was operated by TransCenter for Youth, a small, nonprofit, nonsectarian agency. After my first year, the TransCenter board asked me to become the school's director—a combination of principal, fundraiser, bookkeeper, counselor, spokesperson, policy specialist, and janitor.

In those early years, Shalom ran on a shoestring budget. Nearly all of the students came from families living below the federal poverty level and so could not afford to pay private school tuition. The school survived on government and foundation grants and various fundraisers. Many of the teachers were volunteers. The few full-time staff members were paid low salaries and received no benefits. As director, I was paid $11,000 for my first twelve-month contract. We were essentially doing "missionary work."

The souls we were trying to save were those of the "marginal students" (as they were called in those days) who were not making it through the traditional System. Some of the students were bright and had dropped out because they were bored. Some were behind academically and dropped out because they were lost. Some had family or other personal problems complicating their lives. Nearly all of them had rebelled against the large, impersonal high schools that, with a few exceptions, condemned young people to four years of frustrating anonymity—that is, if they bothered to stay that long.

Some of the students did not drop out, but were thrown out. I remember one young African-American woman I will call "Bonita." Bonita was the perfect student. She was extremely intelligent, worked hard, and received straight "A's." She was an exceptional athlete. More than once, when it was her turn to serve for the girls' volleyball team, she hit fifteen aces in a row. She was a peace-maker. If a fight broke out between other students, Bonita could be counted on to intercede and help the antagonists work through their conflict and find a peaceful resolution.

One day, when she stopped by my office, I could not help asking her: "Why are you here, Bonita? You're every school's dream student." She told me she had been expelled from her previous school for hitting a teacher. "Why?" I asked.

"One of my teachers called me a nigger," she explained. "I reported the incident to the principal, but nothing was done about it. When the same teacher repeated the insult, I told her if she called me that again, I was going to slap her up side her head. Well, she did and I did and I was expelled." Bonita was quiet for a moment, and then she continued: "I know I was wrong. There are better ways to deal with ignorant people than violence." As far as she knew, the teacher was never disciplined for what she had said.

Some of the students did not drop out, but were pushed out. In Wisconsin, at that time, children were required to attend school until they were eighteen unless they had earned their diplomas or had formally "waived out," which they could do at sixteen. Dozens of Shalom's students told me that on their sixteenth birthday, if they happened to go to school that day, they had been met by an administrator who explained to them that if they signed a waiver form, one of which he just happened to have with him, they could legally drop out of school. Many of the students signed.[10]

As I got to know Shalom's students better and listened to their stories, I became obsessed with two questions: Were these young people (and their families) still part of "the public"? And if they were still part of "the public," then why weren't public funds following them to schools like Shalom where they were finding success? I came to realize that the meaning of the phrase "public education" had changed throughout United States history and, with so many students failing in the current System, it needed to continue to change.[11] A new vision was necessary.

I joined other community activists and pressed Wisconsin's Governor (then Democrat Tony Earl) and Legislature to enact what became the Children At Risk statute (WI s. 118.153), which allowed school districts with large numbers of dropouts like the Milwaukee Public Schools (MPS) to contract with private, nonprofit, nonsectarian agencies like TransCenter to support alternative schools like Shalom. The learning centers supported with these contracts were called "partnership schools," which were one of the first parts of an emerging new vision of "public education" in Wisconsin.[12]

Shalom was one of Milwaukee's first partnership schools, and thus converted from "private school" status to being a new type of "public school." When I signed that initial contract in 1985, our budget nearly quintupled. We were able to hire more teachers and pay them decent salaries and offer them health insurance and other benefits. And because all of our energy no longer had to be devoted to just surviving, we

10. When the compulsory attendance law was changed in Wisconsin in 1988, the dropout rate for African-Americans in the Milwaukee Public Schools, for example, jumped by over 5% in one year. The district could no longer hide the fact that it was pushing students out.

11. I invite anyone who doubts this assertion to read David Tyack's *The One Best System* or simply to reflect about how the meaning of "public education" changed from the time of *Plessy v. Ferguson*, when schools could be "separate but equal," to *Brown v. Board of Education of Topeka*.

12. For a fuller description of what evolved in Milwaukee, see my article, "Milwaukee's New Vision of Public Education," in *Education Revolution*.

were able to reflect upon our practice and revise the school's model so that we became even more effective in helping "at risk students" (as they came to be called) stay in school and graduate. This success and the fact that Shalom always had a long waiting list of young people trying to enroll led eventually to TransCenter opening two other schools for at risk students: the Northwest Opportunities Vocational Academy, or NOVA, and El Puente High School for Science, Math, and Technology.

However, contracting with MPS also brought us into an ongoing tension with a large urban bureaucracy. Like all large bodies, school bureaucracies have a huge inertial force and gravitational pull. They want to keep doing what they have been doing and, while they might tolerate some innovations at the margins, they are always trying to pull them back to the conventional way of doing things.[13] Even though some leaders in the school district understood, at some level, that to continue to do the same thing over and over and to expect different results was a species of insanity, the bureaucracy, like the scorpion in the old joke, could not help itself.[14] Every year, we had to fight for our autonomy. This struggle is unavoidable because bureaucracies, by their nature, cannot get the balance between *authority* and *responsibility* right. Examining the choice President Obama and his wife, Michelle, made for the schooling of their children will help clarify this problem.

Shortly after the November 2008 election, it was reported that they had decided to send their daughters to Sidwell Friends School when they moved to the nation's capital in January 2009. Their choice made sense. Sidwell Friends has an excellent reputation.[15]

I heard the news on the radio. The newscaster put it this way: "President-elect Barack Obama and his wife have decided to send their daughters to Sidwell Friends, the same private school Chelsea Clinton attended, instead of enrolling them in the Washington, D.C. public school system." What struck me was that the Obamas chose a *school* for their daughters, not a *system*. I believe one of the reasons so many

---

13. See Christensen, *Innovator*.

14. See Hess, *Same Thing*.

15. I would like to point out that the Obamas made a choice that most poor families can only dream of making. One hopes that, in reflecting about their decision, the President might reconsider his position on school choice. Perhaps, he will be forced to conclude, as I have, that giving resources to poor families must be seen as a progressive public policy.

Confessions of an Apostate from the Religion of "Education"

children fail in school in large urban areas is that "public education" there has been organized into systems.

At Sidwell Friends, decisions about how the school will function are made at the school itself, by the people working there. The parents of the students have to be pleased with the decisions that are made, of course, or they might choose to send their children elsewhere. But, for all practical purposes, the people working at Sidwell Friends have the autonomy to set the school's course and can make adjustments quickly as circumstances require.

By comparison, educators working within large public school systems have very little autonomy. All important decisions are made for them by people "managing the System," either in the bureaucracy or on the school board. The relationship between *responsibility* and *authority* is all wrong.

Consider an analogy. Imagine if the owner of a National Basketball Association franchise told his head coach: "I'm holding you responsible for the team's performance. If we don't make the play-offs this year, I'm going to fire you. However, you have no authority to decide if or when the team will practice; no authority to determine which players will be in the line-up, or which offenses or defenses will be used, or even when to call time-out. I'll make all those decisions from my luxury box. Good luck."

This sounds crazy, doesn't it? Isn't this similar to the situation educators face in our large public school systems? We expect the people working with our children to be accountable for student outcomes, but how can they be responsible when they are not in a position to make key decisions about their practice? And the people with the authority to make the decisions resent being held accountable because they are not the ones working with the students. No wonder that no matter how much money is poured into these systems and how many strategies for "reform" are tried, whether they come from the prickles or from the goo, we do not seem to be able to improve education outcomes for urban kids.

A second major problem with large bureaucracies is that they conflate standardization with having standards because they inevitably confuse *ends* and *means*. This confusion affects not only school bureaucracies, but the larger societal debate about "education reform." As I mentioned, we have yet to reach a consensus about what "education" is—about what we are trying to do. The word "education" has become

A Whole Which Is Greater

what linguist, Uwe Poerksen, calls a "plastic word": words that are "rarely used in a particular, precise, appropriate manner."[16]

Our English word "education" derives from the Latin verb *educare*, which originally meant "to breast-feed."[17] Used properly then, it should refer to well-nourished people, people who have grown to responsible maturity. I think it is good for people to grow up, so for a long time I tried to defend the word. But it had become so entangled with "schooling" I should have seen that it was impossible to save. I often advised people to heed Mark Twain's advice. He once said something like: "Never let your schooling interfere with your education."

Wendell Berry, the Kentucky writer and farmer, was one of the few people whose ideas about "education" made sense to me. Berry once wrote:

> Education in the true sense, of course, is an enablement to *serve*—both the living human community in its natural household or neighborhood and the precious cultural possessions that the living community inherits or should inherit. To educate is, literally, to "bring up," to bring young people to a responsible maturity, to help them to be good caretakers of what they have been given, to help them to be charitable toward fellow creatures.[18]

Most of us would probably support the *end* of helping young people grow "to a responsible maturity." (Different people would phrase this *end* in different ways: humanistic psychologists might say we want children to reach their full potential; those worried about democracy might say our goal should be to help young people become critical, thoughtful, active citizens; business leaders might be hoping we can prepare people to compete productively in the "global economy.") The question becomes: What *means* will help us reach our desired *ends*?

Anyone who takes the time to think about it will realize that we use all kinds of tools to help young people grow up: libraries, museums, science and nature centers, zoos, parks, fairs, carnivals, the media, the internet, travel, summer camps, and swimming, dance, and music lessons. Apprenticeships and internships are at least as effective learning tools as

---

16. Poerksen, *Plastic*, 8.
17. See Pat Farenga's "The Root of Education" in Hern, *Everywhere*.
18. Berry, *Home*, 52.

classrooms. People do not need schools in order to grow up as hundreds of thousands of "home schooled" children demonstrate every year.

But somehow, in the modern industrialized world, most of us have fooled ourselves into believing that only people who have been "schooled" can become "educated." (Is that Mark Twain I hear laughing?) And "schooling" itself has been narrowly equated with the "System" we compel young people to endure (for thirteen years in most states) so they can be treated and indoctrinated. (I'm sorry. I should say "socialized." I want to be polite.)

Drawing on Berry's definition, I began to think of "education" not as a thing that people were born without and needed "to get," but as the process by which a community keeps itself healthy. I argued that keeping communities healthy is the *end* we should be trying to achieve and that the educational process should be analyzed not only in its socio-economic and historical contexts, but in the ecological context as well. In the final analysis, communities cannot be healthy without drinkable water, breathable air, and sustainable sources of food.

The prickly proposals for national standards and merit pay for teachers and the gooey proposals for smaller class sizes and multicultural curricula really are not about "education" at all. These proposals are focused entirely on schooling. And schools do not educate people. Communities do. Schools are just some of the tools communities can use to promote "education."

These are some of the ideas that guided my efforts to keep spaces open for at risk students so that they would have multiple opportunities to find their way to lives worth living and work worth doing.

4

In the fall of 1993, I had the chance to tell these same stories and to make these same arguments to Ivan Illich, the Austrian-born historian and social critic. Illich had invited me to attend a gathering he had convened outside Columbia, Maryland to examine the concept of "hospitality."

On the second day, Illich and I took a walk through the woods near the site of the gathering. We were just getting to know each other and Ivan asked me about my work. So, I told him about Shalom High School and my struggle to keep it open. I told him about the young

A Whole Which Is Greater

people who attended the school and about the ways the System first damaged, then discarded them.

I told him about my efforts to help people understand that what has been meant by the phrase "public education" keeps changing throughout history and will continue to change with the times. I told him of my observation that it was almost impossible to get the relationship between authority and responsibility right in large urban school systems. I told him about the confusion of *ends* and *means* I saw in the ongoing debates about "education." I told him that I thought schools were only some of the tools that a community uses to educate its children.

I told him of my belief that "education" was best understood, not as an individual accomplishment, but as a community practice; not as a thing to be acquired, but as a process in which we are all inevitably engaged. I told him that I thought "education" had to be examined not only in socio-economic and historical contexts, but in the ecological context as well.

Ivan listened patiently to my ranting. When I finished, he looked into my eyes with his characteristically intense but compassionate gaze and said: "Daniel, you are asking the wrong questions. The question you should ask is: Why do we have such a low opinion of ourselves that we think we need to be educated in the first place?"

That question was the beginning of my apostasy. From Illich, I learned that modern people, living in industrialized societies, had turned "education" into a religion.[19] He first came to this realization in the 1950s while he was the vice-rector of the Catholic University of Puerto Rico and served on the board that oversaw the entire school system on the island. In a graduation speech, delivered at the University of Puerto Rico in Rio Piedras in the late 1960s, Illich concluded: "The Church, holy, catholic, apostolic, is rivaled by the school, accredited, compulsory, untouchable, universal. Alma Mater has replaced Mother Church. . . . The school has become the established church of secular times."[20]

Twenty years later, lecturing in Chicago, he developed the analogy: "Education" as an institution assumes that each person is born as an individual into a contractual society that must be understood before it is

---

19. Look at my own language: "missionary work," "savings souls," a school being "converted." Damn.

20. Illich, *Celebration*, 126–27.

Confessions of an Apostate from the Religion of "Education"

lived. According to this construct no one can become part of this kind of society except through some grace provided to him under the guise of education. This education is something for which he must work. But this education is also something that he cannot get except through the mediation of an agency: School, for *homo educandus*, is analogous to Church for the Christian.[21]

Illich observed that educators had become blasphemous to the point that they had come to believe that they could "do what God cannot, namely, manipulate others for their own salvation."[22] But, he also noted these educators inevitably privilege an elite who are destined for heaven, while condemning the vast majority to purgatory, if not hell.

Illich saw that schooling had become the mythopoetic or myth-making ritual of societies "committed to progress and development" and that "progress and development" had come to be defined as perpetually growing levels of production and consumption.[23]

In *Deschooling Society*, Illich exposed what he called "the hidden curriculum of schooling":

> Everywhere the hidden curriculum of schooling initiates the citizen to the myth that bureaucracies guided by scientific knowledge are efficient and benevolent. Everywhere this same curriculum instills in the pupil the myth that increased production will provide a better life. And everywhere it develops the habit of self-defeating consumption of services and alienating production, the tolerance for institutional dependence, and the recognition of institutional rankings. The hidden curriculum of school does all this in spite of contrary efforts undertaken by teachers and no matter what ideology prevails.

In other words, schools are fundamentally alike in all countries, be they fascist, democratic or socialist, big or small, rich or poor. This identity of the school system forces us to recognize the profound worldwide identity of myth, mode of production, and method of social control, despite the great variety of mythologies in which the myth finds expression.[24]

---

21. Illich, *Educational Enterprise*.
22. Illich, *Deschooling*, 50.
23. Cayley, *Ivan Illich*, 67.
24. Illich, *Deschooling*, 74.

A Whole Which Is Greater

To remedy the inevitable injustices caused by compulsory schooling, Illich proposed that education should be disestablished, just as all other religions had been disestablished in the United States. But, his hopes were not realized and schooling has continued to spread across the globe like plague.[25] In the context of Illich's analysis, the ongoing war between the prickles and the goo over "education reform" seems "kind of silly." (I'm quoting Marilyn Snell who was being polite.[26])

Are there alternatives to the religious fundamentalism of education?[27] I think there are, but for these to emerge, we are going to have to learn to see through other modern myths. We will have to give up the idea that there can be unlimited economic growth on a finite planet.[28] We are going to have to realize that consumption beyond certain limits does not lead to increased happiness and that, in Thoreau's words, people are "rich in proportion to the number of things which [they] can afford to let alone."[29] We will have to acknowledge that "progress," as it has come to be defined, is a community-damaging and soul-shredding myth.

Alternatives to a continued, ecocidal, global expansion of industrial society will require a revival of what Illich called "the vernacular,"[30] of what Wendell Berry calls "local economies" and "locally adapted communities,"[31] of what Paul Gilk calls "rural" or "folk culture."[32] Bringing them back is the real work.

The most important question facing our species in the twenty-first century has been beautifully framed by Wendell Berry: "Can we change the ways we live and work so as to establish a preserving harmony between the made and the given worlds?"[33]

25. I invite the reader to check out award-winning filmmaker Carol Black's "Schooling the World: The White Man's Last Burden."

26. Snell, *Invitation*.

27. I revealed how I have tried to deal with my own cognitive dissonance about "education" and "schooling" in "From Untouchables to Conscientious Objectors." See Hern, *Everywhere*.

28. See Mander, *Capitalism*, 81–104.

29. Thoreau, *Walden*, 78–79.

30. Illich, *Shadow*, 57–58.

31. Berry, *Art*.

32. Gilk, *Nature's Unruly Mob*.

33. Berry, *Way*, 72.

Confessions of an Apostate from the Religion of "Education"

I do not think the question Ivan asked me almost twenty years ago was a psychological one. He was a historian. The history of *homo educandus* has yet to be written, but I have a hunch the answer to his question is that we think we need to be "educated" because we have sacrificed "vernacular life" to the god of economics. As Illich's friend David Cayley pointed out, when a society worships economics: "Instead of assuming that learning is innate and depends only on the existence of an interesting and varied world, which we learn from by living in it, it makes the opposite assumption: that the means for learning are scarce and therefore must be constantly pursued in specialized institutions called schools."[34]

As apostasy to the religion of education and the god it serves grows, I hope more and more people will see through the prickly hype about "high performing" schools and look for more than gooey alternatives.

---

34. Cayley, *Part Moon.*

BIBLIOGRAPHY

Berry, Wendell. *The Art of the Commonplace.* Washington, DC: Counterpoint, 2002.
———. *Home Economics.* San Francisco: North Point Press, 1987.
———. *The Way of Ignorance.* Washington, DC: Shoemaker & Hoard, 2005.
Brill, Steven. *Class Warfare: Inside the Fight to Fix America's Schools.* New York: Simon & Schuster, 2011.
Cayley, David. *Ivan Illich in Conversation.* Concord, Ontario: House of Anansi Press, 1992.
———. *Part Moon, Part Traveling Salesman: Conversations with Ivan Illich.* Ideas. Toronto: CBC Radio, 1989.
Christensen, Clayton M. *The Innovator's Dilemma.* Boston: Harvard Business Press, 1997.
Cleaver, Eldridge. *Soul on Ice.* New York: McGraw-Hill, 1968.
Fanon, Frantz. *The Wretched of the Earth.* New York: Grove Press, 1968.
Fromm, Erich. *The Art of Loving.* New York: Harper & Row, 1956.
Gilk, Paul. *Nature's Unruly Mob: Farming and the Crisis in Rural Culture.* Eugene, OR: Wipf & Stock, 2009.
Gregg, Richard B. *The Power of Non-Violence.* Philadelphia: J.B. Lippincott, 1935.
Grego, Daniel. "Milwaukee's New Vision of Public Education" in *Education Revolution*, Volume 20, Number 1, Spring, 2008.
Hern, Matt, editor. *Everywhere All the Time: A New Deschooling Reader.* Oakland, CA: AK Press, 2008.
Hess, Frederick M. *The Same Thing Over and Over: How School Reformers Get Stuck in Yesterday's Ideas.* Cambridge, MA: Harvard University Press, 2010.
Illich, Ivan. *Celebration of Awareness: A Call for Institutional Revolution.* New York: Doubleday & Company, 1970.
———. *Deschooling Society.* New York: Harper & Row, 1971.
———. *The Educational Enterprise in the Light of the Gospel.* Unpublished manuscript of a lecture given in Chicago, November 13, 1988.
———. *Shadow Work.* London: Marion Boyars, 1981.
King, Martin Luther, Jr. *Strength to Love.* New York: Harper & Row, 1963.
Kohn, Alfie. *Feel-Bad Education.* Boston: Beacon Press, 2011.
Kohn, Alfie. "The Folly of Merit Pay" in *Education Week*, September 17, 2003.
Kozol, Jonathan. *Savage Inequalities.* New York: Crown Publishers, 1991.
Mander, Jerry. *The Capitalism Papers: Fatal Flaws of an Obsolete System.* Berkeley, CA: Counterpoint, 2012.
Poerksen, Uwe. *Plastic Words: The Tyranny of a Modular Language.* University Park, PA: Penn State Press, 1995.
Rethinking Schools Online. http://www.rethinkingschools.org/about/index.shtml.
Salomone, Rosemary C. *Visions of Schooling: Conscience, Community, and Common Education.* New Haven, CT: Yale University Press, 2000.
Snell, Marilyn. "An Invitation to Ivan Illich" in *Utne Reader*, January/February, 1995.
Thoreau, Henry David. *Walden.* Boston: Houghton Mifflin, 1995.
Tyack, David. *The One Best System: A History of American Urban Education.* Cambridge, MA: Harvard University Press, 1974.
Watts, Alan. *The Book: On the Taboo against Knowing Who You Are.* New York: Vintage Books, 1966.

9

Worldwide Neo-Liberal Development: A Challenge We Must Meet

John I. Laun

IN FEBRUARY AND MARCH of last year, 2011, tens of thousands of outraged Wisconsin residents converged upon the State Capitol in Madison to demonstrate their rejection of policies proposed by the new Wisconsin Governor, Republican Scott Walker. On one very cold Saturday afternoon my wife and I joined about 125,000 other people in the Capitol square protesting Walker's attack upon unions, disdain for public school teachers, and proposed largess of State funds for businesses. As he famously said after taking the oath of office for Governor, "The State is open for business." We did not know then what we know now: his playbook had been scripted by far right-wing business interests led by David and Charles Koch, who invited Walker and other Republican gubernatorial victors from other states to meetings where the policies they were to undertake were revealed to them. In Walker's case, the Kochs and their business had provided him with very substantial funding for his campaign.

The remarkable thing for me was that so many people responded spontaneously by literally taking to the streets to protest against Walker's measures. Demonstrations occurred in cities across the State, followed by recall campaigns against Republican State Senators who had voted for Walker's union-busting and other measures in the budget bills. Then what began in Wisconsin spread to other states where far-right Republicans had been elected Governors.

A Whole Which Is Greater

More surprising still was that the neo-liberal model against which Wisconsinites reacted also produced similar reactions elsewhere in the world where this model was being applied. In Colombia an estimated 50,000 people took to the streets in late February to oppose a Canadian mining company's proposal to build an open-pit gold and silver mine in an ecologically sensitive area near Bucaramanga, a city of more than 800,000 people in the eastern part of the country. The company, Greystar Resources, Ltd., had been encouraged to develop plans for a mine by the Colombian government of President Alvaro Uribe before he left office on August 7, 2010. (For further details on Greystar's plans and the effective opposition to them, see my report, Exhibit 1 in the Appendix to this article.)

Here's what we are facing: a blind belief in the positive effects of providing wealth to corporations, not principally corporations which produce products in the United States, but rather those which outsource production to save on labor costs. And when the right-wing Republicans and tea party folks cry out against labor unions which have historically protected workers' rights, they act utterly against their own best interests. Only an ignorant populace mesmerized by misinformation in the media could be so irrational as to actively work against their own economic interests.

But it is not only in this country that we find such a perverse reaction to economic policies which hurt the majority of the people. What is happening in the United States is part of a global strategy. Countries are assigned roles to play in the international economy. The United States is more and more dominated by service industries; companies here seeking bottom-dollar labor costs produce their goods overseas in countries where laborers have few rights and their countries' governments take little interest in protection of workers in the workplace and in establishing decent wage levels, health care and education. Meanwhile our captains of industry complain that they cannot afford to pay higher wages, health care costs, and retirement benefits. Speculators on Wall Street drive the economy; officers of the biggest banks are paid obscenely large salaries with valuable stock options, even though these same banks contributed to the collapse of the economy through their loan and investment policies. At the same time the right to a free public education in grade and high schools, the most fundamentally important

Worldwide Neo-Liberal Development: A Challenge We Must Meet

right of citizens in this country, comes under threat as schoolteachers are maligned and public budgets for education are slashed.

Colombia, with Latin America's third largest population, 46 million people, has for the last nine years in its leaders' eyes been the strongest supporter of United States government policies in Latin America. Employers have been encouraged to utilize employment search services or employer-owned "cooperatives" to provide short-term employment, firing workers when their six-month probationary period is up to avoid paying for pensions, health care or other benefits. Unions have been attacked, including by the Colombian Army and Police acting in concert with illegal paramilitary forces. Thus the few rich Colombians become much richer, and the poor much poorer. In this sense, Colombia is now where the United States is headed. We are in a sense seeing the economic and social "Colombianization" of the United States.

The current President of Colombia, Juan Manuel Santos, has established a plan for his country, which he calls a "locomotive engine for growth." Recently, substantial mineral deposits have been discovered in the country. President Santos, like his predecessor Alvaro Uribe Velez, has focused attention on inviting in foreign capital and multinational businesses to build mining operations for gold, silver and other metals, while also expanding oil exploration and production.

A look at the terms of concessions to the multinational companies is revealing. The Colombian nation is given ownership of subsurface minerals by the Colombian Constitution, thus concessions must be sought from the Colombian government. As the former Minister of the Environment, Manuel Rodriguez Becerra, noted in a July 10, 2011 article in the Bogota daily *El Tiempo*, the Uribe Administration granted multi-year tax exemptions to foreign mining companies and charged royalty payments of only four percent on the gold removed by these mining companies, and the percentage charged was not linked to the price of gold, as is done in other countries. Citing a study by a Colombian economist, Guillermo Rudas, Rodriguez observed that: "In 2009 royalties paid were 1.93 billion and exemptions were 1.75 billion. Which is to say, [the Government] practically repaid them their royalties! On this mining locomotive only a few privileged ones are on board." Nor were requirements for creation of jobs made, nor were limits placed upon repatriation of funds from Colombia to the home country of the mining company. Environmental regulations were minimal, including for mining projects in the environmentally sensitive Amazon region or in water-producing highland areas known as *paramos*. Nor were open-pit or mountaintop-removal projects banned. Although the Constitution and laws require consultations with indigenous and Afro-Colombian communities in advance before any mining project can be undertaken in lands where these communities are located, effective prior consultation (*consulta previa*) has rarely been conducted. This is also true for other development projects in these communities' lands.

An example of how the process of project approval has been carried out is the current proposed new highway between the town of San Francisco in the Sibundoy Valley in Putumayo Department and the Putumayo capital city of Mocoa. This road, called the San Francisco-Mocoa *variante* (spur), is to form a part of a superhighway running through the Amazon region from Belem on the Atlantic Ocean in Brazil all the way across the continent to Tumaco, Colombia on the Pacific Ocean. The stretch of road between San Francisco and Mocoa would replace an existing road, which everyone in the area agrees is in bad shape, by proceeding through a water-producing highland area. Several thousand old-growth trees would be cut down to make way for the road. Two indigenous communities which have long lived in the Sibundoy Valley, the Kamentsa and the Inga, are certain the valley will dry out, ending their ability to grow food crops, while displacing their burial grounds and traditional cultural areas, leading to the end of their existence as indigenous communities.

Those who wish the road to be built, including multinational mining interests looking to transport ore out of the region, have received approval of the World Wildlife Fund, which has supported the regional environmental agency, Corpoamazonia, in favoring construction of the new road. The Inter-American Development Bank (IADB) has provided preliminary approval for over $200 million in financing for the road project, without following required procedures for prior consultation with elders of the Camentsa and Inga communities. These procedures must include prior consultation with indigenous communities following the consultation mechanisms of these communities, in this case consultation with a group meeting of the community leaders, known as "*taitas*." Such a consultation has not taken place, and, if it were to take place, most of the *taitas* have indicated their disapproval of the plan. (For more details on the controversy over the road, and the Colombia

Worldwide Neo-Liberal Development: A Challenge We Must Meet

Support Network's role in supporting the position of the Kamentsa and Inga communities, make requests through the wesbsite of Colombia Support Network. As to the World Wildlife Fund's support for the planned new road, see the organization's 2011 report, "The road to development: building a policy case from the grassroots." Interestingly, a coordinator of environmental policy charged with monitoring the San Francisco-Mocoa road project for the World Wildlife Fund (known in Colombia as the Fondo Mundial para la Naturaleza), Juan Carlos Espinosa, is now working for Fedepalma, the federation of African palm growers, which supports large-scale African palm development.)

Besides the invitation to multinational mining and oil interests, the Santos administration has established a plan for a second engine of development, which seeks to open vast parts of Colombia's sparsely settled eastern plains and Amazon rainforest areas to foreign investors to develop large-scale African palm plantations and for other export crops. The Colombian government's vision is that Colombia will fit into the world capitalist system as a producer of gold, silver and other precious metals, as well as oil and coal, and as an exporter of large-scale crops. The bilateral so-called Free Trade Agreement which the Colombian and U.S. governments have negotiated and which was put into effect by President Barack Obama on May 15, 2012, will decimate the small farmers' (campesinos') ability to market their crops, as food crops from the United States will enter without tariffs into Colombia at prices so low that local producers of these food crops will be unable to compete. While the Obama Administration has developed a list of protections for labor leaders and workers, including an end to the employer-sponsored "cooperative" system which effectively relieved employers from obligations to the workers by making the workers employees of the cooperatives, not the businesses in which they worked, this wish list has not lowered the violence against labor leaders and union members. Colombia continues to lead the world in number of labor union leaders killed. (For more detailed information about the Free Trade Agreement and what its effects are likely to be, see the articles collected as Exhibits 2 and 3 in the Appendix.)

But the FTA is unlikely to provide much benefit to U.S. workers either. It will very likely expand the riches of multinational businesses but not substantially increase employment in the United States. Take, for example, the case of Caterpillar, a manufacturer of large construction equipment such as bulldozers and earth movers. The elimination of tariffs by Colombia on U.S. companies' equipment should stimulate sales of Caterpillar products to Colombia. But Caterpillar plans to open several new production facilities in China, where low wage levels will lead to higher profits for the company. So the additional products sold to Colombia will likely be made in China by Chinese workers, not adding to employment of U.S. workers.

This, of course, is the very essence of the neo-liberal model which threatens workers throughout the world. As far as Colombia is concerned, both the Obama Administration and the Santos Administration are anxious to proceed.

But remarkably, resistance to this model has appeared where one might least expect it. The spontaneous opposition of people in Madison demonstrated by the thousands who gathered in protest at the State Capitol was matched by a march of an estimated 50,000 people in the city of Bucaramanga, Colombia, protesting the plan of Greystar Resources to develop an open-pit mine in the environmentally sensitive highlands known as the Santurban paramo. The popular protest by the thousands of people who were concerned that their water supply would be placed in jeopardy by the Greystar project led to a public hearing which thousands of people attended and which caused government officials to deny a permit to Greystar on environmental grounds. This successful protest has led to public protests in other parts of Colombia where multinational corporations had been given concessions by the Uribe government to develop plans for open pit, mountaintop removal mines for gold, silver and other precious metals. Also, indigenous communities, such as the Kamentsa and Inga communities in the Sibundoy Valley, have protested publicly the multinational plans which threaten their communities and their way of life.

Nothing is more important in this struggle against imposition of the neo-liberal model on a worldwide basis than the solidarity of those who are threatened by this model as applied in their countries. We have begun the struggle. The great challenge is to expand and strengthen this opposition to neo-liberalism.

Exhibit 1

REPORT ON SANTURBAN MINING PROJECT OF GREYSTAR RESOURCES

John I. Laun
March 14, 2011

On March 2, 2011, I traveled to Colombia to attend a hearing on March 4 before an official of the Colombian Government's Ministry of Environment, Housing, and Territorial Development.[1] The hearing was held in the city of Bucaramanga, the capital city of Santander Department (Province). The subject of the hearing was a proposal by a Canadian mining company, Greystar Resources Ltd., to develop an open-pit gold and silver mine in an ecologically sensitive area located between 3,000 and 5,000 meters above sea level known as the Santurban paramo. This paramo, like others in Colombia, is a source of water for communities at lower altitudes, including the city of Bucaramanga, which has more than 800,000 residents.

My purpose in making the trip to Colombia was to discuss with environmental protection organizations there, as well as governmental figures, the nature of the threat posed by the mining proposal and whether it might be stopped by convincing Colombian government leaders of the dangers presented by Greystar's proposed mine, named the Angostura Project for a stream in the immediate vicinity of the mine. In developing the mine, Greystar plans to excavate more than 2,700 acres and construct two piles of tailings and a dump at an altitude of 8,500 to 13,450 feet. Heavy machinery will be used to remove the covering of vegetation to expose the soil and rock, which will be removed with explosives.

Greystar proposes to open a hole 656 feet deep and remove 1.075 billion tons of rock, of which 775 million tons will be dumped and 300 million tons will go to two leaching water basins. The plan calls for .25 kilograms of explosives to be used per ton of rock removed per hour. Sodium cyanide at a concentration of 500 milligrams per liter of water will be used in the gold ore separation process. The sodium cyanide used in each water basin would be 4,500 to 5,000 cubic meters per hour.

The cycle is planned to be 60 days long and the time of leaching would be 10 years. Greystar plans to use 250,000 liters of water per hour in the mining process. It proposes to extract 11.5 million ounces of gold and 61 million ounces of silver over 15 years.

The Santurban paramo captures water and supplies it to 20 municipalities in the region, including the City of Bucaramanga. Environmentalists I spoke to in Bucaramanga before the hearing, among them Orlando Beltran Quesada, President of the environmental NGO Adan, stressed the danger to the water supply that the large use of water (250,000 liters per hour) would represent, with the likely consequence of reducing the groundwater supply and diminishing aquifers in the area. This would reduce availability of water for small-scale farmers in the region, diminish water supplies for cattle-raising and other uses in the lowlands which depend upon water from the paramo, and affect the water supply for residents of the small towns of California and Vetas, which lie in the immediate vicinity of the mining operation. And the use of cyanide in large quantities in the process of extracting gold represents in the eyes of many area residents a very dangerous potential threat. Although Greystar officials have minimized the threat to public health from the cyanide they would use in the production process, many opponents of the Greystar project focus their attention on the very large use of cyanide that Greystar has proposed. The Santurban paramo lies in a highly active seismic zone, where tremors are common. What would happen, people living in the region say, if an earthquake were to occur in the Santurban area? The ponds where cyanide is used might break up, releasing the chemical into streams that provide drinking water for Bucaramanga and other communities, killing fish, frogs and other amphibians in the paramo and putting people's lives at risk in these communities. Moreover, containers where cyanide is stored might collapse, releasing the deadly chemical. And trucks transporting cyanide to the mine site might be forced off the roads, already said by those who have seen them to be in poor condition, spilling their poisonous loads.

All of these arguments against the Greystar project were mentioned at the hearing on Friday, March 4. The hearing was held before a very large crowd of perhaps 2,000 people in a large auditorium in the town of Giron, near Bucaramanga. Greystar had set up a display near the entrance to the auditorium, and reportedly bussed in 3 busloads of people from communities near the mine, especially California and Vetas, and provided an ample lunch for them. These folks, whom the company has assured will be the beneficiaries of jobs Greystar says it will bring to the region, as well as funds for schoolchildren and community facilities and programs, appear to be largely in favor of the mining project. The critics of the Greystar project, much larger in number, sat on the opposite side of the auditorium. I sat with them and a request was made on my behalf to allow me to speak on behalf of the international community in opposition to Greystar's plans. I might have been able to do so, had not a spirited shouting match between supporters of Greystar and their opponents broken out and turned very confrontational. The shouting of each side against the other began almost as soon as the hearing began about 9:30 a.m. and continued, with occasional warnings from the official of the Ministry of Environment, Housing and Territorial Development who was in charge of the meeting, Dr. Luz Helena Sarmiento Villamizar, that she might suspend the hearing for lack of security. After 5½ hours, during which only some 40 of the 480 persons who had signed up to speak had been heard, a confrontation occurred between opponents of the project and a supporter who jumped from the stage where he had been speaking to confront the hecklers. At that point Dr. Sarmiento declared the hearing concluded. Later that day we heard that no further testimony would be taken and that a decision on the environmental compliance or lack thereof by Greystar would be forthcoming from the Ministry in two weeks, i.e., on March 18.

There were some very significant developments during the hearing. Public officials were the first to speak. The Governor of Santander, former Presidential candidate Horacio Serpa, who had not stated publicly if he was in support of the project or against it, came out against the Greystar plan. He said his office had studied the proposed mining project in great detail and had concluded that the environmental license should be denied to Greystar. He noted that the Colombian Congress had passed a law outlawing mining in paramos, which he said he supported, and he observed that the great majority of Santander residents are against the mining plan.

Likewise, a representative of the Mayor of Bucaramanga spoke against the plan, as did a representative of the Colombian Procurador's (Inspector General's) office, expressing doubt about Greystar's capacity to manage environmental problems should they arise. And a representative of the Defensor del Pueblo's (Public Defender's) office suggested that Santurban should be made a public park, with no mining permitted there. Next, a representative of the Organization for the Defense of the Meseta of Bucaramanga spoke against the project, noting the potential for natural disaster and observing "Nature never pardons." That brought to mind the fact that at 5 p.m. on the day before the hearing heavy rains had caused an avalanche at the Angostura River, virtually at the place the Greystar project was be carred out, resulting in 3 deaths and five homes being destroyed. As one speaker against the project said, "Nature itself has spoken."

Supporters of the project who spoke included the mayor and the city clerk (personero) of California and the mayor of Vetas, who stressed the area's long history of mining and the government's historical ignoring of their towns and their needs. For these municipal officials, Greystar represents a promise of development and an improvement in their community resources and standard of living.

After these government officials had spoken, Orlando Beltran was given 20 minutes to speak on behalf of environmentalists. He noted the tragic avalanche of the previous day and said it might have been caused by the lack of care of Greystar in carrying on its preparatory works in the area. He cited Eduardo Galeano as opposed to open-pit mining, and noted prohibition in some countries to use of cyanide in mining processes. He criticized former President Alvaro Uribe for promoting the Santurban and other projects of foreign mining companies. He referred to Mining Watch Canada as a knowledgeable Canadian opponent of Greystar's Angostura Project.

Following Orlando's presentation, Greystar was given 20 minutes to present its case in favor of the mining project. A Peruvian representative spoke for Greystar and emphasized that the company was confident that water for Bucaramanga would not be affected. He said there would be water treatment plants. He suggested that Greystar had increased the security in the area (which had formerly been the site of some guerrilla activity). He stressed that the soils were "firm" in the mining area and discounted the likelihood of serious effects from seismic activity in the area. And he said Greystar would manage the cyanide used in its processes in accord with the International Code of Cyanide, and that the ponds would not be affected.

Senator Jorge Enrique Robledo of the opposition Polo Democratico Alternativo Party spoke next. He focused upon the small value that area residents and the Colombian government would receive from the Greystar project. Only some 3.5% of the royalties would remain with Colombia. He pointed out the danger presented by the use of explosives and cyanide in the paramo, and said he favored the law against mining in the paramos of Colombia. And he said when water is put into play, the principle of being especially careful must be followed. Saying the Greystar project must not be approved, he intoned "Today all Colombians are Santandereanos!"

Next, Gloria Florez, the Colombian representative in the Andean Parliament and a Bucaramanga native, spoke out against the Greystar project. She noted that non-renewable resources such as those in Santurban cannot be replaced once they have been damaged, and she suggested it should be made a national park. She acknowledged a commitment to development of communities, but opposed the Greystar project. Senator Jorge Gomez Villamizar followed, noting that Colombia has 49% of the world's paramos and stressing the low level of royalties the Greystar project would produce for Colombia. Another speaker stated that Greystar would wind up with 85.8% of the profits from the Santurban project. He noted that the World Bank and J.P. Morgan had invested in the project and were allies of Greystar in its plan to reap great profits at the cost of Colombia's resources, and said he opposed granting the environmental license to Greystar.

Several other members of the audience came forward to speak, most by far against the project. Then, at 3 p.m., the threat of a fist-fight on the auditorium floor brought the decision to end the hearing.

After leaving the auditorium and in the two following days, I was interviewed twice on television and met with two local reporters, one a correspondent for Bogota's *El Espectador* newspaper. I told them that I opposed the Greystar project because it threatened the water supply for Bucaramanga and some 20 other communities, presented the very real possibility of a catastrophic accident given the substantial, continuous seismic activity in the area, and as an open-pit mining project would scar the land permanently. I also said I favored enforcing the law the Colombian Congress had passed against all mining in paramos. In addition, I indicated that I do not believe the Colombian government has the technical resources or a proper regulatory framework to evaluate the Greystar project. I also discussed the unfair, in fact scandalous, proposed distribution of benefits from the mining project, which would leave Colombia with no more than 12% of the value of the gold and silver taken from the Santurban mine, while enriching Greystar. And I expressed doubt that Greystar, which registered in Colombia with only about $40,000 in capital and which has limited resources and limited experience (Santurban being its only project in the world), would be able to respond financially if its mining activity were to cause a catastrophe. There is one further point that I believe should be taken into account. Water itself is a valuable resource. Any fair calculation of the price for developing a mine should take into account the value of the water being used in the project. The 250,000 liters per hour that Greystar has proposed using in the Santurban mine project should not, in my view, be considered free to Greystar. In calculating how much the Colombian government should charge any international mining company, the price of the use of water and other natural resources in the mining process should be a part of the charge made to the company, in addition to royalties and a tax on profits.[2]

I had intended to visit the mine site on the day after the hearing, but I was told by members of the environmental protection organizations and a reporter who interviewed me that it was not feasible to travel there, because of the poor state of the roads, especially after the March 3 avalanches. I was also told that private security forces or paramilitaries hired by Greystar might prevent me from reaching the proposed mine site. I decided, therefore, not to try to make the trip to the Santurban paramo.

On Monday afternoon, March 7, I met with Colombia's Vice President, Angelino Garzon, at his office in Bogota. He received me very cordially and gave me about 40 minutes of his time. I mentioned to him that I had attended the hearing on the Santurban project and gave him originals of my letters of representation. When I expressed my hope that the Greystar project not be approved, the Vice President told me two things: 1) that the Colombian government was thoroughly aware of the drawbacks of the proposed Santurban project; and 2) that he believed that we who oppose the project do not have to worry that it might be approved. I surely hope the decision of the Ministry of Environment, Housing and Territorial Development proves Dr. Garzon right.

ENDNOTES

1. I carried letters of representation from Mining Watch Canada based in Ottawa, Canada; the Council on Hemispheric Affairs (COHA) of Washington, D.C.; the Center for Alternative Mining Development Policy, based in La Crosse, Wisconsin; the University of Wisconsin-Madison Latin American, Caribbean and Iberian Studies Program; and the Colombia Support Network (CSN), with headquarters in Madison, Wisconsin. I wish to thank all of these organizations for the support they provided to me. I also am indebted to the numerous individual contributors who made my trip possible.

2. In a February 17, 2011 report, Greystar stated that 54% of the income generated by the Angostura Project would remain in Colombia. Its percentage breakdown of these income figures was as follows: Investment on gross Income, 5%; royalties, 4%; Operational Costs, 48%; Colombian Taxes, 23%; Capital Costs, 20%. In a March 7, 2011 news release, Greystar expressed disappointment at the early termination of the March 4 hearing and said it had brought several international experts to the meeting, whom it expected would present "their respective statements and supporting reports but did not have the opportunity to do so." Greystar President and CEO Steve Kesler is quoted as follows: "Clearly there are divisions within communities and within authorities on this project. Greystar will only develop a project with the support of both." If that is true, the Santurban Project would appear far from ready to proceed, even in Greystar's opinion.

Exhibit 2

SOME OBSERVATIONS ON THE COLOMBIA-U.S. BILATERAL TRADE AGREEMENT

The Colombia-U.S. "Free Trade Agreement" (FTA), as passed by the U.S. Congress and being implemented by the two countries, will have several negative effects upon Colombia.

Among these are the following:

1. Colombian campesinos, small scale farmers with very limited economic resources, will suffer the loss of their traditional markets. Subsidized food crops from the United States will undercut prices in Colombia for such products, leaving the campesinos with nowhere to market their products, such as corn, rice and other staple products. This will increase poverty in rural areas, already a very serious concern, since hundreds of thousands of campesinos were forced off their lands during the Presidential terms of Alvaro Uribe Velez from 2002–2010. Colombia has some 4 million internally displaced persons, and the FTA will only add to this problem.

2. Some larger Colombian agricultural producers, such as those of cotton and sugar cane, may find imports from the U.S., subsidized by the U.S. government, threatening their markets, for example for cotton and sugar.

3. Colombian manufacturing businesses will face increased competition from the entry of U.S. manufacturing concerns into the Colombian market on a preferential basis. This combined with intellectual property protections allowed to the U.S. companies will likely force some Colombian businesses to close. For example, Colombian pharmaceutical manufacturers may find it impossible to compete and to market their products successfully.

4. Indigenous peoples in Colombia are very concerned that intellectual property provisions relating to patent rights may have the effect of cutting off their access to traditional medicines, a fundamentally important part of their culture.

5. Preference for products produced in the United States may result in the decline and disappearance of traditional Colombian products. Thus favorable treatment for wheat may undermine local growing of quinoa and other traditional cereal crops.

6. The Colombian government has failed to provide adequate protection for unionized workers and their leaders. While President Obama expressed concern about the large number of union workers being murdered in Colombia—a large number of them by paramilitaries hired by U.S.-based companies, such as Drummond Coal and Chiquita Brands—insufficient steps have been taken to reduce these killings, which continue unabated. And very few murders of union members result in convictions. Without a strong commitment to ending this union-busting-through-murder phenomenon and impunity for these crimes, violence will continue to threaten workers seeking to protect themselves and their employment from employers' repressive actions. And the U.S. should press Colombia to outlaw a procedure permitting Colombian employers to sponsor "cooperatives" as an alternative to labor unions. These "cooperatives" are associations which eliminate a direct employment relationship between the workers and the employer, who is then able to avoid providing benefits to the workers and whose wage payments to them are often scandalously low. While the Colombian government has promised to take steps to reduce or eliminate this phenomenon, few practical results have been demonstrated.

7. As products from the U.S. take market share from local Colombian products, the advertisements for such products will become ever more pervasive, leaving native Colombian culture and mores ever more difficult to preserve.

Exhibit 3

THREE MISCONCEPTIONS ABOUT INTERNATIONAL TRADE

Jack I. Laun

U.S. President Barack Obama and Colombian President Juan Manuel Santos agreed to put the so-called "Free Trade Agreement" (FTA) between the United States and Colombia into effect on May 15, 2012. The provisions of this bilateral accord were debated in the U.S. Congress for several years, with a focus upon labor rights and the extraordinary level of violence against labor leaders in Colombia. Although attacks against labor leaders continue in Colombia and the effectiveness of promised protections for labor organizations, which helped the measure win passage in the U.S. Congress, is questionable, President Obama and U.S. Trade Representative Ron Kirk embraced the FTA with Colombia as a likely source of new jobs for U.S. workers.

The fact is, however, that the expected benefits of this FTA are illusory. This expectation is based upon some important misconceptions about international trade and who benefits from it. For the United States the suggestion that the FTA will benefit U.S. workers fails to take into account certain realities of the current economic system. The fact that Colombian import duties for U.S. products will be reduced or eliminated does not necessarily mean an increase in jobs in the United States, because many U.S.–based companies produce their goods outside the United States, taking advantage of cheap labor and limited or nonexistent environmental and workers' health and safety provisions in the cheap labor countries. Thus, for example, Caterpillar, a company historically based in Peoria, Illinois, may benefit from reduced Colombian import duties on heavy construction machinery the company produces. But Caterpillar has reportedly undertaken construction of new plants for production of its machinery in China, which has low labor costs. What is to prevent Caterpillar from producing the equipment it sends to Colombia in China, thus not increasing employment in the United States? As far as I know nothing is in place to prevent this. And there are plenty of other companies in the U.S. that will behave as I have

Worldwide Neo-Liberal Development: A Challenge We Must Meet

indicated Caterpillar would. The first misconception, therefore, is that elimination of import duties in Colombia must necessarily lead to job creation in the United States.

A second misconception has to do with how businesses operate. We hear that the goal of a corporation is to maximize profits, and that a fundamental part of the work of a company executive and the company's board of directors is to squeeze out the largest possible profits from company operations. This means that companies acting rationally will look to produce their products in the way that results in the largest profit margin, basically looking for the lowest labor costs. In our society it seems even "liberal" commentators take this as a given. But this is a fundamental misconception. A company may operate profitably even if it employs labor at a higher cost than it might find overseas, treating its employees well and providing them with what we have come to call "fringe benefits." Maximization of profits is not, and should not be, the principal goal of business. The goal should be to produce items that are useful for society and to provide a healthy work environment and compensation to employees that will enable them to obtain what they need to live in dignity. This used to be called, with reason, a "living wage."

Which brings us to the third misconception, which is that protective tariffs are ipso facto bad, and that "free trade" is by its very nature good and desirable. Years ago in the United States the goal of this country's participation in international commerce was "balanced trade," not "free trade." This meant that the government would consciously try to protect employment in this country by limiting the amount of products coming into this country at lower cost through application of tariffs to the lower cost products. The glorification of multinational or transnational businesses, which typically have very little commitment to any one country, has led the U.S. government essentially to abandon the concept of balanced trade. We need to re-establish this concept as a guiding principle of U.S. trade policy.

This discussion has not highlighted the extraordinarily negative effects of the proposed FTA on Colombia. These effects are discussed in detail elsewhere, but suffice it to say here that the effects will virtually end market access for food products of small-scale farmers (campesinos), leading to an increase in displacement in a country which already leads the world in internally displaced people with some 4.5 million displaced persons (nearly 10% of Colombia's 46 million people), while not providing significant protection to workers and their union organizations. Nor will the intellectual property provisions of the FTA protect indigenous communities' access to their traditional medicinal herbs or allow numerous Colombian businesses to develop products already produced by multinational businesses, which are the real potential beneficiaries of the FTA.

10

Seeing Our Struggle from Distant Shores

Jeff Leigh

During the 2010–2011 academic year, I took a leave of absence from my professorship in history in the University of Wisconsin system to serve as a professor of cultural studies in the Republic of Lebanon under the auspices of the Fulbright U.S. Scholars' program. While many of my U.S. colleagues were engaged in the struggle here at home to preserve the public sphere (that part of social life wherein the public debates issues of its well-being) and the public sector (those state-run agencies that promote the common good), I was stuck on the sidelines watching not only the efforts made in Madison upon my behalf but also the far more difficult endeavors taking place around me in the Middle East.

Beginning on December 18, 2010, with the self-immolation of Muhammad Bouazizi in Tunisia, the entire Middle Eastern region convulsed with demonstrations by peoples demanding an end to their long-standing oppression at the hands of corrupt, malicious regimes. Within a year, governments in Tunisia, Egypt, and Libya had fallen, those in Yemen and Syria faced civil insurrection, while all others were pushed to promise substantial reform.

While some observers have likened the events occurring in the Middle East to those in the Mid-West and have teasingly quipped about the desire to bring Cairo to Wisconsin, it would, of course, be ridiculous to equate the suffering of peoples in the Middle East and the inherently dysfunctional and mendacious systems of government there with the troubles facing Wisconsinites under Governor Walker. While, as a proud Wisconsin public employee, I certainly had "a dog in the fight" taking place in Wisconsin and therefore sorely missed the opportunity to participate in protecting our common interests, I feel that I benefited even more from the opportunity to see this struggle from distant shores and—through different eyes—I gained a new insight into my duties as a citizen and a new commitment to social action.

In the Middle East, as in much of the world today and indeed in the entire world throughout most of human history, government has been overwhelmingly a force for the preservation of elite interest and a predator upon the weak and vulnerable. While these conclusions about the traditional use of government are usually associated with the traditions of 19th- and 20th-Century European radicalism, exemplified by Pierre-Joseph Proudhon, Mikhail Bakunin, and, in a very different sense, Karl Marx and Vladimir Lenin, they go far back into the Chinese philosophy of Daoism, the conclusions of the Cynic philosophers of ancient Greece, and recurring strands of Jewish, Christian, and Islamic thought wherein the spiritual and material needs of the poor are juxtaposed to the behavior of the wealthy and powerful. These conclusions also occupy a central space in our understanding of the origins of democracy in 6th-century Athens and the rise of republican governance in Rome. In both of these cases new political systems were developed to rescue political stability from the failings of governments dominated by a narrow range of aristocrats. In Athens, under the reforms of Solon and then Cleisthenes, common citizens were first freed from the worst effects of private debt and great economic and social inequality, and then, to ensure that these changes would not be quickly overturned, the political system was reformed to create truly representative legislative bodies. In Rome, through acts of military insubordination, the common citizens (plebeians) won for themselves the right to name tribunes who could veto legislation deemed prejudicial to the plebeian interest, the promulgation of a constitution outlining the rights of all Roman citizens, and the building of popular legislative assemblies. Under Roman law, the plebeians enjoyed the protections of equality before the law, trial by their peers, and a judicial system armed with the powers of interpreting the law and setting of legal precedent.

The rise of modern participatory government was no less attended by the willingness of the common people to take risks in the pursuit of their own interests. The products of the modern history profession have provided us copious examples of the difficulties faced by most of our fellow human beings and all of our ancestors to create what is perhaps the most important of all human accomplishments: government for the people, by the people. They have also provided us lessons of what often occurs as governments, once made responsive to the public interest, are allowed to slide increasingly in the direction of promoting elite rather than popular interests. Democracy in Athens, the Republic in Rome, and many modern democracies have failed in this way.

While in Lebanon, I learned something about the skills and moreover the mindset necessary to maintain a democracy. Lebanon, a parliamentary democracy, still abides by the stipulation established in the constitution of 1926 calling for political representation upon the basis of religious identity. This clause became operative with the 1943 declaration of independence and the National Pact, an agreement among the political elite setting out the conditions and procedures for assuring representation by religion. In this agreement, the Christians—the largest single religious bloc according to the census of 1932—were assured political predominance with 6/11ths of the seats in parliament and control over the office of the president, who would be elected from among Christian candidates by a unicameral legislature made up of all religious confessions. The president then presided over the cabinet. The prime minister would be a Sunni Muslim, but appointed by the president, and the speaker of the parliament would be a Shi'ite Muslim, elected by the parliament. The failure of this system was evinced by the civil war, 1975–1991, which ended with the agreement of the major erstwhile political entities to the Taif Accords, negotiated by the surviving members of the 1972 parliament. These accords solved none of the underlying problems that led to war. They merely altered the ratios in the sectarian system of political representation to create a fairer balance for the Muslims, who now would possess a 50/50 split with the Christians in the number of seats in the parliament. The accords also provided for more representation for smaller religious communities, accommodated by increasing the number of seats in the parliament, ultimately to 128. Similarly, the powers of the Christian president were sharply curtailed. The naming of the prime minister now requires the approval of the parliamentary majority. The president still attends cabinet meetings, but he no longer presides and has no vote in their deliberations. The right to dissolve the parliament was removed from the president and given to the cabinet as a whole. Furthermore, presidential decrees now require the signature of the prime minister. Ultimately, this second republic, stemming from the Taif Accords, is to give way to a third republic which will be marked by the end of political sectarianism. To date, however, there has been no movement towards this goal.

While the political system in Lebanon provides for the representation of minorities who might otherwise find it hard to voice their interests at the national level, it also reinforces the long-standing sectarian divide and the concept of parliamentary democracy as a way to defend specific group interest vis-à-vis those of rival groups. Political power and even career opportunities are circumscribed by sect identity, and religious bigotry remains a common part of social life. A change in the political structure will require a concomitant devotion to the alteration of popular opinion regarding the reliability and worth of members of other religions. As it stands, it is extremely difficult for leaders to emerge from this system with the goal of benefiting the public as a whole since power is channeled first and foremost through singular constituencies defined by religious identity. The system further suffers from gaps in democratic culture: there is not yet a firm attachment to the rule of law, little tradition of loyal opposition, and still no successful political party cast as an alternative to sect interest. The public interest, such as it exists, is divided geographically and in terms of sect identity, and the public sphere—as we would use the term—is manifestly weak, as is the public sector. The primacy of private interest and a strong distrust of others are endemic throughout Lebanese society. Many people hope for something better, but the system is so far immune to change.

Shortly after the demonstrations in Madison began, I was beset by concerned colleagues from many countries who uniformly expressed stunned disbelief that such attacks on the public sphere and public sector should occur in, of all places, Wisconsin. Since Wisconsin enjoys an international reputation for progressivism and good governance, my colleagues, though familiar with the trends of recent American politics in general, were shocked by what they saw. Given the history and culture of Wisconsin, however, I felt confident to assure them that these assaults on the public good would not go unanswered and the losses of today would, in time, be overturned. Still, the inclination to become directly involved was not part of my own background.

Previously, given my employment as a history professor, I had abstained from political action. I had considered my duties to be first and foremost those of a scholar. I could teach my students regarding the solid conclusions of my academic discipline and thereby influence them to more closely investigate current events and to rethink their own positions in light of the evidence they uncovered. I, however, had always thought that I would lose some measure of credibility in the classroom if it were known that I was directly engaging in political action—not that I would be betraying a trust but rather that I would be seen as compromising my academic impartiality in the eyes of those students who did not share my political perspective and indeed might be inclined to see my teaching as a vehicle for political rather than academic ends.

The events of 2010–2011, however, proved a powerful wake-up call to political action. In the Middle East, the single most frequently voiced demand in every country has been that government must accord the people *dignity*. For Americans who possess legal guarantees under the U.S. Constitution, this would not likely be their first demand should they feel their interests threatened. For Americans, terms like freedom, liberty, and demands to redress specific grievances would likely come to mind first. While there is much to complain about in the distance that many of us frequently feel exists between ourselves and our government, the point repeatedly raised in the Middle East, that government has no regard for the dignity of the people, is far from our consciousness. For Americans who have benefited beyond the scope of their imagining from the traditions of the rule of law, the loyal opposition, and the benefits of an educational system that places rational argumentation based upon material evidence as the greatest means of determining the best and most just course of action, this would not likely be a problem they would expect to confront. Still, there is an important lesson in this for us.

As citizens of the great State of Wisconsin, we do not face the personal risks that Middle Eastern citizens face as they struggle for the very things we have the luxury of taking for granted. In terms of rights, opportunities, and obligations, many in the Middle East would gladly trade places with us here. This entails for us a great responsibility. We need to take it upon ourselves to be a role model for others who need a positive example of democratic institutions. We also need to remember that what we enjoy was purchased at great cost by our forebears. Where our responsibility lies is in protecting what has been bequeathed to us. Among the great accomplishments of our forebears was the creation of a broad public sphere, wherein the common interests of all citizens can be debated, and a strong public sector, wherein the citizenry is served by government agencies responsive to the will of the people through their elected representatives. While there have never existed human institutions immune to improvement, we have benefitted greatly from our system of politics and the habits of thought and behavior it relies upon and in turn promotes. Equally, as a result of this system, we are extremely fortunate to possess the public sector we have with its fine fire departments, police departments, school districts, public health authorities, and other services still available to us.

Although many Americans will draw a false distinction between activities that do and do not 'produce wealth,' it is exceptionally important to note that all public sector institutions create value and enhance the ability of the private sector to further create economic benefits. Even the most obstinate self-made men must realize that they did not rise alone. Even those who did not take the opportunity to enjoy a public education benefited from the fact that others—whose services they require—did so. It is a simple truism realizable by all that even those who have never had to call the police or fire department have benefited from the fact that their neighbors could do so. Today's Wisconsinites possess a great advantage over most of our predecessors and global contemporaries in that we can still count on individuals and institutions in our state to advance the public interest.

The demands for a strong public sphere and public sector are not in opposition to capitalism. They are the preconditions for its success. The great philosopher Adam Smith, founder of the theory of capitalism, maintained that while each man could be expected to pursue his own private interest, none could be counted upon alone to look after the public interest. In his words, neither the economic workings of *the hidden hand* nor the fear of public censure could ever be enough to ensure that individuals behave justly. All markets, he maintained, tend towards monopoly. The level playing field upon which true competition can contend is only kept in place by non-market mechanisms, maintained by the public sector. Equally, he wrote that the market could never adequately supply all the services the nation required: foremost among those needs he felt unmet by the market were defense, justice, and education. For all that is not merely a matter of private interest we rely upon a greater service to the common good provided us by the public sector and the means by which we determine our common needs, the public sphere.

What was brought home to me in the Middle East was the fact that our rights as U.S. citizens and our interests as members of the American public are rare and precious possessions, purchased at great cost. As a professional historian, these were not epiphanies. They are part of what I teach every semester. What I remembered, viewing the protests in Wisconsin from the vantage point of the Middle East, however, was that it was my responsibility to protect these rights, not merely to instruct others to do so. In 2011, there were struggles for human dignity that turned bloody in Egypt, Libya, Yemen, which were far from my location, and Syria, which was not so far away. There were protests in Lebanon, but I did not feel it was my place to protest for changes that would affect others greatly but ultimately have little direct bearing on myself. I did not think it was my place to stand up where others should be standing. Moreover, it was certainly not my place to encourage others to undertake actions that could lead to their endangerment. The Lebanese will have to decide when and how to act on their own behalf. I did, however, decide that I had greater duties than I had previously undertaken with regard to my own community in Wisconsin.

It was brought home to me that as U.S. citizens we have been fortunate beyond anything we deserve to live in a country with laws that give us the right to act on our own behalf, and with traditions that emphasize the power of argumentation and civil action. In our shared culture, the voice of reason is not always adhered to but it remains the signal source of authority respected across most of the political spectrum. People have often allowed emotional appeals to override their reason, but rarely has there been a culture such as ours in which this is overwhelmingly considered an unfortunate occurrence. A premium placed upon the pursuit of private interests produces tremendous wealth that, well-harnessed, can lead to a rising standard of living. Alone, however, the pursuit of private interests cannot protect the values I have just identified. These values are a product of the public sphere and the public sector and can only be maintained by a rigorous protection of both. That is our obligation.

11

Can Religion Help Revive the Progressive Tradition?

James F. Veninga

THE LAST SEVERAL YEARS have been good for democracy. In 2011, in one Middle East country after another, citizens took to the streets to demand basic human rights. The "Arab Awakening" continues, and it can teach us much about the human passion for justice, fairness, and economic opportunity. It also teaches us how difficult it is to secure these conditions, for we also have seen, during this Arab uprising, powerful forces that resist democratic movements in order to retain privileges for the few at the expense of the many, and we grieve for the loss of life and injuries to so many who have risked everything to bring about fundamental change.

Here at home, the impact of the "Great Recession" has continued, but we too have experienced anew the power of democratic forces. In 2011, the year began with tens of thousands of citizens gathered in Madison to protest the efforts of newly elected Governor Scott Walker and the Republican Legislature as they acted on an ultra-right platform that included a rollback on worker rights including collective bargaining for public employees, reductions in funding for public schools and universities, a relaxation of environmental rules, a stringent voter identification law, a rejection of significant federal funding that would have improved and expanded railroad lines, and fresh tax breaks for the state's corporations. We have also experienced the Occupy Wall Street movement, begun in September, 2011, which then spread from New

Can Religion Help Revive the Progressive Tradition?

York to cities and towns across the country, exposing the dangerous gap between the wealthy and the poor and the diminishing strength (in dollars and in numbers) of middle-class America.

The Arab Awakening raises serious questions about how a nation's people can create democratic culture where none has existed, where institutions of civil society are not present, and where religious leaders historically have tended to support repressive regimes. What must happen for the revolutionary spirit to take hold, for courageous people to step forward, risking all, to ensure basic human rights and democratic governments? Our own populist movements tell us that even here in the United States, with our more than two centuries of representative government, and with a civil society that nourishes and sustains democratic culture, it still remains a struggle to ensure equal opportunity, equality, and justice. It is a struggle to ensure a vibrant economy with full employment, but it is also a struggle to protect human rights and nourish the American dream—a dream that historically has been tied to a healthy middle class and one that extends help to the poor, those who struggle, and those who are new arrivals.

How can the democratic impulses that have come alive once again in the U.S. achieve positive results? These are important efforts to revitalize democracy, strengthen the middle class, and ensure opportunity for all. In some cases, the protests are over specific policies, while in others the frustration seems more generalized and proposed remedies poorly defined. Yet it is possible to sense in these endeavors a reawakening of the progressive spirit in America.

For those who seek change, who see growing class divisions that undermine American unity and financial interests that are exerting extraordinary influence in American politics, the challenge is one of arriving at well-conceived social and political platforms that offer concrete policy suggestions and institutional reforms. For this to happen, there needs to be an intellectual framework, one based on ideas and values that will provide the vision, the substance, and the rationale to help make constructive change happen.

For guidance on how such an intellectual framework might be developed, we can turn to the Progressive Movement in America during the late 19th and early 20th Centuries. Diverse groups focusing on very different problems were able to come together to achieve great things. They were able to do so because a compelling intellectual framework with defined values pulled these groups together. It is my contention

A Whole Which Is Greater

that powerful religious perspectives helped shape this intellectual framework a hundred years ago, and in many Progressive Movements since that time. If the current expression of American progressivism is to thrive and achieve results, it too would benefit from religious perspectives that offer the overriding justification—the intellectual and spiritual grounding—that can make substantive change happen.

RELIGION AND SOCIETY

As we think about this topic, it will be helpful to note some underlying features about the often complex relationship between religion and society. The objective study of religion and the role religion plays in the lives of societies is a relatively new academic field in university studies.[1] In introductory religious studies courses, the French sociologist Emil Durkheim (1858–1917) and the German economist Max Weber (1864–1920) are often used to help students understand the relationship of religion to society. Durkheim championed the importance of society—institutions, but also various relationships and social structures—in understanding human thought, values, and behavior.[2] Thus religion, along with other human endeavors, could be studied to determine its social dimension. Historically, he argued, religion and society are inseparable. He recognized the fundamental changes taking place in Europe—the challenging of sacred values of the church, the lessening of social controls and the claiming of new freedoms, and the breakup of Europe's traditional social system—but he saw religion, especially through his studies of tribal religion in Australia, as a means for society to secure order and ensure the commitment of the individual to the group. Religious rituals, for example, provide opportunities for individuals to renew their commitment to the community and to push back "profane" and individual concerns which, left unchecked, could destabilize society. Religion helps anchor people to the community. It builds loyalty and keeps people together. Thus we can say that religion historically has tended to be a conservative force, protecting society and the status quo.

Max Weber (1864–1920), trained in history, law, and economics, took great interest in the dramatic economic and political changes that took place in parts of Europe beginning in the 16th Century, and he sought specifically to understand the role that religion played in the development of early capitalism in those countries that came to be

Can Religion Help Revive the Progressive Tradition?

associated with Reformed Protestantism—the tradition founded by John Calvin.[3] Weber maintains that religious ideas can be powerful forces in the evolution of society. Social change involves structural change (new, vibrant institutions replacing decaying institutions, for example) but also changes in ideas, including those we think of as religious. After studying the rise of capitalism in Protestant Europe, Weber studied religion in China, India, and ancient Israel. He recognized that certain material conditions can bring about fundamental changes in a society, but he further developed his belief that religious ideas can play a major role in the evolution of society. Dramatic change often happens as a result of "prophetic" figures who serve as agents who leave behind the old order to claim a new and higher cultural order. Thus Weber argued that religion, counter to what Durkheim taught, can play a powerful role in changing societies—whether for good or ill.

These two emphases come together in the work of contemporary sociologist Peter Berger. In one of his most important books, *The Sacred Canopy: Elements of a Sociological Theory of Religion*, Berger begins with a Durkheimian perspective: Religion historically has tended to secure the world order and has functioned as a powerful and widespread instrument legitimating the existing social order.[4] But like Weber, he also recognizes that religion can shake things up, create powerful changes, and bring about new values and institutions. To understand both tendencies, Berger articulates the fundamental dialectical process by which society—which is a human product—is created. In a never-ending process, human beings are engaged in a creative endeavor—developing new ideas, values, and institutions—a process that Berger calls "externalization." Religion is the farthest reach of externalization, for it secures the world order by creating a sacred cosmos—a sacred world. That which is created takes on a life of its own—it often stands over and against the individual and provides an objective world that creates stability. The third step in this process is that of internalization whereby individuals learn the significance of this objective world, the ideas and values and institutions created, and make them their own. For Berger, then, religion functions to secure the world order and provides the legitimations that make it difficult to challenge the existing state of things. Religion is the ultimate guardian of order and meaning.

Yet we know that the existing state of things is often challenged—and this happens all the time. After all, this process of constructing reality and internalizing it is ongoing, and there are times when individuals and societies begin to doubt and question and wonder if the way things are must necessarily remain the same. Could truth lie elsewhere? Could new values, behavior, and institutions create a different and perhaps brighter future? In times of great societal change, the existing order—and the legitimations that hold things together—become doubted. But during these uncertain and difficult times, religion often calls us to new and deeper realities, to new insights and even to new "revelations" that push societies in new directions. Thus for Berger religion appears in history both as a world-maintaining and a world-shaking force. The first tendency, which Durkheim explored, is the more prominent. But the second tendency, which Weber analyzed, can be seen throughout history: in the Jesus movement of the 1st Century, in the 6th- and 7th-Century prophet Muhammad, in Luther and the Protestant reformation in the 16th Century. New breakthroughs, new insights, new revelations can happen, creating a new objectified world that then becomes grounded in individual consciousness and in society.

Of course we know that such movements can also be regressive. Followers of radical Islam reject much of historical Islam in order to claim new "truths" (or recover perceived lost truths) that create a world of ideas and values that justify striking out against one's enemies. But whether such breakthroughs prove beneficial or harmful, it is clear that religious ideas and sentiments can provide the means for dramatically changing existing cultures and societies.

It is important to recognize these points about the relationship of religion to society. Religion can play a conservative role, protecting the status quo—the "world" that has been created—ideas, cultural values, institutions, and ways whereby human beings relate to each other. But religion can also be a powerful agent of change, providing breakthrough ideas that in the end challenge the existing order and fundamentally transform existing cultures and societies.

THE PROGRESSIVE CENTER

The progressive era in American history, roughly 1890 to 1920, has attracted the attention of many outstanding historians who have long seen this era as transformative. Writing in 1955, Pulitzer Prize-winning author Richard Hofstadter argued in *The Age of Reform* that the Populist-Progressive Movements meant much more than the platforms

Can Religion Help Revive the Progressive Tradition?

of the People's (or Populist) and Democratic parties of the 1890s.[5] Likewise, he noted, progressivism means something far more than the Progressive (or Bull Moose) party of those Republican fighters who endorsed Theodore Roosevelt for the presidency in 1912, and far more as well than the administration of Democrat Woodrow Wilson. Hofstadter maintained that the political platforms of these parties and their legislative agendas were "heightened expressions" of broader impulses in American culture, especially "that broader impulse toward criticism and change that was everywhere so conspicuous after 1900, when the already forceful stream of agrarian discontent was enlarged and redirected by the growing enthusiasm of middle-class people for social and economic reform."

Historians of the progressive era have been consistent in identifying the social and cultural conditions that existed during this time: industrialization, urbanization, an "immigrant invasion" that led to increased diversity and social unrest, political corruption, and the growth of big business and monopolies. But they differ in how to understand and assess the broader social and political movements that sought to address the pressing problems that emerged from these conditions. One of the most recent and most compelling such efforts has come from Michael McGerr in his book, A *Fierce Discontent: The Rise and Fall of the Progressive Movement in America*.[6]

McGerr would most likely not disagree with Hofstadter's insistence on seeing progressivism as a movement that involved very diverse social groups, but he, far more than Hofstadter, emphasizes progressivism as "the creed of a crusading middle class" that sought to offer the American people the promise of utopianism. He argues that the progressives developed a "stunningly broad agenda" that went far beyond the control of big business and the elimination of political corruption. It includes, he says, efforts to transform gender relations, to regenerate home life, to discipline leisure and pleasure, and, surprisingly, maybe out of fear, to maintain racial segregation. Thus it was not just a question of using government to regulate the economy and control big business. Rather, "they intended nothing less than to transform other Americans, to remake the nation's feuding, polyglot population into their own middle-class image." That relates to one of McGerr's most important points, that the Progressive Movement was about expanding the middle class.

McGerr argues that this middle-class activism "began as an unprecedented crisis of alienation amid the extremes of wealth and poverty in America." Industrialized America had created enormous wealth for what was then called the "Upper Ten." But McGerr makes it clear that the "Upper Ten" were really a tiny minority, perhaps one or two percent of the 76 million U. S. citizens. "These were the people who owned the majority of the nation's resources and expected to make the majority of its key decisions." Their ranks included approximately 4,000 millionaires and some 200 families worth at least $20 million. The wealth was concentrated in the Northeast and included "the famous names of American capitalism—Vanderbilt, Whitney, Carnegie, Harriman, and Morgan." And, of course, this group included the man who had the greatest fortune of all, John D. Rockefeller of Standard Oil, thought to be worth a billion dollars by 1913. These people came primarily from English stock, families who had long been in America, and most were associated with "fashionable" Protestant denominations—Episcopalian, Presbyterian, and the Puritan-descended Congregational Church. Few matched Andrew Carnegie's story of rising from poverty to great wealth. The basis of most fortunes was inherited wealth, although many expanded that wealth through entrepreneurship and new economic adventures that flowed from growing wealth.

This one or two percent of American society held fast to a belief in the power of the individual and in the need to protect individual freedom. McGerr argues that they "attributed the hardships of the poor not to an unfair economic system but to individual shortcomings. The remedy was individual regeneration rather than government action." McGerr quotes Rockefeller: "[The] failures which a man makes in his life are due almost always to some defect in his personality, some weakness of body, or mind, or character."

Alex de Tocqueville, writing in the 1830s, saw individualism as a distinctive American trait. But these capitalists of the late 19th Century reworked the idea for the Gilded Age. They were merchants, landowners, corporate executives, and professionals, and most had no reserve or regrets in championing their position in society. This upper-class individualism was about pleasure. It was about sons getting Harvard, Yale, and Princeton educations. It was about building stately mansions, owning yachts and summer homes, and throwing expensive receptions and dinner parties. The pursuit of wealth and pleasure transformed these families, and not always for the good, as seen in the dramatic rise of divorce. Twenty percent of those Americans worth $20 million or more and born between 1865 and 1900 were divorced—a remarkable figure for the time. One consequence of this was the disempowerment of women.

A few of these affluent individuals, John D. Rockefeller and Andrew Carnegie among them, resisted the wasteful and gaudy lives of the "Upper Ten" and offered counter-models, where philanthropy became a redemptive course of action for dealing with unprecedented wealth. Deeply influenced by his Baptist pastor, Rockefeller took the lead in developing new business-like trusts to dispense wealth to the betterment of the public. And Carnegie, in a move that would be replicated by some of America's most wealthy families a century later, pledged to give away most of his wealth. McGerr notes that 90 percent of his wealth was distributed before his death in 1919.

But Rockefeller and Carnegie were exceptions, and from the perspective of the working class, the wealthy lived despicable lives. The gulf between the Upper Ten and the working class was enormous, and McGerr points out that to be a part of the working class inevitably meant "low wages, lay-offs, accidents, limited opportunity, early death." Numerically, the United States was a working-class nation. More than half the country—36 to 40 million men, women, and children—made up the laboring class that "toiled with their hands on docks, roads, and farms, in factories, mines, and other people's homes." They labored eleven or twelve hours a day, often six or seven days a week. Still, their financial resources were extremely limited, and most families required the labor of everyone—children included—to try to make ends meet. McGerr points out that a typical Chicago packing house worker could make just 38 percent of the income needed to support a family of four in 1910. One important response to this situation was the development of economic interdependence—promoting a "family economy" (and "family farm") where everyone worked. Mutualism and association would form the foundation of some populist and cooperative organizations including the trade union. Resentment toward the conspicuous wealth of the "Upper Ten," anger over limited opportunities, and crippling fear over the vicissitudes and unpredictability of working-class life, contributed to enormous friction.

While a majority of those who comprised the working class were Protestants, this largest segment of the population included ten million

A Whole Which Is Greater

Roman Catholics and several hundred thousand Jews. By 1900 some twenty-six million Americans, more than a third of the total population, were immigrants or native-born Americans with at least one foreign-born parent, notes McGerr. Many were from Southern and Eastern Europe, supplanting the German, English, and Irish immigrants who had arrived earlier in the 19th Century. Often this increased diversity in race, ethnicity, and religion "produced suspicion, antagonism, and conflict among workers."

For the growing middle class, approximately twenty percent of the population—some twelve to sixteen million people by 1900—the gulf between wealth and poverty in America, and the subsequent friction that seemed evident everywhere, meant that they "could no longer abide the alien cultures, class conflict, and violence of a divided industrial nation." The middle class was defined primarily by occupation: small proprietors, clerks and salespeople, managers and bureaucrats, and some professionals—most holding "white collar" positions. Most, says McGerr, lived pretty well, although many had to "scrimp and save" to get by. Not all was well with this middle class. There was an unhappiness and discontent. They may have had more opportunities than the generation before; for example, women often pursued education in unprecedented ways, including college education. But this often contributed to uncertainty about gender roles. Still, public opportunities for women expanded as seen in the growth of women's clubs, Chautauqua movements, and literary clubs. Some women, and Nobel Peace Prize winner Jane Addams exemplifies this, discovered new and important callings that would be so central to the Progressive Movement.[7]

McGerr maintains that the progressive era emerged from a middle class struggling with its identity and feeling threatened by a nation divided by wealth and privilege. Important questions emerged regarding the relationship of the individual to society, the nature of men and women, the role of the home, and the value of work and leisure. The middle class sought to provide answers to these questions—and did so by providing a set of guiding values and a new ideology. But it was the widening breech among the classes—evident in violent class conflicts that included the railroad strikes of 1877 and 1886, the Haymarket bombing in Chicago in 1886, the Homestead strike in 1892, and the Pullman strike in 1894—that truly threatened the stability of the middle class. It was caught in a "crossfire" in the struggle between rich and poor.

Can Religion Help Revive the Progressive Tradition?

McGerr argues that many members of the middle class, traveling separate paths, arrived at the same ideological destination. "Increasingly, the fundamental values of the wealthy, deprived of middle-class endorsement, appeared selfish and destructive," he writes. At the center of the emerging ideology was a condemnation of individualism, a critical development, notes McGerr, in the contest for authority in America. In place of individualism, these members of the middle class offered new forms of association and social solidarity. They aimed for significant changes in many areas of individual and public life.

McGerr looks at four significant progressive battles, and it would do us well to briefly summarize these, and to take a look at how they played out in one state, Wisconsin, before we explore the place of religion and religious thought within the Progressive Movement.

TRANSFORMING AMERICANS

Major campaigns included reshaping adult behavior, with alcohol, prostitution, and divorce being the major enemies. But many realized that individuals were not always to blame, that societal conditions—the sins and injustices of society—were also responsible. Poverty and economic constraints often led to vice, as did excessive wealth. Other efforts focused on remaking the classes—the wealthy and the workers. Both led troubled lives. Contempt for the leisure class found expression in politics with Theodore Roosevelt calling for graduated taxes on incomes and inheritances (leading to the Sixteenth Amendment). Efforts to remake the working class included settlement houses, the YMCA, the Salvation Army, soup kitchens, public libraries, evening schools, mail service to rural areas, better schools for children, and better sanitation. Efforts also included improving childhood: getting children off the streets and in school, limiting child labor, and improving public education.

ENDING CLASS CONFLICT

Work stoppages made the U.S. the most strike-torn nation in the world, notes McGerr, and the 1902 coal strike backed by the United Mine Workers with the call for an eight-hour day and increased pay was especially galling to the Upper Ten. For the capitalists, organized labor meant "terrorism, tyranny and lawlessness." Progressives sought to stop the battles and promote interclass harmony. The conflict between labor and capital was a central threat to middle-class prosperity. The progressives demanded that government mediate disputes, and that is what Roosevelt did in regard to the coal strike which had resulted in dramatically increased prices, the loss of heating fuel for many working-class people, and an undermining of the U.S. economy. Roosevelt helped create the settlement—a workday of nine rather than ten hours and a 10 percent increase in wages. Organized labor, collective bargaining, and trade agreements were developed to promote stability and the welfare of workers. Of course, many workers were not part of the unions—Blacks, the extreme poor, and Eastern European immigrants often appeared as economic threats to the organized workers. Meanwhile, capitalists continued to oppose labor and to push for the "open shop." Some progressives joined a minority of capitalists who promoted "welfare capitalism," which included company housing, kindergartens, nurseries, adult education programs, baseball teams, pensions, and in some cases, medical care for workers. But more often than not, capitalists resisted reforms and the unions were led to more radical undertakings as exemplified in the organization of the Industrial Workers of the World—the Wobblies—and the use of boycotts.

CONTROLLING BIG BUSINESS

The push to tame big business stemmed from the emergence of large-scale enterprises (Standard Oil, United States Steel, etc.), economic interdependence (everyone impacted), and a recognition that natural resources needed protection. Progressives sought to break up and regulate big business, using federal power to do so, although some wanted to rely on the power of state governments to provide oversight. This was the era of mergers, conglomerates, monopolies, and new industrial technologies (James Duke produced millions of cigarettes with a machine). The Upper Ten promoted laissez-faire economics, in effect rationalizing self-interest. Some progressives supported socialism, encouraging public ownership of many industries, but especially those natural monopolies such as water works, gas plants, and other utilities. Other approaches sought to preserve competitive capitalism while encouraging government intervention when needed. Antitrust legislation to break up the monopolies and promote competition and regulation led to some remarkable legislative accomplishments: the Food and Drug Act of 1906 and the Federal Reserve Act in 1913. Progressives encouraged increased taxation to ensure that a small portion of the wealth of these corporations would be returned to the community. One can also see the growth of federal power in the conservation movement, championed especially by Roosevelt, as the need to manage the nation's forests, water, and land became more pressing. The Panic of 1907 brought an end to a period of great prosperity and required a bailout of banks and federal efforts to deal with a credit shortage. The big financiers needed government to save themselves—a situation re-experienced a century later. The progressives achieved considerable success in controlling big business, but by the end of the progressive era, many Americans—certainly the capitalists—expressed concern about excessive government and wondered if federal control of business had increased too much. But antitrust legislation and regulation had been legitimated, leaving a lasting legacy.

PRESERVING SEGREGATION

Michael McGerr's careful analysis of the goals of early American progressivism includes a sobering account of the limits of the movement when it came to segregation of Black Americans. With the focus on halting dangerous social conflicts, progressives by and large found it impossible to tackle one of the nation's most serious social problems. They showed courage in dealing with problems of gender, crime, family, class, and the economy—but not of race. For some, it was believed that there was a growing number of Black physicians, lawyers, teachers, and leaders even with segregation and that a segregated society might continue to see modest progress for Blacks. But there was little desire to end Jim Crow. One finds here a fundamental contradiction in early American progressivism, one that would only be dealt with decades later when white middle-class leaders—the clergy included—joined hands with Martin L. King, Jr. and other Black leaders to tackle segregation head-on with the Civil Rights Movement.

Despite the failure to confront racism in America, the progressives had much success in rallying "the people" to support a host of reforms designed to promote harmony and needed social, economic, and political reforms. It found various levels of support from presidents

Theodore Roosevelt, William Howard Taft, and Woodrow Wilson. It often found bipartisan support in the U.S. Congress and in many of the state houses. Success depended in part on its ability to allow very different kinds of groups and elements of the population to focus on different aspects of reform. Progressivism provided a very big tent. Some focused on drinking and gambling; some on monopolies and unbridled capitalism. Some directed work toward controlling child labor and promoting juvenile justice. Others aimed to eliminate poverty and improve sanitation and housing. Still others focused on the condition of women and the suffrage movement. There were fault lines to be sure—gender, race, and religion among them—but the amazing thing is how so many efforts were subsumed under the banner of the Progressive Movement.

PROGRESSIVISM IN WISCONSIN

Of all those states that provided fertile soil for progressive reforms, Wisconsin proved exceptional. This year, 2012, marks the centennial of the publication of *The Wisconsin Idea* by Charles McCarthy, then legislative librarian for the State of Wisconsin and a member of the faculty of the University of Wisconsin.[8] McCarthy wrote this book to document some of the reform legislation that occurred during the progressive era. He did so, he notes in the Preface, because this legislation has attracted national attention and because his department "has been besieged by newspaper writers who have come here to use the files and records."

In an introduction to the book, President Theodore Roosevelt begins by noting that it was the leadership of Republican Senator Robert La Follette that led to the "overwhelming victory" of "genuinely democratic popular government in Wisconsin." Wisconsin had become "a laboratory for wise experimental legislation aiming to secure the social and political betterment of the people as a whole." McCarthy's book, he says, provides "a well reasoned and thoughtful exposition of how sane radicalism can be successfully applied in practice." Roosevelt praises Wisconsin reformers—the nation owes them much—because they had a powerful vision that was then followed with concrete steps to achieve this vision. He writes that real reform efforts must have "many lines of development" and reformers must take great care to plan carefully what is to be constructed before "they tear down what exists."

Can Religion Help Revive the Progressive Tradition?

Political reform, Roosevelt argues, must be accompanied by economic reform, "and economic reform must have a twofold object; first, to increase general prosperity, because unless there is such general prosperity no one will be well off; and, second, to secure a fair distribution of this prosperity, so that the man of the people shall share in it." The nation can learn from Wisconsin's experience in creating "radical" legislation. He concludes by noting how tough it is to achieve real reform, to secure justice, to avoid plutocracy on the one hand and a government by mob rule on the other hand, and "to give the public proper control over corporations and big business, and yet to prevent abuse of that control." Wisconsin had done that.

As McCarthy makes clear, critical to the success of reform efforts was the recognition that until recent times, "men forgot that prosperity exists for the benefit of the human being and for no other purpose. If prosperity does not uplift the mass of human beings, it is not true prosperity. . . . Individual opportunity must be safeguarded, but the corrupting force of concentrated wealth and the shackling power of monopolies must be resisted." McCarthy goes on to state in the first chapter that the reader will not find in this book "perfect legislation" or some clear-cut philosophy, but, rather, serious analysis of problems and the often tedious process of arriving at workable solutions. And that process includes, he notes, serious research efforts. McCarthy quickly gets to one of the major emphases of Wisconsin progressivism, and that is the use of expertise in analyzing problems and exploring solutions. He praises the faculty of the University of Wisconsin, individuals who are eager to put theory into practice. "Behind this Wisconsin movement," he writes, "is a great body of tradition, a tradition of orderliness and of scientific methods, a knowledge that things can and should be done by experts in a careful and diligent manner and that progress must come, slowly but thoroughly." McCarthy's book then goes on to discuss how the expertise of the University of Wisconsin faculty members, working collaboratively with legislators from both parties, produced some extraordinary accomplishments:

- the regulation of big business including the railroads
- ensuring accountability of public utilities
- ensuring sound local government

A Whole Which Is Greater

- regulating the insurance industry
- developing fair taxation and a monitoring system
- developing the primary election
- protecting the rights of prisoners and preventing their abuse while confined
- establishing "Initiative and Referendum"
- passing legislation to allow elected officials except judges to be recalled
- providing financial support to ensure a strong University of Wisconsin free from legislative meddling and with a mandate to serve the entire state by encouraging research and outreach useful to the state
- establishing free libraries including traveling libraries to all parts of the state
- ensuring conservation of natural resources
- giving municipalities the ability to establish public land and parks
- child labor legislation
- passing the first workman's compensation act in the nation
- establishing a commission form of government
- ensuring safe work environments in the growing manufacturing sector
- the passing of laws governing lobbying the legislature
- developing a non-partisan and non-political reference library department to assist legislators in the development of sound legislation
- agreeing on the non-partisan election of judges

Two important points need to be made about *The Wisconsin Idea*. First, McCarthy highlights the non-partisanship of this era of reform. Secondly, he responds to the attacks that he knew would be forthcoming from the most conservative segment, namely, that so much of this progressive legislation is "socialist" and inspired by European-styled socialism. "Shall we always be deceived by the cry of 'Socialism' whenever it is necessary to use the state to a greater degree than formerly?" He goes on to make the case that progressive legislation and good government, whether in Wisconsin or elsewhere in the U.S. or abroad, will in the end protect true individualism and free enterprise. For McCarthy, a *"New Individualism"* (his italics) will best be protected by the kind of progressive legislation recently enacted.

RELIGION AND PROGRESSIVISM

The "big tent" that housed progressives included, among those religiously inclined, ministers, priests, nuns, rabbis, publishers and writers of religiously oriented publications, leaders of various organizations, and professors in the social sciences, humanities, and theology. Working with their more secularly oriented progressive colleagues, these proponents of reform had particular interests: poverty, temperance, woman suffrage, workers' rights, education, welfare of children, and others. But the United States was still very much a Protestant country at this time, and thus the majority of religious proponents came from the ranks of the larger Protestant denominations: Episcopalian, Presbyterian, Congregational and American (or northern) Baptist.

Although some of the more important and effective social outreach work of the Catholic Church did not occur until the 1930s, including the Catholic Worker Movement, the Catholic Church in the U.S. was deeply influenced by Pope Leo XIII's 1891 encyclical letter *Rerum Novarum,* which addressed social justice issues and began the process whereby the Catholic Church sought to relate itself more effectively to the conditions of modern life.[9] Thus it is certainly possible to identify parish efforts to deal with the problems of modern society during the progressive era, even if the theological impulse behind "social Christianity" came essentially from Protestant Christianity and its more moderate to liberal denominations.

The churches of these denominations tended to include more of the "haves" rather than the "have nots"—that is, their parishioners tended to be middle class. But more conservative and "evangelical" denominations and churches, including those in the South and northern urban churches with working-class members, also were involved, including pastors and churches associated with Methodist and Baptist traditions in the South. The difference, of course, is that these individuals, with a focus on personal conversion, regeneration, and piety, tended to focus more on the "sins" of alcohol use and abuse, prostitution, crime, and divorce—personal failings. They are the inheritors of the revivalist tradition in American religion. Yet many of these churches also had social missions and undertook social work; the Women's Christian Temperance Union is one example. Thus these more conservative leaders probably belong within the big tent of religious progressivism, even if they had nothing to do with proposed secular reforms or with the Social Gospel that inspired so many political progressives.

Historian Gary Scott Smith discusses the various attempts by historians to find the origins of social Christianity and the Social Gospel Movement.[10] Some have argued that the Social Gospel was a reaction on the part of many Protestant leaders to rapid industrialization, urbanization, and class conflict that emerged in the last decades of the 19th Century, forcing them to modify orthodox doctrines. Others have placed the origins of the movement in a deep concern that the deplorable social conditions of the time might generate radical secular movements—socialism especially, but anarchism as well—which could tear apart American society and destroy its Christian foundation. Several other approaches have emphasized the changing role of the clergy and their need to maintain a sense of control and prestige in a dramatically changing society. For example, it was important that they deal with powerful new insights provided by the sciences and the social sciences, from Darwin to Freud, and to do so they needed a different kind of theology and biblical understanding.

Still other scholars have found the origins of the Social Gospel in the personal experiences of these religious leaders—witnessing labor strikes, ministering to the unemployed and disheartened, seeing the devastation of poverty and poor sanitation on families, seeing the growing and dangerous gap between the wealthy and the poor—even within a single congregation. These direct experiences told these leaders that churches must change if they are to remain relevant and if the Gospel of Christ is to be heard. For these religious leaders, the meaning and truth of the Christian faith had to be reworked for a new generation, a new time. Gary Scott Smith, summarizing this perspective, puts it this way: "Deeply moved by biblical teaching about service, sacrifice, and stewardship, they marched in the streets, slums, and marketplace, determined to improve social and economic conditions."

Can Religion Help Revive the Progressive Tradition?

Each of these perspectives may offer insights into the origins of the Social Gospel Movement, although the latter perspective, pointing to the personal experiences of Social Gospel leaders and to their rediscovery of the social teachings of Jesus, seems to me to be all-important. What separates these pastors and church leaders from the more revivalist, evangelical component of American Protestantism is recognition that the Christian faith is as much about social transformation as it is about personal salvation.

WASHINGTON GLADDEN

The impact of direct experience, and how this influenced a fresh understanding of biblical teachings, can be seen in the life and work of one of the Social Gospel's earliest proponents, Washington Gladden (1836–1918). With great clarity, historian Paul Boyer describes the impact of experience on Gladden's theology and work.[11] A graduate of Williams College in Massachusetts, Gladden experienced the brute realities of untamed capitalism during his first pastorate in a North Adams, Massachusetts, Congregational Church. When workers went on strike at a local shoe factory, the owners broke it by importing Chinese workers. Boyer notes that this experience shaped his life-long position on "the labor question"—supporting workers and unions. Gladden went on to serve as an editor of the *Independent*, a liberal New York-based religious journal and here he helped expose the corruption of political boss William Tweed. In 1875 he returned to New England, holding a pastorate in Springfield, Massachusetts, a factory town. Here he dealt with the impact of the depression of the 1870s on the workers, encouraging factory owners, says Boyer, to offer assistance to jobless workers.

But Gladden is best known for his long pastorate at the First Congregational Church of Columbus, Ohio, a city that by the 1880s was experiencing its own urban crisis—crime, corruption, and fear of urban disorder. The region experienced one of the worst strikes in American history, when 4,000 coal miners walked off the job at the Columbus and Hocking Coal and Iron Company. They were protesting wage cuts and high prices charged in the company store. The strike was broken when the company brought in 1,500 immigrant strikebreakers. The workers finally caved in and agreed to the wages offered, but had to pledge never to join a union. Gladden, Boyer writes, played a major role one year later when they went on strike again, working toward arbitration which led to a wage increase and reaffirmation of their union membership.

Gladden was a prolific writer. His many books and published sermons expressed the heart of the Social Gospel, that it is the obligation of Christians to help bring about the Kingdom of God here on earth. He defended labor unions; he supported legislation to shorten the work week and end child labor. He believed that public utilities should be carefully regulated. Boyer quotes Gladden: If corporations failed to serve the public interest "their power must be taken from them, at whatever cost," and they must face "a rigid supervision of all (their) affairs." He denounced lynching and racial violence in an 1895 address to Congregational ministers, although Boyer acknowledges that much more could have been done by Gladden on the issue of racism when racial violence and Jim Crowism spread to the north in the early 1900s. But in other areas, Gladden seemed rather radical. In 1905 he urged the Congregational Church to return a $100,000 gift from John D. Rockefeller in support of the denomination's missionary work. Boyer writes that his accusation of "tainted money" was reported widely and led to extensive public discussion on "corporate ethics and the disparities of wealth and poverty in America."

From the perspective of Peter Berger's sociology, the Social Gospel message of Washington Gladden provided "the sacred canopy" that grounded progressive ideals in a fresh interpretation of scripture and Christian thought, thereby legitimating the many reform efforts of the progressives.

WALTER RAUSCHENBUSCH

The most important advocate of mature social Christianity and the Social Gospel Movement was a Baptist, Walter Rauschenbusch (1861–1918). In Rauschenbusch we find a well-developed theology born of real life experience. Through him we can see even more clearly that this movement was not merely the religious wing of progressivism, but rather a powerful religious awakening that provided a theology and a social ethic that supported the secular agenda of the progressives. It is best to see the relationship between the proponents of the Social Gospel and the proponents of progressive reforms as symbiotic, with both groups working together to address real problems and offer real solutions.

Can Religion Help Revive the Progressive Tradition?

Rauschenbusch was born in Rochester, New York, the son of German immigrants "whose Baptist heritage was engrafted upon six generations of Lutheran ministers."[12] His religious background focused on traditional, orthodox doctrines that emphasized individual salvation through the substitutionary atonement of Christ. At age 17, he experienced a spiritual awakening, a conversion experience that was formative in his development, although he would soon realize the inadequacy of a religion that focused on repentance of personal sins without regard for social sins. He studied in Germany for four years and then returned in 1883 when he was 22 to complete studies at the University of Rochester and Rochester Theological Seminary. Here he was exposed to the latest in biblical scholarship which challenged orthodox notions of the inerrancy of the Bible. In 1886 he was ordained as a Baptist minister and accepted the pastorate of the Second Baptist Church located on the edge of Hell's Kitchen in New York City.

This neighborhood, located on the west side of Manhatten, was in Rauschenbusch's time a congested slum area with warehouses and multiple tenements housing mostly immigrants. Here Rauschenbusch encountered overcrowded housing conditions, malnutrition and poverty, inadequate sanitation and health care, unemployment, and rampant crime. A theology that stressed personal salvation from sin was not enough. The church had an obligation to respond to the social and economic ills of the time. Paul Minus, in his 1988 biography of Rauschenbusch, writes:

> Day after day he moved among people whose lives were buffeted and drained by conditions over which they had no control. Three-quarters of New York's population lived in tenements; as many as two dozen families pressed into dimly lit, foul-smelling, five-story buildings. Tenement life was especially brutal to children. In one section of the city it was reported that 68 percent of the deaths that occurred were among children age five and under. Rauschenbusch felt nothing more keenly: "Oh, the children's funerals! They gripped my heart—that was one of the things I always went away thinking about—why did the children have to die?" For him, there was no theological sense in the answer that many pious people gave, that the children died because God willed it.[13]

During his eleven years as pastor of this congregation, he pushed his parishioners to take on the injustices and social evils that abounded.

He fought political corruption, sought improved housing and working conditions, argued for the eight-hour work day, advocated municipal ownership of the new subway, worked toward better schools, created playgrounds for children, and collaborated with a host of organizations to improve the lives of those who lived in Hell's Kitchen.

Rauschenbusch left the Second German Baptist Church in 1897 to teach in the German Department at the Rochester Theological Seminary, associated with the American Baptist Church. Five years later he was a Professor of Church History, teaching in the English Department. His understanding of the Christian faith and the current crisis of civilization deepened as he sought to relate the Gospel to contemporary realities. In 1908 he published his first major work, *Christianity and the Social Crisis*. The extraordinary success of this book meant that Rauschenbusch had become the major spokesperson for the Social Gospel Movement. Invitations to speak across the country followed quickly.

The book explores the consequences of the Industrial Revolution, the loss of power and declining standards of living of industrial workers, the exploitation of children, the rise of poverty throughout the United States, the deplorable working conditions that robbed people of the possibility of finding joy in work, the constant threat of workers being laid off or wages cut, the inevitable crippling strikes that further exacerbated the poverty-stricken lives of the working class, the overcrowding and unsanitary conditions leading to the spread of disease, and the impact of all this on the spiritual well-being of working-class families. He warns that some of the core values of American society, especially the commitment to equality, are slipping away. The extremes of wealth and poverty have created two distinct classes, and the resulting social chasm is widening to such an extreme that democratic life is undermined. Political power is a tool of the dominant, capitalist class that enjoys every luxury life can offer while the working class is cut off from political life and the hope of improved conditions. "To secure special concessions and privileges and to evade public burdens have always been the objects for which dominant classes used their political power," he writes. One percent of the population controls more than half of the total wealth of the nation. He writes at length on the toll that inequality in economic and political matters is having on the American family. He warns of a pending societal collapse if existing dehumanizing conditions continue.

Can Religion Help Revive the Progressive Tradition?

In the last chapter of the book, Rauschenbusch makes the case for a revitalized and reoriented Christianity that has the power to address social evils and the underlying structural flaws of capitalism and "in what main directions the religious spirit should exert its force." It is the function of religion, he argues, "to teach society to value human life more than property, and to value property only in so far as it forms the material basis for the higher development of human life." There is a quiet optimism here, a belief that it is possible to turn things around through religious faith that can provide a powerful moral force in society. "We must repent of the sins of existing society, cast off the spell of the lies protecting our social wrongs, have faith in a higher social order, and realize in ourselves a new type of Christian manhood which seeks to overcome the evil in the present world, not by withdrawing from the world, but by revolutionizing it." But he is also realistic about outcomes. "We shall never have a perfect social life, yet we must seek it with faith." That is the obligation and the hope of the faithful Christian, he says. He who understands the message of Jesus understands that it is impossible to separate religious life from social life. Rauschenbusch believed that the Kingdom of God—the reign of God—required social as well as individual salvation. The Christian message requires a new order that would rest on the Christian principles of equal rights and democratic distribution of economic power.

The success of the Social Gospel Movement was due in part to the large number of periodicals—journals and magazines—that took core ideas and made them available to the masses. One of the most important such endeavors was *The Ram's Horn*, an interdenominational Social Gospel magazine, published in the 1890s and early years of the twentieth century.[14] In the July 25, 1896, issue, the magazine produced a table that showed that there were more than 1,100 religious newspapers and magazines in print, mostly weekly, with combined circulation of 4.2 million. The three largest producers of these publications were Roman Catholic, Baptist, and Methodist. Of course many represented a more conservative religion, but many also were devoted to the Social Gospel. *The Ram's Horn* circulation jumped from 4,200 in 1893 to 52,000 three years later. Its popularity was due in part to the penetrating cartoons of illustrator Frank Beard. Here is one such drawing, titled "Businessman in League with the Devil."

"BEHOLD I STAND AT THE DOOR AND KNOCK."

Rauschenbusch himself contributed to the growing body of Social Gospel literature for the average layperson with the publication in 1910 of *Prayers of the Social Awakening*, "one of the most unique books any American religious writer has produced."[15]

While the growing print industry played a crucial role in the dissemination of the Social Gospel, so did the hundreds of ministers who had opportunity to read serious theological and economic books from scholars and public intellectuals who supported both the Social Gospel and progressivism. In 1912 Rauschenbusch published *Christianizing the Social Order*, an effort designed to provide specific ideas on the application of Christian ethics to economic and political realms. The key issue for Rauschenbusch was how best to draw from the Christian faith in order to successfully democratize an economic system that was creating havoc across America. "Christianizing the social order," he writes, "means bringing it into harmony with the ethical convictions which we

Can Religion Help Revive the Progressive Tradition?

identify with Christ.... We call this 'Christianizing' the social order because these moral principles find their highest expression in the teachings, the life, and the spirit of Jesus Christ.... Christianizing means humanizing in the fullest sense."[16] Rauschenbusch provides moral justification for many of the reforms the progressives were demanding: direct primaries, direct legislation, recall of judges, the popular election of senators, and government regulation of industry on behalf of the common good.

The most sophisticated interpretation of the Social Gospel came from Rauschenbusch five years later with his book, *A Theology for the Social Gospel*.[17] He notes early in Chapter 1 that "If theology stops growing or is unable to adjust itself to its modern environment and to meet its present task, it will die." Rauschenbusch's task, then, is to ground the Social Gospel in a "systematic theology" that will help ensure its permanence. He is convinced that the Social Gospel is here to stay—an optimism that will be heavily criticized two decades later. But at the time, he had good reasons for being optimistic; the Social Gospel was being preached in Protestant churches throughout the United States. "It is no longer a prophetic and occasional note," he says. "It is a novelty only in backward social or religious communities. The Social Gospel has become orthodox."

Rauschenbusch was convinced that a new stage was being reached in the history of Christianity, and that the Social Gospel represented "a new revelation" that sought to make the Good News of Jesus Christ relevant to contemporary society. As a Baptist, he does not shy away from the legitimacy of profound personal religious experience, including conversion, but such experience is only the beginning of the religious life and that life cannot achieve its fulfillment without applying the teachings of Jesus to contemporary social problems. "The Social Gospel is the old message of salvation, but enlarged and intensified," he writes. "The individualistic gospel has taught us to see the sinfulness of every human heart and has inspired us with faith in the willingness and power of God to save every soul that comes to him. But it has not given us an adequate understanding of the sinfulness of the social order and its share in the sin of all individuals within it."

Central to Rauschenbusch's theology is the concept of the Kingdom of God. This concept tends to be absent from evangelical, individualistic theology except in reference to "end times" and the return of

175

Christ. Rauschenbusch's greatest contribution as a theologian of the Social Gospel is the rediscovery of the idea of the Kingdom of God as central to the teachings of Jesus, and that this Kingdom exists in the present. For 2,000 years, Rauschenbusch writes, the idea of the Kingdom of God shriveled in Western civilization as the idea of the Church moved forward; the latter supplanted the former. The consequences have been devastating. Theology lost its contact with the thought of Jesus. The distinctive ethical principles of Jesus—so tied to the idea of the immediacy of the Kingdom of God—disappeared. Worship became more important in the life of the church than social ethics. All concern was placed on the salvation of the individual, none on the salvation of society.

The Kingdom of God is divine in its origin, progress, and fulfillment. Jesus defined the Kingdom for humanity through his life and teachings, but it is up to his followers to help realize the Kingdom and to bring it to fruition. The Kingdom of God is humanity organized according to the Will of God. It is a social order that will best guarantee the freest and highest development of the individual. It involves a progressive reign of love in human affairs, a genuine concern for those often left behind, increased social equality (allocation of wealth), and the progressive unity of people overcoming all those wedges that drive them apart. The Church exists for the Kingdom of God, but the Kingdom is much bigger and transcendent. "The advance of the Kingdom of God," Rauschenbusch notes, "is not simply a process of social education, but a conflict with hostile forces which resist true social order."[18] It demands action: the transformation of economic interests to better ensure fairness, unity, and harmony, and the transformation of political life as well, where the interests of all can take precedence over the interest of the few.

Rauschenbusch died in 1918, one year after writing *A Theology for the Social Gospel*. His most basic question was: What does God want of us? His answer provided the intellectual and spiritual foundation for the Social Gospel Movement and a theological framework—a sacred canopy—for the Progressive Movement. This is surely an historical process that Max Weber would recognize, and from the perspective of sociologist Peter Berger, we see the way in which religion and theology can help legitimate broader social movements seeking to substantively change the direction of a society.

THE SOCIAL GOSPEL TAMED AND TRANSFORMED

By the mid-1920s, the Social Gospel and political progressivism were in disarray. An underlying anxiety emerged from the trauma of World War I, the inadequacy of the new but struggling League of Nations, the perceived over-reaching of the federal government, and the growing Red Scare in the U.S. following the Russian Revolution of 1917. In 1920 Warren Harding won the presidency on the promise of a "return to normalcy," but nostalgia for a simpler time could not translate into a harmonious America. While the economy got on the fast track, with an extraordinary bull market running from 1924 to 1929, America's underlying anxieties and frustrations can be seen in the rise of the Ku Klux Klan, anti-immigration fervor, fear of Communism, the Scopes trial and the emergence of religious fundamentalism. The decade would end with the October 1929 stock market crash, the result of an overheated economy and unprecedented confidence in what seemed to be an ever-expanding stock market that lacked government regulation. Herbert Hoover's proclamation in the 1928 presidential election that there would be "A chicken in every pot and a car in every garage," rang hollow indeed.

Although the Social Gospel Movement was in disarray, liberal clergymen and theologians maintained commitments to social transformation, to making the Gospel relevant to the twentieth century. It is the contention of historian Dan McKanan "that religious practices, ideas, and institutions are thoroughly intertwined with the [political] left" and that "religious threads" can be found throughout the history of American radicalism.[19] This is true, he argues, even in conservative periods, when progressive and liberal thought and work may be outside the public eye, but the work of organizing, planning ahead, and envisioning new possibilities, is nevertheless going on. In moments of triumph—the abolition of slavery during the Civil War, the protection of workers in the progressive era, the establishment of a broad social safety net during the New Deal, and the elimination of racial segregation emerging from the Civil Rights Movement—we find the visible work of religious proponents as well as of leaders of the political left.

The continuation of the liberal religious tradition in the 1920s can be seen in the work of the Fellowship of Reconciliation (FOR), an organization that was committed to pacifism and to "a quest after an order of society in accordance with the mind of Christ," as McKanan notes. McKanan maintains that the continued vitality of the Social Gospel, which continued to be taught in many of the nation's seminaries, attracted the loyalty of somewhere between five and twenty-five percent of all mainline Protestant clergy by 1934. This means, he argues, that "the stage was set for a great expansion of the religious constituency of American radicalism" as the Great Depression unfolded.

But for the majority of Protestant clergy, the Social Gospel had lost its steam. The promise of creating a Christian social order seemed utopian and unachievable. Protestantism lost its hold on much of America in the 1920s and 1930s for many reasons, but its fragmentation certainly stands out. Many churches returned to a more individualized Christianity, while still accommodating to "modernism," accepting science, higher criticism of the Bible, and non-literalism. The remnants of a religion requiring social obligation remained in this majority component of American Protestantism, but it centered itself primarily on individual redemption and regeneration rather than efforts to create public policies that would further change and restructure society.

The more liberal segment of American Protestantism, found primarily in the mainline denominations of the North, continued to press for social transformation, especially in light of the harsh realities of the Great Depression. Many became proponents of Franklin Roosevelt's New Deal, often emerging as key players. The Depression and New Deal brought about a much more diversified liberal religious community, with these Protestants joined by Roman Catholics and Jewish leaders. Many were influenced by a revitalized and active labor movement and others by concrete expressions of caring for the poor and oppressed. The American Roman Catholic Church had remained close to workers as a result of the millions of Catholic immigrants who had arrived earlier from southern and eastern Europe and who provided labor for the Industrial Revolution. Dorothy Day gave up socialism for Catholicism, and, with her friend and mentor Peter Maurin, a former French seminarian, launched a new movement in American Catholicism with their settlement houses, social programs, and the publication of the *Catholic Worker* in 1933. She maintained her commitment to a Catholic Social Gospel, drawing on a growing body of Catholic social teaching, for nearly a half century. An example of the increased participation of the Jewish community can be found in the work of Saul Alinsky who grew

Can Religion Help Revive the Progressive Tradition?

up in one of Chicago's Jewish neighborhoods. His contribution was that of "community organizing," seeking to create social change at the local level, drawing on the power of existing organizations, including unions, churches, and synagogues.

Alongside the taming of the liberal element of Protestantism, we find the emergence of religious fundamentalism. Especially prominent among the urban and rural poor, fundamentalism developed in the 1920s as a rigid response to modernism and as a rejection of the Social Gospel. Core beliefs focused on the inerrancy of the Bible, the virgin birth, the substitutionary atonement of Christ on the cross, and the bodily resurrection and physical return of Christ. Some three million copies of *The Fundamentals*, a series of books containing the fundamentalist theology, made their way to pastors and religious workers across the country.[20] For this group, science was suspect, the Bible supreme. Nine decades later, fundamentalism remains a significant part of the American religious landscape.

As the United States changed, so did its religions. We see the growth of new groups and sects. Pentecostalism gained followers, Mormonism expanded far beyond its western base, and the Roman Catholic Church took on a much more prominent place in American culture. African-American denominations such as the African Methodist Episcopal Church and the National Baptist Convention emerged as important evangelical institutions with a commitment to social and racial justice. One finds in the 20th Century history of the Black church the continuation of some aspects of the Social Gospel, as churches addressed issues related to poverty, race, and economic opportunity.

Despite the changing religious landscape, made even more complex later in the 20th Century with the growing number of followers of other world religions, the Social Gospel and certainly liberal Christianity, never really went away. Dan McKanan devotes an entire chapter in his book to "Mentors of a New Left": individuals like A. J. Muste, a pacifist and Fellowship of Reconciliation leader; Dorothy Day, who influenced so many later activists, including writer Michael Harrington whose work contributed to the War on Poverty in the 1960s; and A. Philip Randolph who led the effort to end segregation in the armed forces during World War II and who organized massive urban rallies in support of that goal. "The themes of direct action against war, resistance to racial segregation, and life in intentional community," says McKanan, "were woven together in the work of these mentors."[21]

New organizations emerged in the 1940s and 1950s through this leadership—the Congress of Racial Equality, the Highlander Folk School in Tennessee (a labor school established by several Union Seminary graduates), and the Fellowship of Intentional Communities. This period also saw the emergence of new publications that sought to bring together diverse groups into new coalitions such as *Liberation*, founded in 1956. Drawing from the populist/progressive tradition as well as the Farm Labor movement, this magazine would contribute ideas that would help guide student activists in the next decade.

A revitalized Christianity emerged in a powerful way in the Civil Rights Movement. With the leadership of the Reverend Martin L. King, Jr., white ministers, often from northern, liberal Protestant churches, and rabbis from Jewish congregations north and south, joined hands with the Black clergy to march, preach, and engage in acts of civil disobedience to remove segregation. But it was the Black community itself, ordinary folk as well as professionals, that led the way, beginning with the 1956 Montgomery bus strike. The commitment to and exercise of nonviolence created a remarkably powerful force that added a new dimension to engaged, liberal religion with its continuing emphasis on many of the principles of the Social Gospel.

One finds the Social Gospel in Black liberation theology that emerged a decade later. Theologian James Cone became a leading spokesperson with the publication of *Black Theology and Black Power* in 1969 and *A Black Theology of Liberation* in 1970.[22] Black liberation theology, drawn in part from Catholic liberation theology that captured the hearts of many priests in Central and South America, had a lasting impact on many Black congregations, as the Black church moved to erase remaining vestiges of racism and discrimination and the lack of educational and economic opportunity in the United States. In the presidential election of 2008, Dr. Jeremiah Wright, pastor of Barack and Michelle Obama's church in Chicago, the Trinity United Church of Christ, was criticized for preaching a radical message of black liberation theology.

The impact of the Social Gospel on the Roman Catholic Church in the U.S. can probably best be seen in the role played by Catholic priests, nuns, and laypersons in the work of Cesar Chavez and the development of the United Farm Workers. After years of struggle, walkouts, and strikes—efforts that Rauschenbusch would have understood fully—to improve wages, reduce hours, and provide better living conditions for migrant workers in California and then the greater Southwest, including Texas, the United Farm Workers could claim 50,000 dues-paying members by 1970 with the ability to negotiate contracts with giant agribusinesses in California and elsewhere.

The Farm Workers movement drew inspiration from multiple sources, but none were probably more important than the social teachings that emerged from Pope John XXIII. In his first major encyclical on social issues, *Mater et Magistra: Christianity and Social Progress* (1961), Pope John discusses the social dimension of property and the need for a more effective distribution of goods in society. He talks about a just wage and the common good and the dangers for society when the rich dominate the poor. He also discusses in this encyclical the condition of agriculture, "in which he touched on issues such as health and crop insurance, price management, agricultural technology, and the relation between market value and the necessity of a just wage for farmers."[23] The encyclical drew the attention of world leaders and most certainly Catholic clergy in the U.S. It opened the doors to ecumenical cooperation in dealing with social issues, setting the stage for Catholic/Protestant work on many domestic issues. The encyclical *Pacem in Terris: Peace on Earth* (1963), built on these themes, emphasizing the rights of all human beings (including the right to a worthy standard of living); the necessity of grounding the authority of the state in a higher moral order, with recognition of the importance of democratic participation of its members; the necessity of eliminating costly arms and nuclear weapons; and, finally, the concept of the common good which transcends the individual person's good.

Vatican II, already underway by 1963, proved to be a watershed for the Roman Catholic Church worldwide, but most definitely for the Catholic Church in the U.S. In the proclamations flowing from Vatican II, we find a new commitment to human liberties, human rights, and issues related to social justice. On American soil, the theology and reforms of Vatican II repositioned the Catholic Church and stimulated commitment to many social and political reforms.[24] Poverty, the conditions of the working class, racial injustices, military interventionism (the Vietnam War), and the disappearance of the common good, became issues that demanded Church involvement. In *Gaudium et Spes:*

A Whole Which Is Greater

Pastoral Constitution on the Church in the Modern World (1965), the Second Vatican Council spoke through the world's bishops to Catholics and non-Catholics alike, providing an "ethical framework for dealing with world problems," while "it urged pastoral action to make its commitments real in Christian life and work." The liberal component of American Protestantism where the Social Gospel was still respected and taught, especially among those "mainline" denominations such as the United Church of Christ, the American Baptist Convention, the Methodist Episcopal Church, the Episcopal Church, the historically Black denominations, and the Presbyterian Church U.S.A., applauded, and in the spirit of Vatican II, new ecumenical endeavors to address the needs of American society, unfolded.

PROSPECTS FOR A NEW PROGRESSIVISM

The history of American interfaith dialogue from the time of Vatican II to the present is complex and difficult, but it is possible to argue that a powerful vision may once again emerge from the religious community as we deal with the problems of the present time. Three important developments need to be noted.

A Gilded Age, Once Again

First, as was the situation a century ago, we are experiencing a very destructive gap between the economic elite and everyone else, with those holding extreme wealth often benefiting through actions of the political elite. Economist Jeffrey D. Sachs provides overwhelming data to document the unprecedented increase of wealth among America's economic elite in recent decades, often occurring at the expense of everyone else.[25] Sachs maintains that the top 1 percent of American households "have never had it so good. They sit at the top of the heap at the same time that around 100 million Americans live in poverty or in its shadow." For Sachs, "the CEO-friendly political environment, the economic effects of globalization, and the tax policy choices made in Washington over the past thirty years have combined to create an inequality of income and wealth unprecedented in American history. We are living through a new Gilded Age exceeding the gaudy excess of the 1870s and the 1920s." Sachs notes that "the last time America had such

Can Religion Help Revive the Progressive Tradition?

massive inequality of wealth and income was on the eve of the Great Depression, and the inequality today may actually be greater than in 1929." The New Deal of the 1930s, the reforms enacted after World War II, and economic conditions and policies led to a significant narrowing of income inequality—what the progressives of a century ago so very much wanted—but that inequality exploded once again in the 1980s and has continued through to the present day.

Sociologist William Domhoff points out that, as of 2007, the top one percent of households owned 34.6 percent of all privately held wealth, and the next 19 percent (the managerial, professional, and small business stratum) had 50.5 percent. Thus just 20 percent of the people owned 85 percent, leaving only 15 percent of the wealth for the bottom 80 percent.[26] Domhoff has written persuasively that this concentration of wealth results in a relatively fixed group of privileged people who are able to dominate the economy and the government. He recognizes that this goes against "the American grain" because we want to believe that American society with its elected officials, multiple interest groups, organized labor, and consumers, provide "countervailing power."[27] But such is not the case. Citing a recent study, Domhoff contends that most Americans have no idea that the wealth distribution (defined for them in terms of net worth) is as concentrated as it is.[28]

As Warren Buffet and many others have pointed out, the wealthiest individuals in the United States are paying unusually low taxes to the federal government. Sachs points to the wide variations in the top marginal tax rates during the 100 years that it has existed: 7 percent in 1913, 77 percent in 1917 (entry into World War I), 25 percent in the 1920s (conservative administrations of Calvin Coolidge and Herbert Hoover), 63 percent from 1933–1937 (during the Great Depression and the New Deal), up to 94 percent from 1942–1945 (during World War II), 70 percent during much of the 1960s (tax cuts of the Johnson administration), 28 percent in 1988 (Reagan tax policies). The marginal tax rate has not reached 40 percent since that time.[29] Buffet, arguing that the tax code is unfair, has said that he paid only 17 percent in federal taxes in 2010.[30]

But it is not just the wealthy who pay unusually low taxes to the federal government. David Kocieniewski, writing for *The New York Times*, noted that "Corporate America is not far behind."[31] He pointed to a study by Citizens for Tax Justice "that found that 280 of the biggest

A Whole Which Is Greater

publicly traded American companies faced federal income tax bills equal to 18.5 percent of their profits during the last three years—little more than half the official corporate rate of 35 percent and lower than their competitors in many industrialized countries." And thirty of those companies had no federal tax liability for a three-year period, thanks to shelters and loopholes in existing tax laws.

Such information helped launch the Occupy Wall Street movement. Begun in September 2011, the movement quickly spread to dozens of cities across the United States. Behind the anger one finds resentment over economic inequality; the excess wealth that sustains lifestyles that few can even imagine; the many Wall Street scandals; the havoc brought to the American economy by all the shady practices of America's largest financial firms; the bailout of large corporations that had failed their workers and American society miserably; corporate executives who have continued to receive huge bonuses and stock options in the midst of the Great Recession that has brought pain to so many; and, last but not least, the disdain that many members of the economic elite seem to express toward the rest of society.

A Middle-Class Crisis

Second, the great gains made by the middle class following World War II seem to many to have been reversed in recent times. We saw earlier how the Progressive Movement a century ago began as an unprecedented crisis of alienation amid the extremes of wealth and poverty in America and had as its focus a taming of excessive individualism to allow for a great expansion of the middle class by increasing opportunities for the working class while at the same time limiting the excesses of the "Upper Ten." Now we are caught in a similar situation. Divided in politics as well as in wealth, Jeffrey Sachs writes that "there can be no doubt that something has gone terribly wrong in the U.S. economy, politics, and society in general. Americans are on edge: wary, pessimistic, and cynical." Two-thirds or more of Americans say they are "dissatisfied with the way things are going in the United States," a figure that is up from around one-third a decade earlier.[32] And a similar proportion of Americans consistently describe the country as "off track."[33]

We are also cynical when it comes to the role of government. Beginning with the attacks of Ronald Reagan in the 1980 presidential

Can Religion Help Revive the Progressive Tradition?

election, Americans have tended to express dismaying views about the role and effectiveness of the federal government, as various polls have shown. This lack of confidence extends to other institutions of society. Banks and financial institutions received a positive rating of only 22 percent of persons polled by the Pew Research Center, with large corporations (25 percent), the national news media (31 percent), and labor unions (32 percent), not too far behind. Colleges and universities (61 percent), churches and religious organizations (63 percent), and small businesses (71 percent), retained public confidence—statistics that might help us chart the future.[34]

The financial meltdown of 2008, the loss of 8.6 million jobs from peak employment in 2007, the nearly nine percent unemployment rate over the last few years, with lower-skilled workers and skilled workers in the manufacturing sector hit the hardest, has impacted Americans in profound ways. Sachs points to various studies that show how the satisfaction level of Americans—happiness—has collapsed in recent years. The 2008 economic crisis "deepened the financial distress of millions of Americans who kept their jobs but lost their homes and savings." For the 2010 year, a record 2.9 million U.S. properties received foreclosure filings.[35] For decades the home had been at the very center of the economic, psychological, and social well-being of the middle class, and the reversal of fortune for millions of citizens in losing their homes has probably done more to create a discouraged population and a disappearing middle class than anything else.

In an era of unprecedented and soaring CEO pay, we have seen in the past thirty years a widening gap in power, compensation, and job security between senior management and professionals on the one hand, and the rest of the workforce on the other. Clerical and production workers have seen wages frozen. Job security has declined dramatically, especially in light of the significant shift toward outsourcing of jobs. In an era of increased vulnerability for the working class, whose goal has often been to enter into or remain in the middle class, the pay of CEOs has soared to obscene levels. Sachs points out that at the start of the 1970s, average top 100 CEO pay was roughly forty times the average worker's pay. By the year 2000, it had reached one thousand times the average worker's pay. Meanwhile, the median take-home pay for male full-time workers has stagnated since the early 1970s, and with that, job satisfaction.

A Whole Which Is Greater

Loss of the Common Good

American politics in recent years has been marked by animosities, deep divisions, and brazen, intractable stances on policy questions. Fueled by the Tea Party, the Republican triumphs in the 2010 election, and the response of Democrats, have made compromise, once the mainstay of American politics, a dirty word. Americans viewing the scene in Washington day after day can only conclude that something is broken, and that it has to do with growing doubt that those in power are working for the common good. Intransigence may be an appropriate response from time to time, but when it becomes a consistent mode of response to major policy issues before the nation, one can only conclude that political and economic interests outweigh the interests of the public at large. The long-cherished tradition, so vital to America's sense of self, of sitting down at a table and working things out—knowing that in the end compromise is essential to constructive action—has seemingly disappeared. The low regard that the public has toward Congress can be traced in part to a perception that members of Congress are unwilling to work together and would rather see major issues go unsettled than to collaboratively solve them.

The loss of the common good in policy debates and discussions in state capitols and in Washington points to a much deeper problem, and that is the concomitant undermining of a sense of national unity and purpose—what it is that America stands for. This sense of community is based on a belief that the nation truly is dedicated to fairness, justice, and equal opportunity, and that everyone, the powerful, the not so powerful, and those without power, must accept accountability for their actions. The accountability factor has taken a huge hit in recent years. Sachs writes: "When something goes wrong—a drug proves dangerous in follow-up tests, a drilling practice proves hazardous, or a paramilitary unit engages in murder or torture—the inevitable response is to lie first, cover up next, and acknowledge the truth only as a last resort, usually when internal documents are finally leaked to the public." The political and economic elite have a special responsibility to demonstrate this accountability.

Sachs sees the cause of this as "the nearly complete impunity of lying or costly leadership mistakes. Almost nobody at the top pays a price for such behavior, even when the truth is eventually exposed. The bankers who brought down the world economy remain at the top of the heap, sitting across the table from the president in White House meetings or dining at state dinners as the president's guests of honor.... Those who are actually found guilty of violating the law typically get off with a slap on the wrist, if that." For average working men and women, whose sense of self-responsibility and accountability is strong, the lack of accountability of the economic and political elite in this country is appalling and has worked to undermine confidence in large institutions and that in turn has led many to say that no one is looking out for the average person. The common interest, the common good, and a sense of community—the belief that we are all in this together—have been greatly diminished.

But there are other causes as well. Bill Bishop and Robert G. Cushing argue persuasively in their book, *The Big Sort: Why the Clustering of Like-Minded America is Tearing Us Apart*, that the loss of community and the demise of the common good has deep cultural roots and reflects changing social and demographic conditions.[36] One has to look beyond the stalemate and division in Washington or state capitols. Americans are self-selecting the groups with which they want to be associated—and they are always groups of like-minded folk. National civic groups and major mainline church denominations have lost significant membership, often replaced by local civic organizations and churches that cater to specific segments of the population. At one time, the three big television networks (ABC, NBC, and CBS) tended to provide Americans with shared stories, values, news, and common reference points. Instead, the new media offer Americans the opportunity to tune in or watch what appeals to them, picking, for instance, Fox News for the conservatives and MSNBC for the liberals. Americans thus tend to inhabit a cultural universe that fits in with their social values and political perspectives. The opportunity for obtaining multiple perspectives has never been greater, but that opportunity is squandered as we gravitate to the like-minded, thereby reinforcing our beliefs and values. But this is only part of the story: this segmentation can be found in so many areas of contemporary life. We move into suburbs and communities of the like-minded. We attend churches of the like-minded. We join groups with the same causes and values. We associate with people in our economic class and tax bracket (except, I guess, Mitt Romney, with his 13.9 percent tax rate). "By the turn of the 21st century," Bishop writes, "it seemed as though the country was separating in every way conceivable."

In politics, Bishop believes that gerrymandering—the redrawing of political districts to help ensure predictable results—has been a significant polarizing force. But it goes beyond this, he says, in the self-selection of individuals and families as to where they want to live. In 1976 the average American was likely to live alongside people of the opposing political party—barely 26 percent lived in counties that went in a landslide for one presidential candidate or another. By 1992 the number had increased to 38 percent and by 2004, nearly 50 percent. Scott Stossel, the deputy editor of *The Atlantic*, in reviewing Bishop's book for *The New York Times*, quotes playwright Arthur Miller as the 2004 presidential contest was underway: "How can the polls be neck and neck when I don't know one Bush supporter?"[37]

In reflecting on *The Big Sort*, President Bill Clinton commented: "Some of us are going to have to cross the street, folks."[38] That is the challenge before us.

In January 2011, powerful new realities—the jarring gap between the wealthy and the rest of America, the crisis of the middle class, job insecurity, and the erosion of commitment to the common good, became especially evident to many Wisconsinites in the political agenda of newly elected Governor Scott Walker and the Republican Assembly and Senate, whose leadership seemed so very dedicated to carrying out that agenda. An unprecedented backlash occurred. To the tens of thousands who marched on the Capitol in Madison day after day, week after week, it seemed as though every effort was being made to deconstruct the public sector; to destroy public unions and the right to collective bargaining and the right to help shape the conditions of employment, including those of public school teachers, and to do so under the guise of a budget repair bill; to undermine the quest for equal opportunity through education with deep cuts in funding to school districts and University of Wisconsin campuses; and to cut the wages, salaries, and benefits of public sector employees. At the same time, the Walker administration rejected federal dollars for an expanded railroad system in Wisconsin that would have brought economic opportunities and jobs, while Wisconsinites saw continued job losses, in excess of the national average. Meanwhile, CEO compensation in Wisconsin tripled in the last decade while the average wage of working people remained flat.

Can Religion Help Revive the Progressive Tradition?

The circumstances leading to the protests and then efforts to recall Governor Scott Walker, Lieutenant Governor Rebecca Kleefisch, and a number of state senators, seems eerily familiar to those who have some knowledge of the Gilded Age and the Progressive Movement that sought to deal with the many social, economic, and political issues noted earlier in this chapter. A good case can be made that we are seeing a revival of progressivism, and just as Wisconsin played a seminal role in that movement a century ago, so it is today with the new progressivism which is seeking to hold on to the many gains made earlier.

STRENGTHENING THE NEW PROGRESSIVISM

For those eager to see a revitalized and transformed progressivism, five points seem especially important.

Building Coalitions

Success will depend, as it did a century ago, on establishing a "big tent" under which numerous groups with particular goals can unite. The Wisconsin protest movement provided a great start: firefighters standing alongside school teachers, farmers standing alongside manufacturing workers, small-town people standing alongside those from Milwaukee and Green Bay and Madison. And it is likely that these thousands of protestors held diverse political and religious ideologies.

The early progressive history is instructive. One of the key elements of success 100 years ago as documented by Charles McCarthy was the willingness of Republicans and Democrats to work together. One of the great losses in modern American political history is the disappearance of moderate Republicans who philosophically were aligned with some of the great names in the history of the Republican party—leaders like Governor Nelson Rockefeller of New York; Senator Charles Percy of Illinois; Governor Harold Stassen of Minnesota and, later, Pennsylvania; and, more recently, Congressman Jim Leach of Iowa. Moderate voices like these were essentially driven out of the Republican Party after 1980 although a few voices (Senator Olympia Snowe, former Secretary of State Colin Powell) and a few moderate Republican organizations (Republican Main Street Partnership and the Ripon Society) are still around. A renewed progressivism may well depend on moderate Republicans once again coming forth, running for office, championing long-term interests (balanced budgets, welfare reform, reasonable gun control laws, environmental regulation, public education, higher education, a less bellicose and more prudent foreign policy), and moderating the influence of the far right.

But that is true with Democrats as well. The liberal element of the Democratic Party has been marginalized in these conservative times, so there is no shortage of conservative Democrats serving in the House, the Senate, and state offices across the country. But there is a special need now for conservative Democrats to step forward and "cross the street" to meet with moderate Republicans. Somehow we must get back to the table—in state capitols across the country and in Washington—with folks who represent the broad spectrum of American society, the political center, to forge a new partnership that can set the stage for American renewal. And we need multiple tables in locations across the country, so that those who are not normally part of the political process in this country can participate and be engaged in shaping the future of the nation.

Some would argue that what is needed is a separate entity within the Democratic Party, the creation of a movement within the party patterning the role that the Tea Party has played within the Republican Party and that the Christian Coalition and Moral Majority played before the Tea Party. G. William Domhoff argues that forging these separate identities has been one reason for the success of the right-wing within the Republican party, and the best way to counter that, for those who support the agenda of "the left," is to create something similar, such as "Egalitarian Democrat Clubs" who would find candidates to run in elections, garner support for their campaigns, and press for a political agenda that incorporates their ideas and values.[39]

My hunch is that efforts made by moderate Republicans and conservative Democrats to move beyond the divisive and uncompromising politics of the past several decades holds more promise, and that Domhoff's approach is only more of the same—more of the segmentation and politics of confrontation that has not served the nation well. The success of the Progressive Movement a century ago depended upon coalition building around particular issues, perhaps more so than even the creation of Roosevelt's Progressive (Bull Moose) Party of 1912 or Senator Robert M. La Follette, Sr.'s Progressive Party of 1924.[40]

Understanding the History

Progressives would do well to learn their own history, to spend time understanding not only what happened in Wisconsin and the country a century ago, but the ways in which the progressive spirit has emerged from time to time over the decades to speak to real issues and to help solve real problems. A study of this history will say something about how progressivism changes over time, and how those who claim to be progressives must be able to adjust core ideas and values to new times and issues and to be able to get things done. It is also important to understand where progressivism failed; most notably, perhaps, the lack of attention paid to racial equality during the Progressive era and, more recently, the inability to be more fully engaged in the global ecological crises (see below).

Expanding the Middle Class

A renewed progressivism must once again seek to advance the middle class. As it did a century ago, the new progressivism must seek to bring more and more working-class families and those who struggle so hard to make ends meet, into the middle class. This is why issues related to the safety net—health care, unemployment insurance, protecting social security and pensions—are so important. It is also why adequate funding for public education and defeating efforts to privatize public education are so vital. The same holds true with higher education; its affordability is essential to the economic well-being of the state and nation and provides a primary means whereby individuals, many of whom are the first in their families to attend college, can be part of the middle class. Over a lifetime, college graduates earn nearly $1 million more than high school graduates.[41]

Progressivism and Religion

Political progressives would do well to turn to religious communities for inspiration and for the vision needed to sustain particular goals and endeavors. While there is some clarity on what it is that the tens of thousands who protested in Madison through the winter and spring of 2011 want from their government, there is far less clarity in other "progressive" movements nationally, including the Occupy Wall Street movement. The common complaint is that it is not enough to speak out against excessive corporate pay, government bailouts of misguided corporations, government inaction, and the loss of jobs, political corruption, and the overall plight of the working class. A vision needs to emerge—one that helps us understand what the America of tomorrow should look like, how we can get there, and how and in what ways it will draw fully from the core values and ideals that have been with us since the founding of the nation.

I have no doubt that such a vision must have a secular foundation—we can't be a "Christian America," despite the wishes of some members of the political right. The founding documents of the United States ensure the nonestablishment of religion while granting the free exercise of religion. Besides, religious plurality in America includes not just those many denominations and religious groups that reflect America's Judeo-Christian background, but many others, including Buddhists, Hindus, Muslims, and Sikhs.

No one has captured the dramatically changing American religious landscape better than Harvard University professor Diana L. Eck, who launched in 1991 The Pluralism Project, a research effort that involves faculty and students from the Faculty of Arts and Sciences as well as Harvard Divinity School and aims to help Americans better understand religious diversity in the United States. Eck's efforts document the fact that, even as the Christian right has tried to place the Ten Commandments in court houses and other public places across the country, and has sought presidential candidates who would support their notion of a Christian America, something of "enormous importance" has happened: "the United States has become the most religiously diverse nation on earth."[42] Building on the groundwork of the Kennedy administration, President Lyndon Baines Johnson signed the 1965 Immigration and Naturalization Act into law at the base of the Statue of Liberty in New York, and in so doing lifted four decades of discriminatory immigration policies, especially those designed to exclude people from Asian-Pacific countries. As the web page of The Pluralism Project notes. "In the past fifty years the religious landscape of the United States has changed radically. There are Islamic centers and mosques, Hindu and Buddhist temples and meditation centers in virtually every American city. The encounter between people of very different religious traditions

Can Religion Help Revive the Progressive Tradition?

takes place in the proximity of our own cities and neighborhoods."[43] To this extraordinary growth of religious diversity, one also needs to point out the growing new vitality of Native American religious practices and the powerful feminist voices, including those from within established religious organizations, that have fundamentally changed the theology, liturgy, and ethics of many of these traditions.

Religion has always played an important role in the cultural and political life of the nation. So here is the question: Is it possible to marshal this religious heritage—including the new diversity which is now adding to this heritage—on behalf of the new progressivism? If so, what would that look like—what vision might emerge?

There are many hopeful signs. Within Christianity itself, evangelicalism has become more diverse. Pat Robertson's Christian Coalition and Jerry Falwell's Moral Majority had their day, although their legacy certainly can be seen in the Republican far right, although the Tea Party, part of that group, has focused on economic and governmental issues far more than social issues. But a counter-evangelical tradition, perhaps best seen in the work of Jim Wallis and the Sojourners community, now has a forty-year history. Wallis, author of numerous books and editor-in-chief of *Sojourner's Magazine*, combines the traditional Protestant emphasis on personal salvation with the Social Gospel concern for social salvation. The Sojourners community seeks "to articulate the biblical call to social justice, inspiring hope and building a movement to transform individuals, communities, the church, and the world."[44] Sojourners is highly inclusive; its followers include Catholics, Pentecostals, Buddhists, and mainline Protestants.

There are many other movements that highlight change among evangelicals. Evangelicals for Social Action was created in 1973 when forty evangelical leaders, including conservative theologian Carl Henry, founder of the magazine, *Christianity Today*, agreed to address issues related to "poverty, racism, sexism, and violence." Its influence waned with the arrival of the Religious Right, but social-action evangelicals have not let up. The National Association of Evangelicals, formed in 2004, represents various denominations with a combined constituency of some thirty million members. This group produced a document titled "For the Health of the Nation: An Evangelical Call to Civic Responsibility," and called upon evangelicals not only to safeguard the sanctity of life and to nurture families (traditional concerns) but also

A Whole Which Is Greater

to "seek justice for the poor, protect human rights, work for peace, and preserve God's creation." [45]

Still, there is a tendency in many of the new Christian megachurches to preach a religion that remains focused on personal salvation and devoutness. These churches, often formed in the past thirty years or so by disenchanted members of mainline Christian denominations, tend to reject the socially engaged new evangelicalism for a new form of the old-time evangelicalism—but it is an evangelicalism without the Social Gospel. Governor Scott Walker's religious pilgrimage seems to highlight this trend toward the old-time religion, one that emphasizes personal salvation but not social salvation.[46]

Yet American Christianity—Protestant, Catholic, and Orthodox—includes a tradition that is rich in regard to social theology and engagement and one that has been supportive of progressive causes, and that tradition remains very much alive. It recognizes, as Walter Rauschenbusch did a century ago, that sin can be structural and organizational as well as individual. We see this tradition in the Catholic Worker movement and in the "Call to Action" conference of 1976 where Bishops of the American Catholic Church, inspired by Pope Paul VI's teachings, met to translate Christian ideals into public policy.

We see support for political progressivism in other religious traditions. We see it in the work of Rabbi Michael Lerner who convened the New America Movement in order to foster a deeper spirituality to deal with the oppression of women and minorities. He launched *Tikkun* magazine in 1986 as a vehicle for prominent liberal Jewish thought with the purpose "to heal, repair, and transform the world." It seeks to build bridges between religious and secular progressives.[47] All these movements display a new alignment of religion and politics in the U.S.

Throughout the 20th Century, as Dan McKanan so ably demonstrates, Jewish, Protestant, Catholic and other religious leaders have always been present, contributing in vital ways to social and economic progress, from the strengthening of workers' rights in the early years of the century, to the establishment of Social Security in the 1930s, to the expansion of civil rights and the creation of Medicare for senior citizens in the 1960s.

To this we are now able to add, thanks to the new American pluralism, the opportunity to draw from the rich teachings of all the major religions of the world. I am convinced that within these religious traditions one can find the stories, teachings, and guidance needed to refurbish and renew the sacred canopy that has helped to sustain progressivism during the past one-hundred years. Hinduism tells us much about unity in the midst of diversity, about the sacredness of human life, about the path of nonviolence. Buddhism offers us the opportunity to understand more deeply how the search for wisdom is the path to true freedom. We learn that happiness consists in something other than our consumer-driven culture; the accumulation of things and wealth cannot be the ultimate goal. Engaged Buddhism, a powerful voice now in the United States, teaches that all sentient beings must be saved, not just oneself. Social projects dear to the heart of progressives is part of engaged Buddhism: feeding the hungry, helping those in prison, caring for the sick and dying, tackling the problem of homelessness. Central to Islam is the prayerful life and the recognition that true peace can come only through submission and commitment to Ultimate Reality—to Allah. Islam's emphasis on "almsgiving" has created important charities in the U.S. to address poverty, disaster relief, literacy, and other social problems. The principles of equality and freedom are central to Sikhism.

Diana Eck makes the point that the presence of these religions in the United States "will require us to reclaim the deepest meaning of the very principles we cherish and to create a truly pluralist American society in which this great diversity is not simply tolerated but becomes the very source of our strength."[48] Beyond that, I would argue that these world religions hold the capacity for us to augment the powerful prophetic message of Judaism and the redemptive message of Christianity. We need now an interfaith dialogue among all those who feel kinship with the progressive tradition.

Progressivism, Religion, and the Ecological Crisis

If there is to be a revived and transformed progressivism for the 21st Century, it will need to address what is perhaps the most important issue of our time, the global ecological crisis—global warming, deforestation, extinction of species, the degradation of land and soil erosion, famine, the loss of habitat, the plundering of natural resources, and diminishing fresh water.

A Whole Which Is Greater

Certainly it can be argued that champions of progressivism have helped lead the way the past forty years in protecting the environment, just as they did in regard to civil rights, gender equality, and shoring up the "safety net" for the poor and disabled. There are many significant legislative achievements that often drew support from both sides of the Congressional aisle.[49] But the ecological crisis continues, and industrial capitalism and an economy based on mass consumerism, marches on. And the United States itself has often failed to promote international environmental law, as seen specifically in the continued lack of will to ratify the Kyoto Protocol that followed from the United Nations Framework Convention on Climate Change (1997). The protocol was designed to stabilize greenhouse gas concentrations in the atmosphere.

In many quarters, blame for ecological deterioration worldwide is placed on religion and, in particular, the Judeo-Christian tradition. The argument is this: If the world's religions have historically tended to provide the worldviews and ethical perspectives that undergird economic systems, cultural values, and societal behaviors, and if these systems, values and behaviors are at the heart of the environmental crisis, then is it not true that religion is to blame? That was indeed a primary point in the widely read essay by Lynn White, Jr., published in *Science* in 1967, "The Historic Roots of our Ecological Crisis."[50] White indicted Western societies for how industry, technology, and science contributed to a degradation of the environment, but he also went deeper, pointing out a Judeo-Christian tradition that emphasized the transcendence of God above nature and the belief that the human community was given "dominion" over nature, which led to a devaluation of nature and its subsequent abuse. White stated that "Christianity bears a huge burden of guilt" by fostering a theology that permitted many Western societies to abuse natural resources and harm the environment for commercial, materialistic ends.

Many religious leaders and theologians recognized that they could not ignore this and similar criticism coming from the environmental movement. For some, this meant a return to Hebraic and Christian scriptures and teachings to reevaluate the moral obligation to care for God's creation. What emerged in some religious traditions was a new ethic of stewardship that provided the foundation for serious thinking about the ecological crisis, the environmental movement, and ways whereby religion might serve as a constructive resource.

Can Religion Help Revive the Progressive Tradition?

Some would argue, with considerable merit, that the religious community has responded too slowly, but we have seen in the past several decades significant engagement in the global ecological crisis by nearly all of the major religious traditions. Activist scholar J. Ronald Engel captured this work very well in a recent article in which he reflects on such endeavors:

> Many of us who began to teach and write in the field [of religion, ethics and ecology] in those years [beginning in the 1970s] were led by our positive experiences in grass-roots activism and community organization, and the more far-reaching national and international social change movements with which they were allied, both inside and outside of the churches, to embrace what we considered the imminent prospect of a democratically legislated 'paradigm shift' away from industrial capitalism to a just, peaceful, and sustainable society. These experiences became the . . . background for our efforts to 'green' congregations, seminaries, and denominational headquarters, marshal communities of faith in the comprehensive cause of eco-justice (justice for all of creation and all human beings), participate in the covenanting processes of the Peace, Justice, and Ecological Integrity theme of the World Council of Churches in the run-up to the Rio Earth Summit in 1992 and in the many ecumenical and inter-faith efforts to create a spiritually and ethically purposive international civil society afterward, through the launch of the Earth Charter in 2000 and Rio+10 in Johannesburg in 2002. They were also the subsoil for the immense intellectual energy we poured during those years into recovering the creation-affirming elements of the Christian tradition and what we hoped would one day be called a New Reformation—history-making reforms of theology, church dogmatics, ethics, biblical hermeneutics, church history, and liturgical practice in light of our new-found recognition of our special place and responsibilities in the evolutionary drama of the planet.[51]

Engle is writing from the perspective of one who believes that advances made have been undercut by the policies of many developed nations, especially the United States. He reflects on what has been learned as a result of the Arab Spring. While Americans have shown enthusiasm for the revolutions underway, we have discovered the shadow side, he says—"America's long-standing ties with repressive dictatorships and royal autocrats." He writes:

> The Faustian bargains we have made in the Middle East confirm our worst fears about what our country has been actually doing in the world. Far from ushering in the new age of ecological awareness, human rights, and peaceful global cooperation and responsibility, the opening years of the twenty-first century have shown us how the United States, often with overt support from Christian church members and leaders, has engaged in a series of betrayals of those values, including, but by no means limited to, our invasion of Iraq, our refusal to take serious action to mitigate climate change, and after the largest financial crisis since the Great Depression, a new capitulation to corporate power and mass consumer culture.[52]

But it is important that we not forget the significant progress that has been made in rallying the religious community on behalf of the environment and sustainability. It is beyond the scope of this chapter to document this work, but it can be illustrated by looking at two very important efforts, the Harvard Project on Religion and Ecology and its follow-up project, The Forum on Religion and Ecology at Yale University.

Begun in 1996, the three-year Harvard project, sponsored by the Center for the Study of World Religions, included a series of conferences that involved a thousand scholars, environmental specialists, and activists from throughout the world. The project was sponsored by the Harvard University Center for the Study of World Religions, which at the conclusion of the project published nine books that drew from the conference proceedings focused on nine major religious traditions (Hinduism, Jainism, Buddhism, Confucianism, Daoism, Indigenous traditions, Judaism, Christianity, and Islam). A concluding volume summarizes key findings.[53] According to the project leaders, professors Mary Evelyn Tucker, John Grim, and Lawrence Sullivan, this project responded to worldwide appeals for the world's religions to embrace environmental concerns, including the "World Scientists' Warning to Humanity," issued in 1992 by the Union of Concerned Scientists and signed by 1,575 scientists (including 99 Nobel laureates) from sixty-nine countries. The project was, according to the organizers, "an important step in transcending differences among religions and allowing them to act in concert to broaden a view of nature that goes beyond simple economic ends. Religious values are critical in establishing a

Can Religion Help Revive the Progressive Tradition?

new balance of human-earth relations . . . one that acknowledges human needs for resources, but restrains human greed."[54]

Key findings of the three-year project were released October 20, 1998, at a press conference held at the New York Office of the United Nations Environment Programme, which was followed by a conference at the United Nations where project leaders reported their findings to the United Nations community and non-governmental organizations.

Out of this project, a new effort unfolded, The Forum on Religion and Ecology, an international, multi-religious endeavor based at Yale University that has included conferences, publications, a remarkable PBS documentary, *Journey of the Universe*, and the development of extensive internet resources in order to help "identify the ethical dimensions by which the religions of the world can respond to the growing environmental crisis." [55]

Project leaders Tucker and Grim write:

> Clearly religions need to be involved with the development of a more comprehensive worldview and ethics to ground movements toward sustainability. Whether from an anthropocentric or a biocentric perspective, more adequate environmental values need to be formulated and linked to areas of public policy. Scholars of religion as well as religious leaders, and laity can be key players in this articulation process. . . . The alliance of scholars, religious leaders, and activists is creating common ground for dialogue and creative partnerships in envisioning and implementing long-range sustainable solutions to some of our most pressing environmental problems. This is critical because the attitudes and values that shape people's concepts of nature come primarily from religious worldviews and ethical practices.[56]

Tucker and Grim recognize that religions, "through intolerance and exclusive claims to truth, have often contributed to tensions between peoples, including wars or forced conversion." And to that, we can add, religions have contributed to the intellectual framework supporting economic systems and policies that have been destructive to the environment. But, as we have seen, religions have also contributed mightily to reform legislation, to regulations and oversight of many industries, to civil rights, and to the protection of the poor and oppressed. So there are reasons to be optimistic, that, on the one hand, political progressivism will become a more powerful force in protecting the environment and in encouraging nations to adopt policies that promote true sustainability, and, on the other hand, that progressivism will draw from the deep and rich perspective of the world's religions, including those of indigenous peoples, to develop an intellectual and moral framework that encourages and provides credibility for significant policy initiatives. Tucker and Grim put it this way: "The moral imperative and value systems of religions are indispensable in mobilizing the sensibilities of people toward preserving the environment for future generations."[57]

Religion is also responding to the "deep ecology" movement which seeks to move far beyond an agenda that only encourages specific legislative or policy solutions to particular environmental problems. Instead, deep ecology points to the need to develop an ecological consciousness and cultivation of the insight that everything in the world is connected. This awareness involves "a process of ever-deepening questioning of ourselves, the assumptions of the dominant worldview in our culture, and the meaning and truth of our reality."[58] Deep ecology calls out for an even richer conversation between religion and ecology, perhaps leading to an environmental ethic that confronts our consumer-driven culture with spiritual and religious belief.[59] A strong inter-faith, ecumenical stance drawn from the world's religions may offer the best hope for cultural and social transformations among the world's most technologically driven and industrialized societies that deal with fundamental problems: mass consumerism, materialism, overconsumption, displacement of workers, and the accumulation of wealth for the benefit of the few.

CONCLUSION

Progressivism can stand alone as a political platform, but the prospect of grounding progressivism in not just the best ideals and ethics of Christianity, as was the case a century ago, but also in the diverse religions of the world now prominent in the U.S., including indigenous traditions that have been here long before the age of exploration and colonization, is indeed exciting. It might be possible to develop a "sacred canopy" for our times, one that will light the fires of our collective imagination and allow us to revision the progressive tradition to ensure its relevancy to 21st Century America and the world community. There is much work to be done. We might discover anew the value of working together,

Can Religion Help Revive the Progressive Tradition?

building that big tent that allows for diversity but commitment to ultimate truths, and that draws from the intellectual and moral wealth of the world's religions, so that we can create a vision for America that is inclusive, uniting, and transformative.

ENDNOTES

1. Documentation on the development of religious studies as an academic discipline can be found in *Explaining Religion: Critical Theory from Bodin to Freud*, by J. Samuel Preus (Scholar's Press, 2000).

2. See *Seven Theories of Religion* by Daniel L. Pal (Oxford University Press, 1996) which contains an informative chapter on Emile Durkheim. For further reading, see Durkheim's *The Elementary Forms of the Religious Life* (The Macmillan Company, 1915).

3. Max Weber, *The Protestant Ethic and the Spirit of Capitalism* (CreateSpace, 2010. First published 1904).

4. Peter L. Berger, *The Sacred Canopy: Elements of a Sociological Theory of Religion* (Anchor Books, 1969, 1990). This book is grounded in social science theory. Concerned that readers might see it as contributing to the "god is dead" movement of the 1960s, a sort of treatise on atheism, Berger wrote *A Rumor of Angels: Modern Society and the Rediscovery of the Supernatural* (Anchor, 1970), to support the idea that in the end the social sciences may not have the last word, and that the experience of transcendence claimed by religious practitioners must be taken seriously. Many additional books published by Berger later in his career reflect his Christian orientation.

5. Richard Hofstadter, *The Age of Reform* (Vintage Books, 1955).

6. Michael McGerr, *A Fierce Discontent: The Rise and Fall of the Progressive Movement in America* (Oxford: Oxford University Press, 2003).

7. Sadly, Hull House in Chicago, the most important contribution of Jane Addams, closed its doors on January 27, 2012, after 120 years of service. In recent years it has been providing child care, medical assistance, job training, housing assistance, and a host of other services to 60,000 people a year in the Chicago area. Agency leaders blamed the closing on excessive demands for services while

donations and other forms of support had dropped due to the recession. Tammy Weber, "Hull House shuttered after 120 years," *Austin American Statesman*, January 28, 2012.

8. Charles McCarthy, *The Wisconsin Idea* (MacMillan Company, 1912).

9. References to *Rerum Novarum* and other Papal encyclical letters and Catholic documents are taken from *Catholic Social Thought: The Documentary Heritage*, edited by David J. O'Brien and Thomas A. Shannon (Orbis Books, 1995). This book is a great resource in understanding the development of Catholic social thought from the Papal encyclicals of the late nineteenth century to the statement of U.S. Catholic Bishops, "Economic Justice for All," in 1986.

10. Gary Scott Smith, *The Search for Social Salvation: Social Christianity and America 1880–1925* (Lexington Books, 2000).

11. Paul Boyer, "An Ohio Leader of the Social Gospel Movement," *Ohio History*, Volume 116, 2009.

12. Some of the biographical information on Rauschenbusch is taken from Chapter 1, "An American Prophet: A Biographical Sketch of Walter Rauschenbusch," in A *Gospel for the Social Awakening: Selections from the Writings of Walter Rauschenbusch*, compiled by Benjamin E. Mays with an Introduction by C. Howard Hopkins (Association Press, 1950).

13. Paul M. Minus, *Walter Rauschenbusch: American Reformer* (Macmillan Publishing Co., 1988), as quoted by Donald W. Shriver, Jr. in his Introduction to the 1997 republication of Rauschenbusch's *A Theology for the Social Gospel* (Westminster John Knox Press, 1997).

14. Information on *The Ram's Horn* and the image can be found at http://www.history.ohio-state.edu/projects/Ram's_Horn/Default.htm

15. C. Howard Hopkins, op.cit.

16. Quotations of Rauschenbusch in this paragraph are taken from excerpts of the book published electronically by the National Humanities Center, Research Triangle Park, North Carolina in 2005. http://nationalhumanitiescenter.org/ps/gilded/power/text9/rauschenbusch.pdf

Can Religion Help Revive the Progressive Tradition?

17. Walter Rauschenbusch, *A Theology for the Social Gospel* (Westminster John Knox Press, 1977). Introduction by Donald W. Shriver, Jr. The first edition was published in 1917 by The Macmillan Company.

18. This quote is taken from Walter Rauschenbusch's *The Social Principles of Jesus*, published in 1916, and republished by Wordstream Publishing, "In Celebration of the 15th Anniversary of Rauschenbusch Metro Ministries, New York City," 2010. This book, written for college students, contains the clearest teachings of Rauschenbusch on the message and life of Jesus. The reprint includes a Foreword by J. David Waugh.

19. Dan McKanan, *Prophetic Encounters: Religion and the American Radical Tradition* (Beacon Press, 2011).

20. *The Fundamentals: A Testimony to the Truth*, was originally published from 1910–1915. Ninety writers contributed to the twelve-volume series. Many volumes were distributed for free to ministers and other religious workers. By the 1930s, *The Fundamentals* had gained wide exposure and had become the definitive work defining fundamentalist theology and thought for that period. An excellent resource on American fundamentalism is *Fundamentalism and American Culture*, by George Marsden (Oxford University Press, 2006).

21. Dan McKanan, op.cit.

22. James Cone, *Black Theology and Black Power* (Orbis, 1997, first published 1969), and *A Black Theology of Liberation* (Orbis, 2011, first published 1970).

23. David J. Obrien and Thomas A. Shannon, op. cit.

24. The influence of the Social Gospel can be seen in the long political career of former Congressman David R. Obey who represented the 7th Congressional District in Wisconsin from 1969 until his retirement in 2011. On a number of public occasions, as well as in private conversation with him, Mr. Obey, raised Catholic, has commented on the powerful influence of the Social Gospel on his legislative goals and career in politics. See David R. Obey, *Raising Hell for Justice: The Washington Battles of a Heartland Progressive* (University of Wisconsin Press, 2008).

25. Jeffrey Sachs, *The Price of Civilization: Reawakening American Virtue and Prosperity* (Random House, 2011).

26. G. William Domhoff, "Wealth, Income, and Power," from the website "Who Rules America?" http://www2.ucsc.edu/whorulesamerica/power/wealth.html. Domhoff teaches in the Sociology Department at University of California Santa Cruz.

27. G. William Domhoff, "The Class-Domination Theory of Power," from the website "Who Rules America?" http://www2.ucsc.edu/whorulesamerica/power/class_domination.html

28. Domhoff cites the study "Building a Better America—One Wealth Quintile at a Time," by Michael Nort and Dan Ariely in *Perspectives on Psychological Science*, a journal of the Association for Psychological Science (2010), in "Wealth, Income, and Power" (op. cit.) Domhoff writes: "When shown three pie charts representing possible wealth distributions, 90% or more of the 5,522 respondents—whatever their gender, age, income level, or party affiliation—thought that the American wealth distribution most resembled one in which the top 20% has about 60% of the wealth. In fact... the top 20% control about 85% of the wealth.... Even more striking, they did not come close on the amount of wealth held by the bottom 40% of the population.... The lowest two quintiles hold just 0.3% of the wealth.... Most people in the survey guessed the figure to be between 8% and 10%..."

29. Jeffrey D. Sachs, op. cit.

30. Warren E. Buffett, "Stop Coddling the Super Rich," *The New York Times*, August 14, 2011.

31. David Kocieniewski, "Biggest Public Firms Paid Little U.S. Tax, Study Says," *The New York Times*, November 3, 2011.

32. Jeffrey Sachs refers to a Gallup Poll survey, May 5–8, 2011, op. cit.

33. Jeffrey Sachs quoting a Rasmussen Report, "Right Direction or Wrong Track," March 2011.

34. Pew Research Center for the People and the Press, April 2010, as referenced by Jeffrey Sachs.

35. RealtyTrac, January 12, 2011 http://www.realtytrac.com/content/press-releases/record-29-million-us-properties-receive-foreclo-

sure-filings-in-2010-despite-30-month-low-in-december-6309.

36. Bill Bishop with Robert G. Cushing, *The Big Sort: Why the Clustering of Like-Minded America is Tearing Us Apart* (Houghton Mifflin Company, 2008).

37. Scott Stossel, "Subdivided We Fall," *The New York Times*, May 18, 2008.

38. http://www.thebigsort.com/home.php

39. G. William Domhoff, "Fresh Start for the Left: What Activists Would Do If They Took the Social Sciences Seriously," Who Rules America website, March 2005. http://www2ucsc.edu/whorulesamerica/change/science_freshstart.html

40. But these two efforts, and even the Progressive Party campaign of 1948, continued to press forward on key elements of progressivism. In 1912 it was social insurance for the elderly, disabled, and unemployed; minimum wage for women; the eight-hour workday; a federal securities commission; workers' compensation, inheritance tax and a proposed constitutional amendment to allow a Federal income tax; disclosure requirements on political campaign contributions; initiative and referendum by popular vote; and judicial recall. In 1924, with the base in Wisconsin, the revised Progressive Party called for public ownership of the railroads and strengthening of programs to benefit the working class. In 1948, the U.S. Progressive Party advocated, under the leadership of former Vice President Henry A. Wallace of Iowa, desegregation, full voting rights for African Americans, and universal health insurance, while opposing military conscription as the Cold War got underway. The campaign, which critics saw as influenced by the Communist Party, was notable for correcting one failure of early progressivism: African American candidates campaigned alongside white candidates, even in the segregated South.

41. See Robert Longley "Lifetime Earnings Soar with Education," in which he writes about a U.S. Census Bureau report, "the Big Payoff: Educational Attainment and Synthetic Estimates of Work-Life Earnings." High school graduates can expect, on average, to earn $1.2 million over a life time; those with a bachelor's degree, $2.1 million, and people with a master's degree, $2.5 million. From the

website http://usgovinfo.about.com/od/moneymatters/a/edandearnings.htm

42. Diana L. Eck, *A New Religious America: How a "Christian Country" Has Now Become the World's Most Religiously Diverse Nation* (Harper/San Francisco, 2001).

43. The Pluralism Project. http://pluralism.org

44. See homepage for Sojourners. http://www.sojo.net

45. See http://www.nae.net/government-relations, the webpage of the National Association of Evangelicals.

46. The son of a Baptist minister, Walker's religious journey has taken him from a mainline Protestant denomination, the American Baptist Church U.S.A., to Meadowbrook Church, a nondenominational conservative evangelical church in Wauwatosa. This is a journey that tens of thousands of Americans have made as they have left mainline congregations for nondenominational evangelical churches, often located in suburbs of large cities. Scott Walker's youth was spent at his father's church, the First Baptist Church of Delevan, Wisconsin. A comparison of the web pages of these two congregations is instructive. Although clearly conservative, the First Baptist Church of Delevan appears more open, proclaiming that it is a congregation that respects diversity of thought. Its ministry and outreach programs include a wider range of efforts, including that of serving as one of six congregations in the county to provide shelter and food to homeless individuals. It also contributes to the local food pantry. The web page of the Meadowbrook Church puts much more emphasis on its core beliefs which are representative of Christian fundamentalism. The church's statement of faith focuses on inerrancy of scripture and personal salvation through the atoning death of Christ: ("We believe the shed blood of Jesus Christ and His resurrection provide the only ground for justification and salvation for all who believe and only such as receive Jesus Christ are born of the Holy Spirit and thus become children of God. . . . We believe in the personal and imminent return of our Lord Jesus Christ, and this has a vital bearing on the personal life and service of the believer. . . .We believe in the bodily resurrection of the dead of the believer to everlasting

blessedness and joy with the Lord, and of the unbeliever to judgment and eternal separation from God.") http://www.meadowbrook-church.com/about/faith.cfm.

Walker's faith has been an item of journalistic interest. His religion seems consistent with white evangelicals who have supported the Tea Party. According to various news accounts, Walker feels called to serve as Governor and believes God is directing his life, and that his obligation is to "trust and obey" (words from a hymn popular in evangelical circles). The religion of the Meadowbrook Church is one that Baptist Walter Rauschenbusch would recognize but deeply regret, as it focuses on personal sin at the expense of understanding corporate and social sin, and personal salvation at the expense of social salvation. Mathew Rothschild explores the connection between Walker's personal faith and his unwillingness to compromise in the political arena in "Scott Walker Believes He's Following Orders from the Lord," March 7, 2011. http://www.progressive.org/print/157986.

47. See the homepage for *Tikkun* magazine: http://www.tikkun.org./nextgen.

48. Diana Eck, op. cit.

49. For example, the creation of the Environmental Protection Agency (EPA) by Executive Order from President Richard Nixon in 1970, the various Clean Air Acts (1970, 1977, 1990), the Endangered Species Preservation Act (1966, 1969, 1973), and the National Environmental Policy Act (1969).

50. Lynn White, Jr., *Science* 155, 1967.

51. J. Ronald Engel, "Democracy, Christianity, Ecology: A Twenty-First-Century Agenda for Eco-Theology," *Crosscurrents*, June 2011.

52. J. Ronald Engel, ibid.

53. *The Religions of the World and Ecology* series was published from 1997 to 2003. The books are available from Harvard University Press. Information on the series can be found at http://hds.harvard.edu/cswr/resources/print/catalog.html

54. "Three-Year Harvard Project Calls on Religions to Help Solve Environmental Crisis," United Nations Environment Programme,

New York Office, October 28, 1998 press release. See http://www.nyo.unep.org/harvrel.htm

55. Forum on Religion and Ecology website: http://fore.research.yale.edu/information/about/index.html. The companion book by Brian Thomas Swimme and Mary Evelyn Tucker, *Journey of the Universe*, was published by Yale University Press in 2011.

56. Mary Evelyn Tucker and John Grim, "Overview of World Religions and Ecology," Forum on Religion and Ecology, Yale University, 2009 http://fore.research.yale.edu/religion

57. Mary Evelyn Tucker and John Grim, ibid.

58. Bill Devall and George Sessions, *Deep Ecology*, Gibbs Smith Publisher, 2007, Chapter 1, "Nothing Can Be Done, Everything is Possible."

59. See David Landis Barnhill and Roger S. Gottlieb, eds., *Deep Ecology and World Religions: New Essays on Sacred Ground* (SUNY, 2001).

12

Gandhi, King and 99% Spring

Brian Terrell

"99% Spring" has been declared. "This spring, we will ... rise up in the tradition of our forefathers and foremothers. We will not be complicit with the suffering in our families for another year. We will prepare ourselves for sustained non-violent direct action." The organizers of this effort list the many economic injustices and perils faced by America today and propose to train 100,000 activists "to join together in the work of reclaiming our country" with methods of nonviolent direct action: "We will take non-violent action in the spirit of Martin Luther King, Jr. and Gandhi to forge a new destiny one block, one neighborhood, one city, one state at a time."

99% Spring will address such crucial issues as shrinking pension funds, skyrocketing student loans, foreclosures, budget cuts to schools, a poisoned environment, diminished collective bargaining rights, all "a result of rampant greed—the deliberate manipulation of our democracy and our economy by a tiny minority in the 1%, by those who amass ever more wealth and power at our expense." Some other critical matters, however, will not be addressed by 99% Spring.

The organizers of 99% Spring do not find room in their list of our country's problems to include the wars in Afghanistan and Iraq, spiraling military spending, new nuclear weapons built, or the role of militarism and colonialism on the economy and the toll it exacts on America's working people in general. They pledge that they "will not be complicit with the suffering in our families," but do not express the same refusal to be complicit in the suffering of families in Afghanistan, Colombia, Palestine or the many other nations blighted, threatened and murdered by the same forces that 99% Spring decries here at home. Not to give the war as much as a footnote is a startling omission, especially as recent polls show that a growing majority of Americans are against it. This omission may define 99% Spring more clearly than the proclamations surrounding it.

I know that neglecting to mention militarism might be justified as a deliberate strategic choice. Of course, no one can do everything and no one can address every injustice. I accept, too, that in building a coalition that includes some labor unions that promote armaments contracts and organizations like MoveOn.org that regularly support candidates for office with decidedly pro-war agendas, silence on the threat of the military-industrial-congressional complex is required for the sake of unity. However prudent it may seem, though, this omission raises serious questions.

What is all the more disconcerting is that 99% Spring claims the spirit of Martin Luther King, Jr. and Gandhi. Neither of these teachers held that justice at home was possible in a country engaged in murder and thievery abroad.

Gandhi's life work was to free his country from British colonialism and he warned his English opponents and friends that they would never enjoy peace and prosperity at home while holding and tormenting India and their other foreign colonies. Is it conceivable that in this country today a movement can take action in Gandhi's spirit without using the most decisive and clear language and action against US imperialism?

In 1967, Dr. King was asked why he, a civil rights leader, criticized the Vietnam War, a move that threatened to polarize the civil rights movement. "Now it should be incandescently clear that no one who has any concern for the integrity and life of America today can ignore the present war," King said from the pulpit of Riverside Church in New York. He had come to realize that it was not possible to condemn the violence and oppression suffered by America's poor without "first speaking clearly to the greatest purveyor of violence in the world today—my own government."

If it was true in 1967, as Dr. King noted then, that "America can never be saved so long as it destroys the deepest hopes of (people) the world over," is it possible that 45 bloody years later, America can destroy the deepest hopes of the people of Afghanistan and yet be saved? Has something fundamental changed, so that unlike in Dr. King's time, a movement can now be concerned for the integrity and life of America and yet ignore the present war?

Along with the spirits of Gandhi and King, 99% Spring invokes the example of Occupy Wall Street, a movement in which in many ways the words and work of these two prophets do resonate. In their *Declaration of Occupation of New York City*, adopted by General Assemblies around the world, OWS lists these among the crimes of corporatism: "They have perpetuated colonialism at home and abroad. They have participated in the torture and murder of innocent civilians overseas. They continue to create weapons of mass destruction in order to receive government contracts."

"The time comes when silence is betrayal," and Dr. King confessed that he was "moved to break the betrayal of my own silences and to speak from the burnings of my own heart." Condemning the destruction of Vietnam and the wasting of fortunes and lives for an arms race in the face of poverty at home and abroad was not a strategic choice he could make or not, nor is it for us. Dr. King recognized that he and others would find that "the calling to speak is often a calling of agony." Despite this, he insisted, "we must speak." No one, Dr. King said, was exempt from the responsibility to protest the war in Vietnam. No one today is exempt from the responsibility to protest the war in Afghanistan—our credibility in all matters and our humanity depend upon this. Silence is betrayal.

I hope and pray that 99% Spring is more than successful in its goals, which are certainly worthy ones, even if limited. I fear, though, that its silence on the root of the problem, the military-industrial-congressional complex, will prove fatal to its ends. A movement that engages in "non-violent action in the spirit of Martin Luther King, Jr. and Gandhi to forge a new destiny" is desperately needed in America in 2012. That movement will necessarily be one that demands economic justice at home and that clearly and unequivocally condemns the war in Afghanistan, nuclear weapons, militarism and imperialism in general. 99% Spring, unfortunately, is not that movement.

13

Who's Awake in Clark County?

Mike McCabe

LET ME START BY saying that joining a union in the workplace is a basic human right. That's not just my opinion, it is a statement of fact. That right is found in Article 23 of the *Universal Declaration of Human Rights*, approved by the United Nations General Assembly on December 10, 1948 with the United States voting yes.

Unions have fallen on hard times in recent years in America, and their declining fortunes have been a significant factor in the Democratic Party's struggles. Some of organized labor's wounds were the doing of powerful and vengeful enemies; others were self-inflicted.

Unions have had a tendency to be insular, often not talking to or working with each other much less communities of like-minded non-union people. That's curious, considering the value organized labor places on solidarity and brotherhood.

I grew up on a dairy farm in Clark County in west-central Wisconsin, with the Black River flowing right down the middle of the county from north to south. My dad had an 8th-grade education. In his view of the political world, as he told me more times than I can count, the Democrats were the party of the poor and the Republicans were the party of the rich.

If he were alive today, he would not be able to make heads or tails of the tea party movement. He would be confounded by the fact that some of the poorest Americans are among the Republican Party's most

Who's Awake in Clark County?

faithful supporters. That's not conjecture, it is fact. In the 2010 election for governor, Scott Walker carried eight of the 10 counties with the lowest per capita income. He lost in Menominee County, where only 752 votes were cast on the Indian reservation. And he narrowly lost Crawford County. But overall Walker won by a 13-percentage-point, 8,400-vote margin out of just over 66,500 votes in Wisconsin's 10 poorest counties.

In Clark County, one of the state's five poorest, Walker got 61% of the vote. For years Clark County was represented by Frank Nikolay, one of the truest progressives ever to serve in Wisconsin's legislature. Nikolay was followed by Tom Harnisch, a moderate Democrat. Today, Clark County is represented by a rabid right winger—tea partier and American Legislative Exchange Counsel (ALEC) co-chair Scott Suder.

Today's Democrats have broken the sacred political law of universality. They may say we're all in this together and need to look out for each other, but people in places like rural Clark County don't see Democrats practicing what they preach. Most people in such parts of Wisconsin see today's Democrats standing for health and retirement security and better pay for a few, but not for most. This has created an opening for Republicans to build a *rich-poor alliance* . . . and a governing majority in Wisconsin.

Liberals dwell on how Republicans have used social issues like abortion, gay marriage and gun rights as wedges to splinter off low-income rural voters who used to vote for Democrats and now reliably support Republicans. The left overlooks the economic wedge the right has skillfully exploited.

Republicans ask people in places like Clark County if they have pensions, and the answer is invariably no. "Well, you are paying for theirs," they tell them. Do you have health insurance? No. Well, you are paying for theirs. Are you getting pay raises? No. Well, you are paying for theirs.

For years now Democrats have not plausibly made the case that they will deliver better health or retirement security or higher pay to all. Only the state's few government workers have so benefited from the Democrats' toil. What is the modern equivalent of the GI Bill that offers every family a path to vocational training or an affordable college education? Where is the digital age's equivalent of rural electrification or the interstate highway system?

A Whole Which Is Greater

We have one party that is scary and another that is scared. If one is paralyzed and afraid to lead, people will opt for the one willing to act even if the actions are overly extreme for most people's tastes. It doesn't mean they hold that party in high esteem or fail to see its faults. The truth is most people hate both parties. The ranks of the politically homeless are growing fast. More Americans refuse to align with either major party than at any time in the last 75 years.

In defeat there is still opportunity for the Democrats. But not if they continue to ignore the law of universality and fail to muster the nerve to really lead. And not if they remain resistant to the obvious remedy for their brand problem. The Democratic Party is the party of government, and most people hate the government. Why? Because increasingly they see it as corrupt, run by people they view as crooked. They don't believe government is working for them, and if it's not going to work for them, then they'd prefer to keep it as small as possible.

One party is seen as standing for big government, the other for no government. But neither is seen as truly working for the people. Both are seen as captive parties that owe allegiance to their big donors and ceaselessly cater to those wealthy interests.

For the Democrats, there is a clear way out of the trap they are in. Maybe their defeat in the recall election will be the wake-up call they need. When the scapegoating finally subsides, maybe they will finally come to terms with the cancer that is growing in the body of democracy and see the impact that disease is having on their party's brand.

I'm not holding my breath. After all, in the nearly 15 years I have been doing this work, a Democratic governor reached out to the Democracy Campaign and asked to meet with us only once . . . to read us the riot act for shining light on his campaign money. In all those years, a Democratic state party chair sought to meet with us one time. That was to ask if we would support legislation to significantly *increase* the limits on campaign contributions to candidates and parties.

A few years ago, Tom Frank wrote the book *What's the Matter with Kansas?* It could just as well have been called *What's the Matter with Clark County?* As with Frank's bestseller, Clark County is full of stories that help explain its journey from a hotbed of progressive politics to a mainstay of turn-back-the-clock conservatism.

When I was a teenager, the farm economy was bottoming out and one of our neighbors was facing foreclosure. Just before the family was thrown off their land, the farmer was found hanging from a rafter in a shed. His wife and an adult son were left to pick up the pieces of their shattered life. There was no union standing in solidarity with that family as their way of life—and husband and father—was taken from them.

Today, Clark County is full of people who've never known the brotherhood of a union. They've only grown full of resentment for having to pay for others to have things they don't have themselves. And they have turned their county red. They've drunk the tea.

All of which leaves the Democratic Party trapped. The party of the poor no longer has the poorest in our society with them. The unions that supplied them with a power base have been under siege, first in the private sector and now in the public. With union power dwindling, and union money drying up, Democrats now get way more of their campaign money from business interests than from labor unions. The combination of their reliance on the 1% for donations and their allegiance to what's left of the unions is alienating them from the poor in places like Clark County. Democrats will never win in the rich counties like Ozaukee, Waukesha and Washington. Republicans have built a rich-poor governing coalition in Wisconsin, in Kansas, and all across the country. For Democrats to mount a counteroffensive that has any kind of impact they can't just focus on what—or who—they want to stop. They'll have to think long and hard about where they want to start.

When the Democrats won the hearts of a majority of people in the past, it was because the party had a big hand in creating things that tangibly benefited everyone or at least directly touched every American family in a major way. Social Security and Medicare. Rural electrification. The GI Bill. The interstate highway system.

Some Democrats blame President Obama for their party's defeat in Wisconsin, gnashing their teeth over his refusal to come in and campaign with Tom Barrett. Some blame the DNC for not jumping in the race with all its might. Some blame the unions for wasting millions of dollars trying to anoint Scott Walker's opponent in a primary fight. Some blame Russ Feingold for not accepting a role as savior. Some blame young people for not going to the polls in droves the way they did in 2008.

When the scapegoating subsides, certain realities are left. The Democratic Party proved unable to beat Wisconsin's most polarizing political figure in living memory, one bankrolled by millionaires and billionaires, some of whom could vote in the election and most of whom could not. The nation's worst job-creation record and a mushrooming cloud of scandal and criminal investigations were not enough to prompt the majority of voters to find the Democrats' standard bearer preferable.

When the scapegoating subsides, the real question remains: Will the Democratic Party finally be forced to come to terms with how damaged its brand really is?

To most eyes, the Democratic Party is the party of government and government employees and their unions. Most people hate the government. How do you build a governing majority with a brand people hate?

You don't.

14

Empire's Children: An Afterword

Paul Gilk

IN THE FINAL (OR almost final) pages of *The Nation*, dated May 30, 2011, there's a review—well, not so much a review as a retrospective—on the life and books of John Kenneth Galbraith. It's called "Countervailing Powers." The author is Kim Phillips-Fein.

What jumped out at me most powerfully from "Countervailing Powers" was this: "Today, the gulf between the richest and the poorest has grown wider, with the policies that support such inequalities buttressed, in part, by the intellectual project of modern conservatism, which Galbraith once called 'one of man's oldest exercises in moral philosophy: that is, the search for a moral justification for selfishness.'"[1] Later we're told by Phillips-Fein that in the nineteenth century "economists exalted competition as a civilizing force,"[2] and then, in a section dealing with the central theme of Galbraith's *The Great Crash*, we are introduced to the

> . . . impotence of people with power when in the grip of ideas that leave them no way of confronting reality. They endorse and protect a consensus that conceals what is objectively true. One of the most caustic passages in the book describes the "no-business meetings" held by [Herbert] Hoover in the wake of the [1929] crash, which assembled prestigious businessmen at the White House, to great fanfare from the press. No proposals emerged from Hoover's meetings. No action was taken. No one intended that anything should be accomplished. And yet

> by gathering men of wealth and undeniable social importance, Hoover intended to give the impression that something of importance was being done while doing nothing at all. They were, Galbraith wrote, a "practical expression of laissez faire."[3]

This is an amazingly compact summing up: conservatism as the search for a superior moral justification for selfishness, based on a doctrine of competition as a civilizing force—or as Phillips-Fein also says, a Victorian moral code of "hard work, private initiative and a relentless emphasis on increasing productivity"[4]—leading to intellectual impotence in the grip of ideas that leave no way of confronting reality.

Well, this does indeed seem to be our moment. This is where the entire world is—in the global grip of selfishness driven by intense competition, a muscular wringing out of social budgets, a relentless emphasis on increasing productivity, and a protected consensus concealing what is true—a circumstance and situation in which ecological disaster is accelerating at an astonishing rate, the totality of it capped with an always-imminent, hair-trigger capacity for nuclear extermination.

The omission or flaw in this analysis, however, is that it appears to let liberalism off the hook. If conservatism, in its search for a moral justification for selfishness, can be epitomized by the Christian doctrine of world conquest in behalf of the True Faith and God's Will, such as Western European powers exercised in their colonizing frenzy from the fifteenth century onward, then liberalism is conservatism's "enlightened" son, no longer believing in fusty religious doctrine, maybe even embarrassed by it, and instead transforming the primal drive of religious conviction into a far more finely articulated rational and even scientific plan for the secular transformation of the entire world in an image of utopian civility.

In this view, conservative and liberal are much less opposite or opposing worldviews than they are a kind of generational and characterological male conflict played out through ideology, a struggle over how to manage the secular business brought into being by the raw force of civilizational theocracy. "Dad" is stuck in his old laissez-faire, invisible Hand-of-God presumptions, while "Sonny" itches to streamline the technology and introduce some new economic toys and financial procedures. Therefore the impotence of people with power in the grip of ideas that leave them no way of confronting reality is not just a witty, mocking, and condescending caricature of Good Old Blundering Dad

Empire's Children: An Afterword

living in Do-Nothing Hooverland but, even more deadly, a right-on-the-money description of the Bright Young Obama Boys who intend to run the business of too-big-to-fail utopia with up-to-date scientific management.

In late May of 2011, I went to a "Fighting Bob Fest" here in northern Wisconsin. A former Democratic gubernatorial candidate by the name of Ed Garvey seems to have been the spark plug for this event. All previous Bob Fests (named after "Fighting" Bob La Follette, a former Wisconsin Governor and U.S. Senator) have been held in southern Wisconsin in the fall. It took a while to realize that this spring event was cleverly organized to aid in the building of "progressive" enthusiasm for Democratic Party candidates in the upcoming (2011) recall elections aimed at dislodging a few of the Republican state senators who voted in lockstep with Governor Walker's program to, among other things, disband public sector unions in Wisconsin.[i]

At any rate, there was at Bob Fest a lot of bashing of conservatives and Republicans—most of which was accurately aimed, wittily expressed, and richly deserved—but self-criticism was in short supply and hardly to be heard. "Liberals," you see, were trying mightily to recapture the helm from the "conservatives" so that the ship of state (at least the leaky rowboat that is Wisconsin's senate) could be in "progressive" hands once again, working mightily toward "full employment," with lots of "jobs," and with clear, strong hope for the "restoration of middle-class prosperity."

Oh, really? Has no one mentioned to liberals that they, too, are integral to the cluster of power people whose spiritual and intellectual impotence leaves them no way of confronting reality? To mention only two things of apocalyptic magnitude—nuclear weapons and climate change—we "liberals" are to charge full speed ahead in behalf of continuing, intensifying, and evermore complex forms of economic growth? Are we really to keep believing there's no connection (or, at least, no connection of significance) between our economic ideology, our religious convictions, our apocalyptic weapons, our male-dominated "public" realms of business and governance, and the ecological

---

i. There were, in all, nine senate recall elections in the summer of 2011. All three incumbent Democrats kept their seats, while two of the six Republicans lost theirs. The state senate, however, remained in Republican control by a margin of seventeen to sixteen. More senate recalls were held in June of 2012. The Democrats picked up one seat and regained control of the senate, at least for the time being.

"externalities" and political "blowback" of corporate and military globalization? Shall we call in the psychoanalysts for an assessment? Or are the psychoanalysts either too "liberal" or too "conservative" to offer anything more than partisan psychotherapy? Are we locked into this utopian nuthouse? Is there no way out?

It was this sort of quandary that sparked solicitation of essays for this book.

II

James Botsford's essay was the first submitted. I'm not sure if I've ever seen a less hesitant, more compact condemnation of all the "great organized religions of the world," with the "possible exception" of vipassana meditation, a method for getting out of or beyond our "spiritual malaise." Consequently, when James wonders about the religious underpinnings of our culture—including the religious underpinnings of our culture's politics—he's implicitly dismissive of so-called "conservatives" (those who conserve almost nothing) while holding out little hope for the deck-chair rearrangement offered by "liberals." If I understand James correctly, his question is: Can we shed the conservative/liberal baggage? Can we live there?

Oddly enough, the June 2011 issue of *The Sun* magazine arrived almost exactly with James' essay. In *The Sun* interview, conducted by David Kupfer, Peter Coyote (socialist, actor, Zen Buddhist) says he's "not sure the *system* has to change. People have to change. If people behaved with self-restraint, generosity, and compassion, even capitalism could work. We are never going to create *a system* that generates fairness, equity, good will, and justice."[5] I think this could be right in the sense that system tinkering without elemental spiritual transformation is just the politics of deck-chair rearrangement. But it's misleading to conclude that any system is as good as any other, as if systems were somehow ethically neutral and not creations of consciousness and will. Distorted consciousness and perverse will also generate distorted and perverse systems. We might therefore come to the tentative hypothesis that wise consciousness and compassionate will could conceivably combine to create a wise and compassionate system—or at least one not so uncompassionate or so stunningly unwise as the one we now have.

Empire's Children: An Afterword

One hopes the testing of this hypothesis will occur in the not-so-distant future.

III

The second essay in was Maynard Kaufman's. If James Botsford is a fiery public-sector lawyer advocating on behalf of Native Americans since the 1980s (he was also, for a while, the youthful protégé of religious historian Huston Smith), Maynard is an American peasant with a prestigious Ph.D. who knows more than he tells here about Lewis Mumford's sense of eutopia or Norman O. Brown's psychoanalytical resurrection of the body. To the discerning eye, Maynard's essay is packed with his erudition, his keen understanding, and his vast reading. If Wendell Berry deserves his reputation (I think he does) as a major American advocate for rural culture, Maynard does not deserve his comparative obscurity in the same field of advocacy. He is a treasure of insight and wisdom (he and his late wife Sally founded a School of Homesteading in southwestern Michigan), and any truly serious discussion about the future of small farms and agrarian culture should always keep open a place at the table for my dear friend Dr. Kaufman, who is a nearly perfect blend of peasant groundedness and scholarly competence.

Well, forgive my running off at the mouth about Maynard when I should be commenting on his essay. It seems to me that the core thought lying at the heart of Maynard's remarks is not simply that industrial affluence is ending but that the more agrarian, cooperative, ecological, and frugal life he sees ahead is a good life, a happier and more connected life, a more joyous life, a culturally richer, grounded, and more wholesome life. It is this happier, eager, and wonderfully positive anticipation that so keenly distinguishes Maynard's vision from the usual doom and gloom of many observers (perhaps like James Howard Kunstler in *The Long Emergency*) who remain intellectually and spiritually addicted to looking at the future through the distorted keyhole of civilization-as-our-eternal-savior-from-primitivity-and-backwardness.

In regard to Maynard's essay, I wish to make a couple of remarks in a specifically challenging mode—because all the rest I simply agree with—and those remarks are: I don't think the origins of linear time can be laid on the ancient Hebrews, and I don't think American democracy has ever shaken itself free of aristocratic presumptions. Both constructs—linear time and aristocratic presumption—converge (as Mumford teaches) in the origins of civilization. That is, the imposition of extractive coercion on the agrarian village by bandit aristocrats at the dawn of civilization (which is what I call the "first farm crisis") is the essential origin of linear time. I say this because extractive coercion was unrelentingly permanent; its bondage promised no release or relief; it was unending and therefore evocative of the linear. Coercion may not have exactly ended the peasant experience of cyclical return or eternal recurrence—aristocratic exploitation couldn't undo nature's cycles—but it imposed an enormously heavy, depressive weight and hugely deadening restraint on the relatively free-flowing creativity of folk evolution. Linear time was, in a sense, a religious or metaphysical consequence of the aristocratic (i.e., bandit or civilized) oppression of the agrarian or non-civilized village. In relation to the still-evolving culture of the Neolithic, civilization acted like a powerful herbicide or terminator seed. Civilization is the dead weight sitting on top of cyclical time or eternal recurrence. The ancient Hebrews, with their strict Father God, may have somehow provided the theological cork, but civilization had already fabricated the jug in which eternal recurrence was to be impounded.

The very nature of peasant oppression and borderline destitution meant that escape from agrarian bondage became an endemic yearning; and, cruelly paradoxical, the dominant image for ease and comfort was contained within the aristocratic lifestyle. Progress, in this analysis, derives its core energy from a perverse blending of undeserved peasant suffering seeking release through undeserved aristocratic affluence. (The doctrines of Manifest Destiny and American Exceptionalism are simply loaded with this largely unconscious contradiction. Just think of all the ethnic European pioneers who, at least in part to escape the power and control of Eastern money and established families, pushed west into the "wilderness," beyond the "frontier," and—wittingly or unwittingly—served as the cutting edge of the very civility they thought they were escaping, fighting with and ultimately overpowering the ancient indigenous cultures with which they inevitably came into contact and conflict and with whom—could they only have had the time and gentleness of spirit to slowly, patiently, and carefully integrate—they might have developed a wholly new cultural configuration. This very real possibility—one thinks of Pennsylvania Quakers—was brutally thwarted by relentless energy radiating out of Euro-American civilization, with its emphasis on pagan suppression and religious conversion.)

For democracy to be ecological, ethical, compassionate, and free, it must break its bondage to aristocratic models of consumption and to civilizational structures of governance, for both are products of coercion, predation, extortion, and murder. Democracy must also come to spiritual reconciliation with non-civilized cultures. That's how deep this impending transformation runs. We who are so civilized need to learn to be ecologically and culturally uncivilized. Add into this the restoration (or resurrection) of pre-civilized, agrarian, feminine spirituality, and we can begin to realize that eutopia is rising to enfold us—unless utopia manages to blow us all to hell first.

IV

As the self-appointed lead editor for this wobbly essay project, I found my initial essay (something roughly revolving around Manifest Destiny) shot down by my coeditor David Kast and my old friend Maynard Kaufman. They unhesitatingly edited the editor. Although I accepted the literary wounds and intellectual bruises as gracefully as possible, I was not content with mere editorial coaxing and grooming. So I decided to do an Afterword—which, needless to say, I'm in the midst of, mired in, and mucked up by, even as the essays continue to trickle in.

When my *Nature's Unruly Mob* was first published in 1986 by tiny Anvil Press out of Millville, Minnesota (which also published the *North Country Anvil* quarterly), I asked Anvil editor Jack Miller to write an Introduction to the *Mob*. He did, and I accepted it, even though (among some nice things said) Jack pinned my ears to the wall over positive things I'd said about feminism and negative things I'd said about institutionalized Christianity. I say this now because it's apparently my temperament to do a little ear pinning, too.

But let's be clear. Jack, as Anvil editor, had a firm point of view. He wasn't picking on me. He wasn't being mean. He was, I'd say, brushing the perceived knots out of my perspective with the curry comb of his perspective. And that's what I find myself doing here. The situation is urgent enough—I mean The World Situation—that I'd be (or at least feel) irresponsible not to brush out some knots or to unpack some overly discreet allusions.

Here's an example of what I mean.

Last week David Kast came to supper at the log house, and he brought with him a copy of a paper by Chris Hedges entitled "Endgame Strategy." It was an Internet doomsday piece, the details of which are mostly familiar and, as far as I can tell, quite accurate. The world's going to hell in a hand basket and it's up to us to "rapidly create small, monastic communities where we can sustain and feed ourselves." What I find wanting in the piece is some hint of deeper analysis of how we got into this pickle besides the usual language of "American empire" or "bankrupt corporate power elite" or "unfettered corporate capitalism." That is, if we're faced, as Hedges says we are, with the "catastrophic breakdown of globalization" (which could also mean the catastrophic breakdown of global ecology),[6] I really want to know the etiology of this disaster, for I believe its roots and guiding energy lie much deeper than modern corporate capitalism. How are we to address this crisis in anything resembling adequate proportion if we don't know or grasp its fuller magnitude in history?

If we are to accurately assess this monstrous assault, we need a diagnosis that fits the bill. Anything less is to toss an aspirin at a nuclear bomb. I'm not saying that a fuller diagnosis will necessarily stop this beast. Diagnosis is not treatment or cure, exactly, although true understanding does have subtle but powerful healing properties. Truth does help set us free. Since these essays are in the diagnosis business, our job is to shed as much light as possible on the subjects under discussion. That's also the job of a mere Afterword scribbler who doubles as an editor.

Perhaps we have to goad one another (or pin each other's ears back) simply because the situation is so dire. I don't mean to be mean. Call it compassionately demanding. Tough love. Perhaps this is what James Botsford means by behaving more holistically.

V

Well, having unburdened myself of all that, Rhoda Gilman's essay arrived. In an early letter to contributors, I'd urged them to be personal, to tell their stories, and Rhoda did just that. Her closing paragraphs remind me of Warren Johnson's *Muddling toward Frugality*, with its quasi-Taoist conviction that we will muddle through to a far more

Empire's Children: An Afterword

localized, peaceful, and just steady-state economy. Of course Johnson recognized—in the late 1970s!—that prudent change avoided or perennially postponed would serve to intensify the growing crisis and increase the likelihood of violence—what Rhoda calls "surviving the chaos of a crumbling civilization."

Rhoda opens her essay with a remark about the United States descending into fascism. It just so happened that Eric Yonke agreed to take on the subject of fascism, and his essay came in just after Rhoda's. As might be expected, there's ambiguity in the term. "Fascism" is a word (perhaps like "pagan") that elicits or provokes raw emotional reactions. One could therefore say the term should be avoided. I would say all the more reason to explore its volatile and even dangerous energy.

In a book published in 1971, we are given a glimpse into the founding of the Italian Fascist Party. In *Duce! A Biography of Benito Mussolini*, Richard Collier says it was on a rainy Sunday morning on March 23, 1919, in Milan, in a "hot little hall," that Mussolini and a "handful of men met as founders of the newly-formed Fascist Party—so styled from the fasces, the bundle of elm rods coupled with an axe, bound by red cord, that in ancient Rome had symbolized a consul's powers of life and death."[7]

This brief etymology of "fascism" is more than a linguistic relic or an interesting but largely irrelevant anachronism. That the term derives from an explicit symbol depicting the murderous authoritarianism of ancient Rome should tell us that a kind of super-vigilant politics packed with edgy violence—namely Italian fascism—had chosen its name carefully and well. It's not a term lacking historical context or disguising its brutal intent. And, as Richard Collier says explicitly of Mussolini, he was a "man who saw revolution and social change only in terms of violence."[8]

If I might put it this way, I would say that fascism is a kind of secular theocracy, its virulent order deriving in principle from the sacred hierarchy of the nation (as Eric points out) rather than directly from the church or from God. Richard Collier says Mussolini's mother had a portrait of the Virgin Mary over the big double bed she shared with her husband, while his father hung alongside the Virgin a "glowering likeness of his lifelong hero—the Republican liberator of Sicily, General Giuseppe Garibaldi." Mussolini's mother "yearned for him to be a priest," but Benito "saw his father's lifelong war with authority as headier stuff."[9]

A Whole Which Is Greater

Mussolini was also, for a while, a socialist. But his propensity for reckless male violence—both as street action and as overarching ideology—caused him to leave the antiwar socialists at the outbreak of World War I. Insofar as blind nationalism is a kind of civil religion, it's not psychologically inaccurate to talk of secular worship; and, in the context of this sort of liturgical idolatry, it's also possible for its practitioners to wander freely back and forth—as much of the American Christian Right seems to wander—between civil and religious worship, between flag and cross. When God (the divine) is explicitly identified as male, defined as King of kings, then authoritarian hierarchy can itself become holy or sacred, even if "holy" and "sacred" are alternately asserted in secular terms or in a secular context.

Richard Pierard, in an article entitled "Protestant Support for the Political Right in Weimar Germany and Post-Watergate America: Some Comparative Observations," burrows right into this political (but permeable) membrane between the religious and the secular:

> Since churchmen had convinced themselves that God was on Germany's side in the "holy war" against the Allies, the events of 1918–19 were simply beyond their comprehension. Even more distressing to them because of the long-held belief in the sanctity of the crown was the abdication of the Kaiser and various ruling princes. The link between throne and altar, territorial ruler and territorial church reached back to the Reformation, and the power of the crown was regarded as "sacred" since the office was derived from God's will and grace and was to be exercised according to his command. For them the representatives of the new republic, president and parliament, could not replace the fallen symbol of authority. The revolution was a sin because its architects had struck down an authority sanctified by God and history and egotistically tried to improve on God's work and occupy his place.[10]

We have a firsthand account of this link between throne and altar ("Every attempt to break through was prevented by the unavoidable guilt consciousness produced by the identification of the parental with the divine authority"[11]) from no less a thinker than Paul Tillich:

> The structure of Prussian society before the First World War, especially in the eastern part of the kingdom, was authoritarian without being totalitarian. Lutheran paternalism made the father the undisputed head of the family, which included, in a

> minister's house, not only wife and children, but also servants with various functions. The same spirit of discipline and authority dominated the public schools, which stood under the supervision of the local and county clergy in their function as inspectors of schools. The administration was strictly bureaucratic, from the policeman in the street and the postal clerk behind the window, through a hierarchy of officials, to the far-removed central authorities in Berlin—authorities as unapproachable as the "castle" in Kafka's novel. Each of these officials was strictly obedient to his superiors and strictly authoritative toward his subordinates and the public. What was still lacking in discipline was provided by the army, which trespassed in power and social standing upon the civil world and drew the whole nation from earliest childhood into its ideology. It did this so effectively in my case that my enthusiasm for uniforms, parades, maneuvers, history of battles, and ideas of strategy was not exhausted until my thirtieth year, and then only because of my experiences in the First World War. But above all this, at the top of the hierarchy, stood the King of Prussia, who happened to be also the German emperor. Patriotism involved, above all, adherence to the king and his house. The existence of a parliament, democratic forces, socialist movements, and of a strong criticism of the emperor and the army did not affect the conservative Lutheran groups of the East among whom I lived. All these democratic elements were rejected, distortedly represented, and characterized as revolutionary, which meant criminal. Again it required a world war and a political catastrophe before I was able to break through this system of authorities and to affirm belief in democratic ideals and the social revolution.[12]

It's worth remembering that it was Augustine who justified the merger of the Christian church with the Roman Empire, and also that Martin Luther was an Augustinian priest. Roland Bainton, in his life of Luther called *Here I Stand*, says that Luther's *The Sermon on Good Works* is "built, not around the Beatitudes, but around the Ten Commandments, the core of the law of Moses equated with the law of nature. Like those before him Luther extended the command to honor father and mother to include reverence for all in authority, such as bishops, teachers, and magistrates. His domestic ethic was Pauline and patriarchal, the economic ethic Thomistic and mainly agrarian, the political ethic Augustinian and small town."[13] The Western affiliation with theocracy (or to some "two-kingdoms" facsimile) is deeply embedded in the church's multi-millennial partnership with civilizational governing structure or with what Lewis Mumford called the "traumatic institutions" of civilization.[14] If Jesus in the famous temptation scenes in Matthew 4 and Luke 4 refused partnership with the Devil in running the kingdoms and empires of the world, Augustine in *The City of God* (Book V:1) simply announces that "human kingdoms are established by divine providence."[15] And that has been the guiding principle of church/state relations in Western civilization ever since. Augustine took Jesus' "reign of God" proclamation—which, given all the gospel stories and teachings about leastness and not lording it over, is an overwhelming anti- or non-civilized construction—and turned it into its opposite: a theocratic merging of church and state. What the Devil couldn't do, Constantine did, and Augustine wrote the metaphysical rationale.

Although Rhoda doesn't define her use of "fascism," while Eric prudently warns us against careless use of the term, it may just be—using the Roman *fasces* as our template—that the manic, righteous imposition of vicious order is what human beings, males particularly, do when threatened by cultural change or when offered a radically different worldview (ecological socialism, for example) for which they have no spiritual preparation or emotional resonance. (Christians have been raised primarily on the metaphysics of *The City of God*, not on the ethics of the gospels.) On the part of established authority, violence may simply be a rational tool dispassionately deployed for achieving a desired policy goal ("diplomacy by other means"), while for the rest of us violence may be a reaction generated by fear, including the fear created when inherited order is threatened by change. Such change can quickly get identified as decadent and permissive, deserving only to be stamped out: revolution as sin, democratic ventures as criminal.

In our context, however, the situation may be more closely in accord with these observations by Richard Pierard:

> Despite disclaimers about big government and the evils of bureaucracy, many people today are prepared to give allegiance to authoritarian leaders who promise to enhance their sense of national pride and personal "self-worth." They have little commitment to such ideals as world peace through disarmament, assisting hungry and needy people around the globe, or granting full civil and economic rights to minorities in the United States. Americans are clearly subject to the allurements of a self-centered fascism, but urban affairs professor Bertram Gross

suggests that it will be a benign or "friendly fascism" rather than the violent type of Hitler or Mussolini. This he defines as a "more concentrated, unscrupulous, repressive and militaristic control by a Big Business-Big Government partnership that, in order to preserve the privileges of the ultra-rich, the corporate overseers, and the military brass, squelches the rights and liberties of other people both at home and abroad." Unlike the "unfriendly fascism" of the 1930s, which relied on repression and the mobilization of the masses, the new fascism depends more upon public apathy and the use of scapegoats (such as racial conflict, school-busing, homosexuality, abortion, and the Equal Rights Amendment) to distract attention from the increasing integration of big government and big business. In this way a totalitarian order is ushered in almost by stealth, while the "silent" or "moral" majority has been manipulated to fight over tangential issues that do not impinge significantly on the vital interests of those who occupy bastions of power in the United States.[16]

Perhaps an answer to Bertram Gross's pondering of "friendly fascism" (his book of that title was published in 1980) can be found in Naomi Klein's 2007 *The Shock Doctrine: The Rise of Disaster Capitalism*. In her highly detailed study, Klein documents how "free-trade" capitalism, especially as it radiated out of the Chicago School of Economics (with its guru, Milton Friedman), dovetailed with authoritarian, antidemocratic political forces from Pinochet's Chile to Thatcher's England, to Yeltsin's Russia, to Bush II's Iraq. She shows repeatedly how, in more vulnerable countries, explicit military coups or invasions were used to usher in "free trade," while in more settled democracies the imposition of "free trade" arrived piecemeal, with "liberals" often promoting and voting for "deregulation" right along with "conservatives."

With the American "culture wars" (which are really about clashing spiritualities, with a morality of traditional righteousness pushing up against an ethic of openly increased personal expressiveness and expanding social inclusion), "wars" brought about by the upheavals of the Vietnam era (not only the war itself, but also civil rights, hippies, feminism, environmentalism, and same-sex partnerships), there emerged the Republicanization of the South and, with deindustrialization and the weakening of unions, the steady drift of many working-class whites into the "traditional values" camp of the Republican Right. Fortified with culture-war anxieties and lacking opposition from unions, the so-called "conservative" Right began to ascend to giddy political heights, magnified and accelerated by the collapse of the Soviet Union, with the apparent success—the complete and total success—of the capitalist worldview. The current "budget crisis"—obscene Pentagon budgets in behalf of Empire America, out-of-control healthcare costs, an absolute legislative refusal to tax the rich or address global warming—has given us the Scott Walkers of this political landscape: utopian capitalists who openly worship at the shrine of Milton Friedman. (This is a shrine—if I might whisk us briefly back to Kim Phillips-Fein's article on John Kenneth Galbraith—at which is endorsed and protected a "consensus that conceals what is objectively true.")

In other words, Rhoda's seemingly casual remark about our descending into fascism may be more perceptive than we care to realize. Or, to take us off the deep end—whether deep in an insightful way or just plain loopy depends on the discernment of the reader—we might take the ancient Roman *fasces*, with its axe and rods as emblems of state violence, as a symbol applicable to all civilized governing structures, for all have used institutionalized violence to attain and maintain their power. And that would imply a very alarming and unsettling thought: that the essence of state violence (supra-legal and therefore "sacred") lies exposed in the *fasces* symbol. To "come into power" means, ultimately, to come into possession of the state's sacred violence. And that would further imply that state violence is always and everywhere embedded in civilizational structures of governance and control. And that means "fascism" is far less an aberration than it is an underlying norm. And that may be more than we care to recognize, think about, or acknowledge.

VI

I have a weakness for what might be called a witty turn of phrase, the dropping of an amusing irony; but Al Gedicks doesn't seem to have that vice. I've known Al distantly for twenty-five years or so and, from the first, he's impressed me as a man with a mission. He's always come loaded with facts and with an analysis that explains those facts. He's both an astronomer and cosmologist of industrial mining. His essay is vintage Al.

When you get to the place in Al's "Resisting Resource Colonialism in the Lake Superior Region" (a third in, roughly) where he talks

Empire's Children: An Afterword

about "removing overburden" on something like 22,000 acres in the Penokee-Gogebic Range just south of Lake Superior, it might be worth your while, if you have difficulty visualizing what this means, to see the movie "Dirt" or pull up on your computer an on-line free movie called "Home." Neither movie is totally about removing "overburden" (or, as it's also called in Appalachia, "mountaintop removal"), but each movie has such a graphic section of mountaintop removal in it, and they're enough to make you sick.

If this book, and Al's essay, find traction with the general public, especially here in Wisconsin, I dearly hope some of that traction wends its way up to the Bad River band of the Lake Superior Ojibwa, for much of that 22,000 acres, with its 650 feet of "overburden," lies in the headwaters of the Bad River which, as Al says, constitutes "one of the largest freshwater estuaries in the world and crucial spawning grounds for Lake Superior fisheries."

How big does an issue have to get before we decide to stand for protected ecology and a clean Earth? Is this one big enough?

VII

Next in was Margaret Swedish with her look into "What's Really Going On In Wisconsin?"

Margaret reminds us that consciousness can change, the mold can be broken; and she uses her very own Republican childhood and youth as an illustration, with the assassinations of Martin Luther King and Bobby Kennedy as one "bookend" of her transformation and the Kent State shootings as the other—what she calls her "own personal 'great turning.'"

One can sense in Margaret's essay that "the fact that all three branches of our state government are in the hands of corporate-backed rightwing politicians and judges" must remind her psychologically of her childhood in general and her father's Joe McCarthy Republicanism in particular. So when she says that government "exists to provide services," she is reflecting her bookend transformation in the sense that government, for her, is no longer vigilant militarism ready to violently defend privileges and prerogatives but, rather, the institutionalized and peaceful facilitation of human well-being. If this is socialism, Margaret's great turning doesn't stop there.

A Whole Which Is Greater

Living Beyond the "End of the World" is the title of Margaret's 2008 book that is not only about equitable, institutionalized sharing among human beings the world over, but also about realizing that Earth's ecology cannot sustain or endure the prevailing industrial level of production and the consumerist standard of consumption. Margaret carries this message into her present essay when she says we are going to have to learn "to live within the balance of nature before it can no longer hold us." This, of course, implies what we might call ecological socialism, although we might push both words into italics—*ecological socialism*—or, just so we pay attention, into caps: ECOLOGICAL SOCIALISM.

Here we arrive at the heart of Margaret's essay: the "irreconcilable trajectories" of our prevailing economic structures and lifestyle expectations over against accelerating ecological dysfunction and bizarre climatic behavior. To address the latter in anything resembling an adequate way (which requires an enormous, common effort on our part, both spiritually and intellectually) means we absolutely need to radically reconfigure our economic structures. But such a reconfiguration (Michael Slattery, in his essay, crunches a lot of useful budget numbers for us) demands a massive change of consciousness. And this, needless to say, is a giant nut to crack.

Well, climate scientists and oil-supply analysts are basically telling us that nature will most certainly crack our nut of consciousness—or at least its institutional underpinnings—if we refuse to do the cracking ourselves, methodically, carefully, and voluntarily. But what does this mean? What are the particulars of this nut that needs cracking? Margaret calls it, in her final paragraph, the "challenge of creating a new way of life," and that seems a rather hefty project.

Michael Slattery, meanwhile, opens and closes his essay with reference to Hebrew and Christian scriptures, with their "preferential option for poorer classes," and with firm insistence that "the reign of God [is to be] realized in the here and now." When he goes on to say that "Fiscal management of public-sector budgets is a moral issue," he has already shown us that morality rests, finally, on ethical and spiritual foundations. (Plus, for those who read Michael's budget analysis carefully, it's clear the Walker budget deficit was largely fabricated in order to justify a little homegrown cheesehead shock doctrine, with guidance—and funding—from the Koch brothers.) Therefore, politics and economics represent morality—or immorality—in action. The question then becomes: What's

Empire's Children: An Afterword

the moral basis of the prevailing system? We know it claims to be moral, but on what ethical foundation, exactly, does it stand?

What's hard, of course, and certainly confusing, is penetrating the paradox that so many of the reality deniers (say in regard to Global Warming/Climate Change) and fierce advocates for American empire (say "free trade" and military budget enthusiasts) are also "conservative" or fundamentalist Christians. That is, we have on the one hand the American way of life held up by righteous Christians as an example to the world, and, on the other hand, we have biblical scholars like Michael pointing out that the true ethical and moral content of the same religious tradition leads "liberals" to an entirely different understanding, conviction, and practice.

If Michael is correct (I believe he is), how did the "conservative" camp get to be so strong and wrong? And what does it mean—if Margaret is right, what will it mean—to crack the nut of "conservative" consciousness? What would gospel ethics look like if unfolded socially and ecologically? What will it take for convinced, righteous Christians to repent of their moral righteousness? What will the post-civilized world of frugal, steady-state Green socialism be like?

It would be wonderful to live long enough to find out.

VIII

First off, with Dan Grego's title ("Confessions of an Apostate from the Religion of 'Education'"), I either hear or think I hear echoes of the title of John Perkins' fairly famous *Confessions of an Economic Hit Man*. In his book, Perkins describes how, on behalf of U.S. financial institutions, he persuaded or simply suckered various poor countries into taking on debt burdens that could never be repaid and that therefore made those countries pliable to U.S. political pressure and commercial interests. (Naomi Klein's *The Shock Doctrine* is of course on the same theme, only far more detailed and systematic.)

Well, prickles and goos. Tough-minded versus tender-minded. Let's try to be both here, simultaneously. Or at least dialectically. If people do not necessarily need schools in order to grow up, do people need a *system* of economics in order to feed, clothe, and shelter themselves?

Of course the answer to both parts of that question is a resounding and obvious NO! (If it were YES! that would mean we'd be extinct, for the simple reason that the vast bulk of human history saw neither schools nor economic systems. But, by golly, here we are!) So it's civilization, especially and particularly industrial civilization, that apparently needs systems. Folk culture by contrast makes do with what we might call "patterns." Culture has patterns; civilizations have systems. Anyway, schools are not necessary in order for human beings to grow up. The vast historical record is clear about that. But let's also say, in principle, that schools of a certain type, with certain modes of learning, are desirable. That thought easily generates two additional questions: Why do we have the types of schools we do? What would a post-civilized, post-industrial Green school look like?

I'll wiggle into an answer to those questions by taking off on the question Dan says Ivan Illich threw at him in the Maryland woods in 1993: "Why do we have such a low opinion of ourselves that we think we need to be educated in the first place?" This question is very much like the one Lewis Mumford asks in *The Transformations of Man*: Why were peasants willing to submit to the compulsory routines imposed by aristocratic civilization?[17]

Well, obviously, there is the word "compulsory" staring us in the face. We submit largely out of fear of the power that lies within the *compulsory* institutions; and these compulsory *institutions* are backed, in the end, by a kind of physical force that absolutely relies on male will and male violence. Peasants didn't happily bring the bulk of their harvests—their so-called "surplus"—to the sword-and-knife wielding aristocrats out of eager or cheerful voluntarism. Parents haven't always sent their kids to school out of a deep conviction that compulsory regimentation is best for their growth and maturation. (Sending kids to school now, in order to get them out of their parents' hair, is a simple if tragic fact; but it's a fact that speaks volumes about the atomized, cultureless life we live. Here *Growing Up Absurd* by Paul Goodman, as well as his later work *Compulsory Miseducation*, are very much apropos.)

So this "low opinion of ourselves" (with its deeply resentful acquiescence) is tied tightly into fear of authority (or, in Tillich's words, the "unavoidable guilt consciousness produced by the identification of the parental with the divine authority"), and it is in its deep historical conditioning a fear held by the relatively nonviolent peasants when faced with threatening aristocrats who rely on violence or intimidation as the essential force by which to create and sustain consistent compliance.[ii] Schooling may be, as Dan says, a "mythmaking ritual" committed to progress and development, but it is also—and I would say primarily—a social-control conditioning process. That is, the strict hours, precise class periods, and regimentation of schedules; the way the chairs are arranged to reflect authority and expected obedience; the buzzers and bells; the subjection to electronic screening and sudden searches—all this and much more train and condition young people for an "adult" world largely filled with similar routines and restrictions, only modified by a thoroughly instilled and completely resigned "voluntarism." School conditions us in utopian resignation. We become addicted to prevailing utopian order. We don't know what to do without it. We have had our eutopian self-directedness driven into deep repression; and, as an internalized overlay, we've been fed a steady, almost unrelenting diet of compulsory utopian systems and commercial propaganda.

If that's a partial answer to the question Why do we have the schools we do?, a groping answer to What would a post-industrial school look like? is, obviously, a tough thing to mentally negotiate precisely because eutopian consciousness has been so powerfully suppressed in us simultaneously with the imposed, relentless conditioning that's inherently part of compulsory, utopian institutionalization.

This entire collection of essays is, as far as I am concerned, an exploration into the crises-causing institutionalization represented by the globalization—the shock doctrine—of civilization, even if we're using Wisconsin as our provisional laboratory. Of course, "breaking out" can also be criminal jailbreak or kids playing hooky, a kind of impulsive, directionless rebellion without larger purpose and therefore lacking in constructive intent. To actually live a post-civilized, post-industrial Green life is what we're now called upon to do. It's the only way out of our predicament. And while there's a huge literature available on "how-to" do practically anything or everything, what holds us back from Deep Green Living is not our technical incompetence but our atrophy of eutopian will. We don't know what to do. We're locked in. We're scared. To recall, regain, and reconfigure eutopian will is in some ways our most critical need. But getting there in our utopian-ridden lives is a matter of great physical, emotional, intellectual, and spiritual

---

ii. See also "The Wisconsin Blues and a Failed Progressive Narrative" by George Lakoff and Elisabeth Wehling at www.commondreams.org/view/2012/06/12?key=0.

effort. Material comfort supplies an easy nest for our laziness. We may think of ourselves as "progressives," but we are still very much Empire's children, and most of us have an almost involuntary sense of "lifestyle" entitlement—or at least no intention to get (voluntarily) poor now in order to avoid the (involuntary) rush.

All this is why crisis-provoking breakdowns are inevitable. We are numb with conditioned habit and habituated comfort. The real question is: How much unavoidable pain and comfort disruption will it take for us to get off our utopian butts? What's the threshold of distress before we begin to get beyond the paralyzing grip of our detached, otherworldly voyeurism? Where's the tipping point?

IX

Next in was John I. Laun's "Challenge"—the great challenge to expand and strengthen opposition to what Jack calls "neo-liberalism," which I take to be pretty much what Naomi Klein calls the shock doctrine and what I (following Mumford) prefer to call utopian civilization.

Virtually everyone who's contributed to this essay project (at least so far) is on the liberal or Left side of the political spectrum. That's a generality, but it's true. Yet we need to bear in mind that the utopian project (which asserts, both implicitly and explicitly, that it's only a step below the righteousness of God) has both "liberal" and "conservative" aspects. "Conservatives" may be more Augustinian in their belief that it's God who bestows kingdoms and empires, while "liberals" may be more Aristotelian in asserting that it's the cream (not the scum) that rises naturally to the top. Either way, utopia is a system generated by a dominant minority, but a system with a universal agenda, a globalization, created and maintained by the risen cream, lifted into elite dominance either by God (Augustine) or nature (Aristotle). It's hubristic precisely because it is so righteously self-assured (humility is not prominent among its virtues), to the point where its technologized violence is thoroughly rationalized—even spiritualized— as a virtuous struggle against backwardness and evil.

If it's morally permissible to even use the word "evil" here, I would glue it to the utopian project not only because it is so stupendously destructive but also because it is so stunningly and blindly righteous. Perhaps we need to recall that Lucifer, the evil one, is not some stinky,

Empire's Children: An Afterword

dark-skinned, shifty-eyed, greasy guy with a tangled, dirty beard, but the light-bringer, the morning star, Apollo with a city plan, clean-shaven and freshly scrubbed. The outstanding, unanswered question is whether it's possible to achieve eutopian "civilization" on Earth, though to put "eutopian" and "civilization" in such a tight relationship might be a bit oxymoronic. Is it possible to build a functional engagement globally in a mode that's fundamentally peaceful, ecological, and sustainable? What would be the spiritual and ethical basis for such a "system"? How would its politics function? Who is capable of describing what an ecologically healthy economy would look like?

When Jack says "Only an ignorant populace mesmerized by misinformation in the media could be so irrational as to actively work against their own economic interests" I both agree (as in Thomas Frank's *What's the Matter with Kansas?*) and disagree. Or, if I don't exactly disagree, I have reservations about putting the problem that way. Yes, there is an abundance of misinformation. There's no doubt about that. And people do vote against their economic self-interest. That's true, too. But a lot of this—perhaps the bulk of it—is not simply "misinformation." This sort of "misinformation" carries the cosmic glow of Manifest Destiny, the Divine Right of Kings, the total superiority of civilizational utopianism, and even of Christianity as the only True Faith. "Misinformation" of this sort floats in a powerful cultural mythology with ancient pedigree.

To break out of this mythology, especially for those raised within it, is hard and even painful spiritual work. "Misinformation" is the numbing poison secreted by the tentacles of this octopus. Let me put it this way. With explicit globalization, utopian civilization brings the world to a truly tangled mess of deadly crises. These crises cannot be resolved with utopian tools or methods precisely because the crises are the slowly accrued consequences of those very tools and methods. Only eutopian tools and methods will be effective in the amelioration of these crises. But to choose the eutopian toolkit constitutes spiritual therapy at the social level, for it confronts or at least calls into question the unsustainable destructiveness of the utopian trajectory. It requires the letting go of utopian spirituality and utopian mythology in both "liberal" and "conservative" modes. It's this letting go that's so hard to do. On the "conservative" side, it feels like an abandonment of God (the religious Right fiercely articulates this point); on the "liberal" side, it's felt as the unbearable loss or disintegration of all that's so preciously "civilized."

A Whole Which Is Greater

Should we be surprised there's so much befuddlement? Or that "Colombia is now where the United States is headed"? In other words: Where is the new vision? Who is articulating the eutopian worldview? What is its spirituality? Is it either catastrophe, neo-aristocratic restoration, or an entirely new level of democracy with both ecological and spiritual dimensions, a vision that has yet to be adequately uttered? How soon will we hear its voice?

X

I would like to walk one main idea from Jeff Leigh's essay over to Jim Veninga's. That idea or assertion of Jeff's is this:

> In the Middle East, as in much of the world today and indeed in the entire world throughout most of human history, government has been overwhelmingly a force for the preservation of elite interest and a predator upon the weak and vulnerable. While these conclusions about the traditional use of government are usually associated with the traditions of 19th- and 20th-Century European radicalism . . . they go far back into the Chinese philosophy of Daoism, the conclusions of the Cynic philosophers of ancient Greece, and recurring strands of Jewish and Christian thought wherein the spiritual and material needs of the poor are juxtaposed to the behavior of the wealthy and powerful.

For those who know my writings (especially *Green Politics Is Eutopian, Polemics and Provocations,* or *The Kingdom of God Is Green*), this critique of Jeff's—government traditionally as a force for the preservation of elite interest—is also the conclusion I came to as I followed agriculture's tracks backwards into the far distant past. ("Why are small farms dying?" is the question that goaded me.) So, if we dare put the word "civilization" in the place of "government," and then ask what the "democratization" of civilization implies, we are left with the realization that Jim's list of ecological crises—global warming, deforestation, extinction of species, degradation of land and soil, loss of habitat, plundering of natural resources, diminished availability of fresh water—is the consequence of civilization in its globalized, industrial mode.

To reference Kim Phillips-Fein's piece on John Kenneth Galbraith once again, aren't we dealing here with the "impotence of people with power . . . in the grip of ideas that leave them no way of confronting reality"? People who "endorse and protect a consensus that conceals what is objectively true"? Meanwhile, we continue blithely on with "one of man's oldest exercises in moral philosophy; that is, the search for a moral justification for selfishness." Only I would say this search has both "conservative" and "liberal" ancestry. This seems to be the gorilla in the room we're not supposed to notice or talk about. Yet if we open our eyes to this furry beast, we can't help but conclude that to try to bring or think it's desirable to bring more and more of the world's working class into the middle class—not to speak of bringing more and more of the world's middle class into the upper class—that is, to bring more, more, and yet more people into the income range, general affluence, and habits of consumption that characterize the class above—is, given the already-existing condition of world ecology, a desire of pure unadulterated utopian madness. The search for a moral justification for selfishness will have to conclude its effort by camping out on the toxic landfill that Earth will become.

I like Jim Veninga's essay. His compacted histories of Wisconsin progressivism and the social gospel are wonderfully lucid and helpful. But we need to seriously consider what it means (as Jim says Walter Rauschenbusch asserted) that the "idea of the Kingdom of God shriveled"—not enlarged, *shriveled*—over the two thousand years of Christian history. If the ethical core of the "kingdom of God" proclamation consists of radical servanthood and radical stewardship, then in our world its political nature has to manifest itself as compassionate but frugal ecological socialism. It's this that constitutes the "sacred canopy" even as the sacred canopy contains or reveals a spiritual realm for which servanthood and stewardship are the ethical portals.

We might, in principle, say that the ecologically ruinous globalization of civilization—that is, the globalization of elite interest and its correspondingly opulent lifestyle—provides us with three major options: ecocide or something just short of ecocide; the ruthless restoration of explicit aristocracy (i.e., the unembarrassed restitution of naked elite interest) as the brutal core of global power; or, turning decisively away from civilized criminality and its utopian rationalizations, the embracing of democratic, libertarian, ecological socialism.

Actually, I can't see why it's so democratically difficult to make the obvious selection. Or are we, as empire's children (like Thomas Frank's Kansas?), so utterly addicted to empire mythology, to empire consciousness and empire religion, that we are psychologically and spiritually incapable of politically choosing the "kingdom of God"? Are we really that hornswoggled by inherited utopian mythology and its associated behaviors that we will take Creation down with our toxic technologies and "democratic" consumerism, and commit suicide in the process, because of our perverse blend of pride, fear, and stupidity—our search for a moral justification for selfishness?

XI

It's a horse apiece as to whether Brian Terrell's "99% Spring" or Mike McCabe's "Who's Awake in Clark County?" got across the electronic finish line first. Call it a tossup. It's also possible we might've had—probably would've had—an even deeper and more comprehensive analysis from both Brian and Mike, except that there are only so many hours in the day, only so much energy and attention span in any person's life. We should've asked earlier. But what we got is, I think, very good.

Brian's piece first appeared in the April 2012 issue of *Voices for Creative Nonviolence*—a newsletter, really. But, with his involvement in the walk from Madison to Chicago in May to call attention to the 2012 NATO summit (held in Chicago), and other things like keeping his Iowa farm functioning, any hope for an expanded essay steadily evaporated. Similarly, Mike gave Dave Kast and me permission to use the compact essay originally published in the April 26-May 3, 2012, edition of the *Wausau City Pages*; and then, swept up in the tumult of the Walker recall election and its politically roiled aftermath (i.e., the Democratic defeat and its painful explanation), he could only offer samples of his blogs for us to use, if we chose, as material to dice and splice.

So what we have here is Brian's original piece and original title and Mike's *City Pages* essay with two of his blogs spliced in, all of that retitled as "Who's Awake in Clark County?"

Brian's essential point is that even the so-called cutting edge of protests—99% Spring—avoids addressing Empire America's global militarism and financialized colonialism and, instead, only articulates complaints about shrinking pension funds, skyrocketing student loans, foreclosures, budget cuts to schools, and so on. As Brian goes on to say in regard to the work of Mohandas Gandhi and Martin Luther King, "Neither of these teachers held that justice at home was possible in a

Empire's Children: An Afterword

country engaged in murder and thievery abroad." Exactly. To believe differently is to presume that residents of empire's home country deserve their full share of the booty.

One could say (and presumably should say) that that criticism be directed as well at Mike's diced and spliced piece. But Mike's contribution here consists of specific pieces of writing, focused and compact; they weren't intended as an essay for this collection nor as comprehensive "movement" proclamations. We suspect that Mike is far from oblivious about the consumerist implications of Empire America.

What's not in Mike's piece is an analysis of how and why Democrats have "broken the sacred political law of universality."

Well, first it needs to be said that universality is an appealing construct; but it also has a history of being chimerical. (The word "chimera" has Greek origins, meaning "fabulous monster." Single-party nation-states—and even multiparty industrial states—have been known to resemble *chimaera*.) So let's back off "universal" just a bit and ask, perhaps more modestly, where or in what way the Democratic Party lost touch with the working class.

Well, if we say "working class" we should also say "unions," and if we say "working-class unions" we should clearly indicate the following: After the Second World War, the Red Scare (McCarthyism and all the rest) caused unions to repudiate their radical leftist roots and class analysis. We were now one big and happy (white) family, all of us busily waving flags on the Fourth of July as gas-guzzling cars with big fins cruised by. I would say Grant Park in Chicago, during the Democratic National Convention in 1968, was the big watershed event. When Mayor Daley's cops—"police riot"—beat antiwar demonstrators, those cops—under the political control of a big-city Democratic machine mayor and representative of the moral fist of white industrial unions—those cops declared war on the "unpatriotic" analysis of Empire America simultaneously with civil rights (i.e., people of color), women's liberation, any and all gender-bending sexuality, steady-state and no-growth environmentalism, and anything to the left of Cicero, Illinois. White Empire entitlement was the name of the game. This triggered an avalanche of political realignment and political reformulation, with the white working class (at least much of it) taking its hardhat and flag decal over to the Republican Party and the Democratic Party left with contending, aggravated "special interest" groups whose (un)integrated analysis was apparently too radical, unconventional, and confrontational to be openly articulated in public.

Humphrey lost to Nixon. McGovern lost to Nixon. Carter squeaked one out over Ford but was perceived as milk toast and then lost to Reagan. By then it was explicit: "Democrats for Reagan." Union busting. Deindustrialization. GATT. WTO. NAFTA. A new round of covert and then, with Bush I, overt war.

I sort of take turns joining in the brawl on Democrats and trying to get the rabbit punchers to back off. (Perhaps these essays are a momentary pause in the brawl, with an occasional backhand so as not to totally lose the lubricating sweat.) But, I think we can safely say that the Republican Party is, overall, representative of extremely calculating and extremely powerful Empire interests. Just consider one of the more audacious political moves the Right has made in recent years. No, I'm not talking about Colin Powell's dog and pony show at the United Nations in 2003, as he purported to prove the existence of Saddam Hussein's WMDs, with—presumably—Dick Cheney and Donald Rumsfeld watching offstage and smirking. I mean the way the bulk of congressional Republicans voted *against* the bank bailouts in 2008, knowing Democrats would buckle at the brink and vote *for* bailout, so that the Republican Party could thereafter posture as standing with the "little guy" against Wall Street. Next up was Tea Party formation to take full advantage of this cynical ploy. It was audacious, cunning, brilliant, bold, and—from the perspective of humane, open, and honest democracy—totally vicious and immoral. (But, of course, its public relations face is one of complete sincerity and utter righteousness.)

And, lest we forget, it was in this last fifty-year period, more or less, that Thomas J. J. Altizer (and lots of other radical theologians) announced the death of God even as right-wing Christianity proclaimed that scriptural prophecies are perfectly on track and that God's about to burst into the world, round up all the liberal pagans (or is it the pagan liberals?) and, with great joy and satisfaction, march them kicking and screaming into the furnaces of Hell. Just, you know, a sort of cosmic finale to the overcoming of evil. Righteousness totally wins. Degeneracy totally gets what it's got coming forever and ever, amen.

Where I disagree with Mike McCabe—or maybe I think I disagree because his examples are somewhat yesterday—has to do with what the Democratic Party *should* be advocating. The interstate highway system

Empire's Children: An Afterword

was a colossal ecological mistake from the beginning. Unrestrained rural electrification helped to wipe out the household hearth, a piece of cultural stability and natural connectedness going back thousands upon thousands of years. Social Security, however, enables us creaky old geezers to live in the woods with modest independence and immodest dignity. Medicare for all would—if cleanly formulated—be humane and cheap and a great boon to democratic depth and stability. (And, not too incidentally, it would lift an impossible burden off small business.) Add in publicly owned mass transit. Socialism for the natural monopolies, in other words, anything "too big to fail" or maybe just too important to fail, with free enterprise for the small-scale. Farms, shops, cafes. All of it with a painfully realized ecological reverence.

But saying all this doesn't really address the political problem that is simultaneously psychological, cultural, and spiritual. Back in the Neolithic days of '68, the white working class—when things got emotionally difficult—chose to go with White Big Daddy. We could say that now the problem is the conversion of the white working class: If only the white working class would return to the Democratic Party there would be sufficient electoral traction to achieve Medicare for all, etc., etc.[iii] Or, alternatively, the steadily rising demographics of those not white will, in twenty years or so, tip the electoral scale against the Right through sheer voter numbers.

Perhaps. I have a friend who has organized residents of trailer parks with encouraging results. But one should not misunderestimate the importance of working class ambience here. That is, the organizer has to resonate with the unorganized poor; and, as a rule, the leadership

---

iii. The July 2/9, 2012, issue of *The Nation*, in its lead editorial ("Labor Pains") on page 3, says that 38 percent of union households voted for Republican Scott Walker in the recent recall election that Walker, of course, won. In the August issue of *The Progressive*, editor Matthew Rothschild and political editor Ruth Conniff continue to wring their hands over the election result ("After Defeat," page 4; "Austerity Politics," pages 8 and 9; "Breaking the Rich-Poor Alliance"—with reference to Mike McCabe and Clark County—on page 14). But, overall, this is old, old news. Robert Reich, for example, in his 1997 book *Locked in the Cabinet*, an account of his years as Bill Clinton's labor secretary, shows over and over again how Clinton and his chief advisors repeatedly avoided taking on issues that would've confronted the bloating of corporate America and that greased the slide for subsequent disasters. (See especially pages 193 through 221 of Reich's book for a lively and very readable rendition of events and conversations just before and immediately after the 1994 mid-term elections in which Republicans swept both houses of Congress.)

within the Democratic Party seems far more comfortable in the Republican country club than in the local bar or labor temple, not even to speak of trailer parks. In addition, one should not *misunderestimate* the capacity of the Right to reconfigure its protean net. (I truly love the word "misunderestimate." It's George W. Bush's only lasting legacy.) Nor should we misunderestimate the reflexive tendency of the brilliant insiders of the Democratic Party to be deficient in long-term understanding, lavish with spiritual timidity and old political habits.

But climate change heaped on top of the imminent threat of nuclear mammalian wipeout should, perhaps, give all policy mongers pause. How far do you bright snarky fellas—both "conservative" and "liberal"—want to push this game of sharp-elbowed *realpolitik* and endless economic growth? Will you choose to stop only at that point where its momentum is unstoppable?

I therefore conclude—"a consensus that conceals what is objectively true"—that we have ourselves a bit of a metaphysical problem here, a metaphysical problem related to truth and caring and compassion, a metaphysical problem that has both spiritual and cultural ramifications—ecological ramifications—mammalian survival ramifications. How big does a problem have to get before we consent to acknowledge its existence?

It's my immodest assessment that these essays can help us burrow into the prevailing metaphysical consensus. There's truth to be gleaned and assimilated. But the real question is: Has mythological consensus become impervious to truth? Politics over the next few decades will decisively answer that question, even if it's spiritual transformation that constitutes the hidden interior energy.

Paul Gilk, June 21, 2012

ENDNOTES

1. Phillips-Fein, "Countervailing," 45.
2. Phillips-Fein, "Countervailing," 45.
3. Phillips-Fein, "Countervailing," 44.
4. Phillips-Fein, "Countervailing," 44.
5. Kupfer, "Against," 6.

6. Hedges, "Endgame," adbusters.org/magazine

7. Collier, *Duce!*, 54.

8. Collier, *Duce!*, 46.

9. Collier, *Duce!*, 34.

10. Pierard, "Protestant," 250–51.

11. Tillich, "Autobiographical," 8.

12. Tillich, "Autobiographical," 7–8.

13. Bainton, *Here*, 232.

14. Mumford, *Pentagon*, 199.

15. Augustine, *City*, 142–43.

16. Pierard, "Protestant," 247–48.

17. Mumford, *Transformations*, 45.

BIBLIOGRAPHY

Augustine, *The City of God*. New York: Random House, 1950.
Bainton, Roland. *Here I Stand: A Life of Martin Luther*. Nashville: Abingdon, 1950.
Collier, Richard. *Duce! A Biography of Benito Mussolini*. New York: The Viking Press, 1971.
Hedges, Chris. "Endgame." Adbusters.org/magazine
Kupfer, David. "*The Sun* Interview." In *The Sun*, June 2011.
Mumford, Lewis. *The Pentagon of Power*. New York: Harcourt, Brace & Jovanovich, 1970.
———. *The Transformations of Man*. New York: Harper & Row, 1956.
Phillips-Fein, Kim. "Countervailing Powers." In *The Nation*, May 30, 2011.
Pierard, Richard. "Protestant Support for the Political Right in Weimar Germany and Post-Watergate America: Some Comparative Observations." In *A Journal of Church and State*, Spring 1982.
Tillich, Paul. "Autobiographical Reflections of Paul Tillich." In *The Theology of Paul Tillich*, edited by Charles W. Kegley and Robert W. Bretall. New York: The Macmillan Company, 1952.

List of Contributors

James Botsford

James Botsford is an attorney who has practiced exclusively in Indian Law since 1984. He specializes in Indian religious freedom issues and the development of tribal courts. He is the author of *You Should Write That Down: Stories Along the Way*, published in 2011 by Sandyhouse Press. That book and a forthcoming *History of the Wisconsin Tribal Judges Association* are available through thebigsandy@gmail.com.

Al Gedicks

Al Gedicks is an environmental and indigenous rights activist and scholar. He is Emeritus Professor of Sociology at the University of Wisconsin-La Crosse and has written extensively about indigenous and popular resistance to extractive resource projects. He is the author of *The New Resource Wars: Native and Environmental Struggles Against Multinational Corporations* and *Resource Rebels: Native Challenges to Mining and Oil Corporations*.

Rhoda Gilman

Rhoda Gilman began a 34-year career at the Minnesota Historical Society in 1958. During those years she worked as an editor, researcher, and administrator and wrote several books and many articles on midwestern history. They included a textbook of Minnesota history for middle school students published in 1989 and later issued as a trade edition under the title *The Story of Minnesota's Past*. She joined the Twin Cities Greens in 1986, helped to organize the Green Party of Minnesota in 1994, and was its candidate for lieutenant governor in 2002. Her newest book, *Stand Up! The Story of Minnesota's Protest Tradition*, was published in the spring of 2012 by the Minnesota Historical Society Press.

Daniel Grego

Daniel Grego is the Executive Director of TransCenter for Youth, Inc. in Milwaukee. He lives with his wife, Debra Loewen, the Artistic Director of Wild Space Dance Company, on a small farm in the Rock River watershed in Dodge County, Wisconsin.

Maynard Kaufman

After receiving his doctorate from the University of Chicago, Maynard Kaufman taught courses on Religion and Environmental Studies at Western Michigan University. His response to the energy crisis of the 1970s was to become a part-time farmer and establish a School of Homesteading. As a lifelong advocate of local food and organic farming, he organized Michigan Organic Food and Farm Alliance in 1991. In 2001 Maynard and his wife Barbara moved into their off-grid house that is powered by renewable energy. They enjoy gardening and earth-centered rituals that celebrate the seasons.

John I. Laun

John I. Laun is an attorney and president and co-founder of the Colombia Support Network, based in Madison, Wisconsin. He lives near Verona, Wisconsin, and has taken many delegations to Colombia, where he lived and taught for several years.

Jeff Leigh

Jeff Leigh, Ph.D., is currently an Associate Professor of History at UW-Marathon County where he teaches European, Middle Eastern, and World History. He is a Fulbright Scholar, a past president of the Wausau School Foundation, and past Director of the Marathon County History Teaching Alliance. His current endeavors include an in-progress monograph in European History and various projects to expand Middle Eastern studies in central Wisconsin.

Mike McCabe

Mike McCabe is one of Wisconsin's leading whistle blowers. He shines light in dark places at the Capitol as executive director of the Wisconsin Democracy Campaign (www.wisdc.org), a nonpartisan watchdog group that tracks the money in state politics, fights corruption and works for clean, open and honest government. Along with being a leading voice for political reform in Wisconsin, the Democracy Campaign manages the state's only searchable online database of contributors to state campaigns. Before joining WDC's staff in 1999 and becoming its director in 2000 Mike was the Madison Metropolitan School District's communications director and legislative liaison for six years. He also formerly worked as a newspaper reporter and state legislative aide. He grew up on his family's dairy farm in central Wisconsin and went on to graduate from the University of Wisconsin-Madison with degrees in journalism and political science, and later served in the Peace Corps in the West African country of Mali.

W. Michael Slattery

W. Michael Slattery worked as a missionary in Japan for 10 years, has a doctorate in international relations and a masters in sacred theology. He worked as a financier in New York for a Japanese bank for 12 years, helped to establish and for six years ran finance-related businesses (bond insurance, life insurance, asset management, etc.) in Japan for a large US finance company, and was actively involved in economic analysis and strategic planning for both corporations. Since 1999, he and his wife have operated a family farm in northeast Wisconsin, raising livestock, cash cropping, and selling limited garden crops. He is active in a Christian peace group, Pax Christi, that promotes non-violence and advocates justice issues; he is energetically engaged as a state board member in supporting the interests of small- and medium-scale farming for the Wisconsin Farmers Union; along with his wife, he as a board member of Call to Action promotes progressive positions in the institutional Roman Catholic church; he is a principal in the Wisconsin Green Party; he and his wife are leaders in an inter-faith justice group seeking to make structural changes to correct local and state injustices. He is also a frequent contributor and commentator in various publications.

Margaret Swedish

Swedish was director of the Religious Task Force on Central America & Mexico from 1981-2004, a national office in Washington, DC that helped coordinate the work of faith-based solidarity, connecting national religious leadership to a broad network of grassroots organizations working for just U.S. policies and in defense of human rights in that region. Since 2007 she has spoken in dozens of communities on topics related to the ecological crisis and the role of spirituality in re-inventing our human presence on the planet. She is the author of two books: *Like Grains of Wheat, A Spirituality of Solidarity* (2004) and *Living Beyond the 'End of the World,' A Spirituality of Hope* (2008), both published by Orbis Books, Maryknoll NY. Her current writing is focused on the deep cultural roots of Wisconsin's political upheavals, with lessons for the nation.

Brian Terrell

Brian Terrell was born in Green Bay, Wisconsin, 55 years ago and lived in the vicinity until he was 19 years old. Since then, he has been an activist with the Catholic Worker Movement, living in New York and Iowa. He is an advocate for nonviolent direct action and has been arrested and jailed many times. Brian lives and works at Strangers and Guests Catholic Worker Farm in Maloy, Iowa, and is a co-coordinator of Voices for Creative Nonviolence.

James F. Veninga

James F. Veninga is the former Campus Executive Officer and Dean at the University of Wisconsin—Marathon County (Wausau). He helped to establish the Wisconsin Institute for Public Policy and Service housed in the new UW Center for Civic Engagement, located on the Wausau campus. Prior to joining the UW Colleges in 2000, he served for 23 years as the Executive Director of the Texas Council on the Humanities. He has held teaching positions at St. Thomas University (Houston), the University of Texas at Austin, Baylor University, and the University of Wisconsin Colleges. He is the editor or author of six books including, *The Humanities and the Civic Imagination: Collected Addresses and Essays*. He holds a Ph.D. degree in Religious Studies and History from Rice University.

Eric Yonke

Eric Yonke is a Professor of Modern European History at the University of Wisconsin-Stevens Point. Over the past twenty years, he has developed and taught courses on modern German history, International and Peace Studies, and human rights history. He currently serves as the University's International Programs Director, helping develop global citizens through over thirty programs of study around the world.